THE GROWTH

OF

THE KINGDOM OF GOD

The Growth

OF

The Kingdom of God

BY

SIDNEY L. GULICK, M.A.

MISSIONARY OF THE A.B.C.F.M. IN JAPAN

FLEMING H. REVELL COMPANY

NEW YORK　　　　CHICAGO　　　　TORONTO

Publishers of Evangelical Literature

PREFACE

———◆———

THE contents of this volume can alone justify its existence and publication. A word, however, as to its birth may serve to explain and account for some of its characteristics. The germ of the book consisted of an address delivered to an audience of wideawake Japanese young men. The aim of the address was to lead the hearers to give the Christian religion an impartial study, by telling them briefly of its growth and influence in the world, and the transformations it had wrought in the life and thought of the Western nations. By many of my associates it was thought that, in pamphlet or book form, the argument should be put before a larger Japanese audience. With this end in view, the successive chapters were prepared and translated into Japanese.

In general, the book may be called an apologetic for Christianity, based on a view of its varied forms of growth,—growth in numbers, in understanding, in practice, and in influence. Chapter III. was not a part of the original plan; but, for obvious reasons, it seemed desirable that, for English readers, there should be a chapter devoted to a study of the growth of the Kingdom in England, and it has accordingly been prepared. No one is more keenly alive than the author to the extreme difficulty of a satisfactory treatment of the subject. He has tried to do his best with the materials accessible, and the limited time at his disposal. A satisfactory treatment would require many months of closest application and an entire volume for the presentation of the evidence. In spite of the comparative length of the chapter, he does not pretend to have treated the subject in any exhaustive way. Indeed, this may be said with equal truth of the whole book. Rather than a minute examination of the facts, he has sought to take a bird's-eye view of the outstanding features, the more conspicuous movements and growth of Christianity.

The primary purpose, the Japanese audience, and the practical, rather than the theoretical interest and aim of the book, will thus account for certain of its features, which, if produced under different circumstances, it might not have had. Its value, however, may possibly be increased rather than diminished by these factors and features.

His indebtedness to various writers and his sources of information are sufficiently indicated in the course of the successive chapters. His thanks are due to personal friends and kindred who have rendered very material assistance in the forms of stimulus, suggestions, and correction of the manuscript.

The defects incident to the attempt to cover so much ground in a single brief work, none realise more than the author. Among such a mass of statistics, errors are inevitable. None will be more glad than the writer to have such pointed out and corrected.

That this volume may find its niche of usefulness, and may help onward the growth of the Kingdom, is the one desire of its author.

SIDNEY L. GULICK.

CONTENTS

———+———

CHAPTER I

PRELIMINARY CONSIDERATIONS AND DEFINITIONS

CHAPTER II

GROWTH IN NUMBERS

CHAPTER III

STATISTICAL EVIDENCES OF THE GROWTH OF THE
KINGDOM OF GOD IN ENGLAND AND WALES

PART I.—GROWTH OF THE POPULATION OF ENGLAND
AND WALES

CHAPTER IV

STATISTICAL EVIDENCES OF THE GROWTH OF THE
KINGDOM OF GOD IN THE UNITED STATES

CHAPTER V

GROWTH IN UNDERSTANDING CHRISTIANITY

CHAPTER VI

GROWTH IN PRACTICE

CHAPTER VIII

GROWTH IN INFLUENCE—*Continued*

CHAPTER IX

THE SIGNIFICANCE OF THE GROWTH OF CHRISTIANITY
AND OF CHRISTENDOM

CHAPTER I

Preliminary Considerations and Conditions

'So many wild claims are made in these days about the decline of Evangelical religion—claims based on ignorance, and upheld by the hopes of Freethinkers, Agnostics, Romanists, and other opponents of Protestant Christianity—that a few stubborn facts seem to be called for. The cry of the Agnostic scientist is for facts. He will find here an abundant supply, from the best sources, which he may with profit read, mark, and inwardly digest.'[1]

'There have been periods, since the conquest of the old Roman world by Christianity, when some friends have entertained grave doubts whether it would not soon go down in darkness and wholly disappear. Many times have its enemies confidently predicted such disaster. But at present no intelligent person can doubt whether Protestant Christianity is a setting or a rising sun. . . . Christianity is now far beyond its dawn. Higher and higher is Christ's sceptre lifted. Willing nations, rejoicing in the day of His power—

"To Him all majesty ascribe,
And crown Him Lord of all."'[2]

'All that we call modern civilisation, in a sense which deserves the name, is the visible expression of the transforming power of the gospel.'[3]

---

[1] *The Growth of Christianity during Nineteen Centuries*, Introduction by Dr. Schauffler.

[2] *The Problem of Religious Progress*, revised ed., 1894 (Daniel Dorchester), p. 670.

[3] Froude's *Short Studies*, ii. p. 37.

CHAPTER I

THE question of the relation of religion to
civilisation and the higher development of the
human race is one of profound interest and great
importance. Different classes of thinkers take very
different views. Some think that religion helps, while
others think that it hinders, the healthy growth of
civilisation. Some think that religion is a relic of
barbarism ; others that it is the most perfect flower of
the most highly developed races. Some think that
religion is rapidly passing away, and that it will cease
to exist when civilisation shall have reached its full
development ; others think that religion is ever growing
with the growth of man, being at once the product and
evidence of man's growth thus far, and the mightiest
factor of his future evolution ; and that it will reach its
fullest development only in proportion as the human
race approaches perfection.

In the following pages I propose to study the general
question. To give this study greater definiteness and
vividness, however, I shall devote the main part of my
work to the search for an answer to the primary question
of fact, as to whether or not the Kingdom of God is
growing. Before it is possible to know whether religion
has any real relation to civilisation two steps must be
taken ; we must first know what the nature of true
religion is ; we must have clear definitions. And,

secondly, we must know the actual facts. We need to ask whether, as a matter of fact, religion and civilisation are found to be growing together, and whether the type of civilisation accompanying the most highly developed religion (Christianity) is in any way superior in kind or degree to that accompanying the other religions. We need further to inquire whether, as a matter of fact, the qualities of character conferred on those who become Christians add to or detract from the ability of the nations of which they are members to compete success-fully in the struggle for supremacy with those nations in which Christianity has a slight hold.

Not until answers to these questions have been secured from the field of actual life, shall we be able to take up with any degree of thoroughness the theoretical and scientific aspects of the problem ; for facts must determine theories. Having gained a real knowledge of the facts, we may then ask with profit why religion and civilisation have such an intimate connection, and how the religious factors act in determining the development of man and civilisation. For the present, therefore, we shall put aside all questions as to the theory, and shall strive to confine ourselves to the practical one of fact. We shall study the primary and fundamental question, as to whether or not true religion, in other words, the Kingdom of God, is growing. In the present chapter we shall consider a few preliminary matters ; we shall also strive to make clear what we mean by the leading terms. The relations of the Church and of religion to Christianity and to the Kingdom of God will be dwelt on in their appropriate places.

1. *The problem.*—There are many who think that the world is growing worse, and not better. Many

assert that Christianity is rapidly declining; that not only is the influence of Christ's teaching growing less outside of the organised Church, but that even within it the Christ-spirit is yearly losing its hold on individual lives. They say that love of wealth and fame and power has taken hold of Christians; that the Church no longer exists for Christ's sake, for the purpose of spreading the Christian faith, but rather for the purpose of giving its members social position and official rank; that its efforts at propagation are not prompted by love to God and man, with the sole aim of making men sons of God, but, arising from love of sect, the aim is to assert and enforce man-invented dogmas, creeds, rituals, and policies; that, therefore, missions are essentially a failure; that as a rule even pastors and evangelists have entered on their sacred work from sordid motives, and are blind leaders of the blind. Outside of the Church the wicked seem triumphant; by their very wickedness the wicked flourish and grow rich. Seldom does punishment overtake them. A true view of the world, say the critics, but shows that it is growing worse and worse.

Sweeping assertions like these are made, not only by non-Christians, but even by many who claim to be Christians. It becomes, therefore, important to ask whether these statements are true. If true, then the religion of Christ is a failure; some new power must be sought to save the world from the impending ruin toward which it is surely and rapidly descending. If they are false, then the truth should be made clearly known, for error is always a most powerful obstacle to the realisation of the blessedness and prosperity which naturally follows the reign of truth. The first and fundamental problem, then, for which we seek a clear, convincing answer is, ' Is, or is not, the Kingdom of God on earth growing ? '

2. *The method.*—We naturally seek the answer of our question along four distinct lines of inquiry, namely—(1) Growth in numbers, (2) growth in understanding, (3) growth in practice, and (4) growth in influence.   In the consideration of these various topics, we must adopt the comparative method.   The growth both of society and of the Church is a matter of centuries, and only a comparison of their past and present conditions can afford us a proper estimate of the actual tendencies and directions of development. It is likewise necessary to compare, not only the different ages, but also the different countries ; thus alone can the effects of different systems of religious thought, because resulting in the different degrees and kinds of civilisation, be properly estimated.   We shall compare, not only Christian with pagan nations, but also the various Christian nations one with another.

3. *The standpoint.*—After the most careful study of all the facts and statistics that have been accessible, the conviction of the author has become firm and clear, that both the world and the Church are growing better from generation to generation.   He would by no means assert, as it is not his intention to attempt to prove, the perfection of either the Church or the world.   But he most firmly believes that there has been steady and real growth of the Kingdom of God on earth, and that the will of God is being more fully carried out by this than by any previous generation.

4. *The purpose.*—In the following chapters (II.–VIII.) I wish to present some of the outstanding facts which

abundantly prove that the Kingdom of God *is* growing, and that it is conferring inestimable blessings on all its members, and even on those who, though not members of the Kingdom, are more or less closely associated with those who are. I do not, however, have the presumption to suppose that I can, in so brief a treatment as this must be, convince carping critics. My only desire is to satisfy those who are in doubt, and who yet wish to know the facts. To do this is important; for if the truth is as we suppose it to be, the sooner it is clearly shown how hasty and ill-formed many criticisms are, the sooner will the truth reign triumphant. I do not propose to defend the truth. I only wish to set forth the facts, which have been patiently gathered from many sources.

5. *The sources.*—The authorities on which I have relied are perhaps sufficiently indicated in the footnotes. For convenience, however, it may not be amiss to give here a list of the more important ones, which have been more or less consulted.

1. Dorchester's *Problem of Religious Progress* (revised edition, 1895).
2. Schauffler's Charts on *The Growth of Christianity during Nineteen Centuries.*
3. Dr. Josiah Strong's *The New Era.*
4. Dr. A. N. Johnston's *A Century of Christian Progress.*
5. American Church History Series, vol. i., *The Religious Forces of the United States,* by Dr. H. K. Carroll.
6. United States Educational Census, 1890–91.
7. The Congregationalist's *Handbook of Forward Movements.*

8. The Hibbert Lectures for 1888, by Dr. Hatch, on *The Influence of Greek Ideas and Usages upon the Christian Church*.
9. *The Place of Christ in Modern Theology*, by Dr. Fairbairn.
10. *The Incarnation of the Son of God*, by Dr. Chas. Gore.
11. *The Statesman's Year - Book* and *Whitaker's Almanack*.
12. Census of England and Wales in 1851, 'Religious Worship.'
13. Official Year-Books of the Church of England.
14. Congregational Year-Books.
15. Baptist Handbooks.
16. 'Religion in London in 1865,' from the *British Quarterly Review*.
17. *The Sunday-School Army*, by F. J. Hartley (1889).
18. The Religious Census of London, 1886.
19. *The Conflict of Christianity*, by Uhlhorn.
20. *The Social Results of Christianity*, by Schmidt.
21. Macaulay's *History of England*.
22. Lecky's *History of Rationalism*.
23. Lecky's *England in the Eighteenth Century*.
24. Lecky's *History of European Morals*.
25. *The Divine Origin of Christianity*, by R. S. Storrs.
26. *Gesta Christi*, by C. Loring Brace.

6. *Definitions.* — Much confusion of thought and many fallacies of argument with reference to the religious condition of Christendom are caused by the failure to distinguish between the various meanings of the three important words, 'Christianity,' 'Church,' and 'Religion.' It is needful, therefore, that the various ways in which

these terms are used shall be clearly defined at the very beginning of this study of the question as to the growth of genuine religion.

Webster loosely defines Christianity as 'the religion of Christians, the system of doctrines and precepts taught by Christ.' In this definition there are two distinct things — (1) 'The religion of Christians' must include, not only a system of belief, but also a Church organisation, a ritual, and many customs. Yet these differ greatly in the different lands and in different sects. (2) On the other hand, 'The system of doctrines and precepts taught by Christ,' at least as given in the New Testament, does not include the ritual or the Church organisation. Furthermore, each branch and sect of Christian believers maintains some distinctive interpretation of the teaching of Christ; just exactly what Christ's teaching originally was, is a matter still in dispute. For the purpose of argument, therefore, Webster's definition is insufficient.

The word 'Christianity' is used sometimes with a view to doctrine, sometimes to ritual, and sometimes to organisation. Doctrinally, 'Christianity' is often used to mean—

(*a*) The pure, simple, original teaching of Jesus.

(*b*) The apostles' understanding and teaching of Christ's teaching.

(*c*) The general doctrine contained in the Old and New Testaments, viewed as a self-consistent whole.

(*d*) The interpretation and understanding attained by any subsequent age or sect. In this sense it may be said that Roman Catholic Christianity differs from the Greek. Nineteenth century Christianity differs from that of the eighteenth in important respects. The

Christianity of each age differs more or less from that of every other.

(*e*) Those doctrines believed in common by all Christians of all ages, all lands, and all sects.

'Christianity' is also often used to mean—

(*f*) The religious practices and customs of the believers. These of course also vary in the different ages, lands, and sects.

(*g*) The collective body of all those who claim to be followers of Christ, of whatever branch, denomination, or sect.

It must be evident that with so many and such different usages, confusion may easily arise. Statements about Christianity in one of the above senses may not be true of Christianity taken in another sense. It is often said, for instance, that 'Christianity' is the product of evolution. If by this is meant that the religious beliefs and practices of modern Christianity are the product of these nineteen centuries of development, the statement is self-evident, even a platitude. But if it means that the teachings of Jesus were the product of evolution, as distinct from being in any sense a revelation ; that they grew by the natural operation of Christ's mind on previously existing beliefs and practices with which He was acquainted—then the statement is of very doubtful truth, one which many dispute. Dr. Lyman Abbott's famous Lowell Lectures on *The Evolution of Christianity* are seriously defective just at this point ; he fails to define in what sense he means 'Christianity' to be understood : even in the body of his work he is often ambiguous.

The word 'Church,' also, is used in various senses. It may mean—

(*a*) A building set apart for Christian worship.

(*b*) A local body of Christian believers formally organised into a society with a common place of worship.

(*c*) A collective organised body of Christians observing the same rites and ceremonies, and obedient to the same ecclesiastical authority ; such as the Roman Catholic Church, the Presbyterian Church.

'Church' is also used to mean—

(*d*) The whole number of true believers, of the redeemed, both those on earth and those in heaven, men or angels, whether members of the visible organised Church or not. This is the Church invisible. This Church invisible has two parts—that in heaven, or the Church triumphant, and that on earth, or the Church militant.

(*e*) The Church militant. This is composed of all true believers on earth, whether members or not of any of the many general or local churches. Here, too, accurate usage is manifestly important. For example, it is often asserted that 'the Church is losing ground.' If by 'Church' is meant some particular Church (see (*a*) (*b*) or (*c*) above), or some system or ceremonial or custom, the proposition is a platitude. There are multitudes of church members who rejoice that 'Churchism' is dying out. But if the proposition means that the number of church members, or the power and influence of Christian thought, or the Christ-spirit and the Christian life, is decreasing in the world, a little careful study will, I believe, prove this to be an error.

The word 'Religion,' too, has been defined in many different ways. Like 'Christianity,' sometimes it refers to systems of thought, of doctrine, of philosophy, and sometimes to ceremonials, rituals, customs. Different thinkers have defined religion in different ways. In the words of Dr. Fairbairn, we define religion as the 'thought of a person conceiving the cause, or order, or highest law under which he stands, and the way in which he feels and acts toward him or it.'[1] Religion is thus the intellectual, spiritual, and moral attitude of a man toward the universe ; it includes his conceptions of the origin and destiny of himself, as well as of the world, and shows itself in his feelings, as manifested in his moral, social, and ceremonial life. Religion, therefore, is not only or chiefly ceremonial or church oganisation : these are only some of the manifestations of religion, nor are they essential manifestations. Religion is the regulation of life through the dominant ideas. If the dominant idea is of many conflicting, limited, immoral gods, then the religion is a low polytheism, with fetich worship and immoral service. If the dominant idea is of one, omniscient, omnipotent, all-holy, all-righteous, all-just, all-loving God, who is best known as Father, then the religion is correspondingly high, and becomes the 'application to all things, and all events, of the great spiritual, moral, ethical, rational elements contained in that idea.' Accepting this as a correct definition, it follows that religion creates the organic churches and ceremonials in order to satisfy the spiritual longings and needs of the human soul. It shows itself not only in temples and priests, ministers and church buildings, but also in the commercial and social laws and customs of communities and nations. In the study, therefore, of religion we need to observe, not only the external ceremonies

[1] *Religion in History and Modern Life*, p. 86. Cf. the whole chapter, pp. 65-93.

and the formulated doctrines, but also, as being much more important, the moral standards of the nations, whether explicit or implicit, together with the actual moral and social life of the common people. Viewed in this broad way, the best estimate of the development of a people is obtained by a study of its religion ; for it is the religion that has the greatest influence on the development of the people, and that also reveals the degree of that development.

In the following pages, it is hoped that these pivotal words have been so used as to make their meaning clear in each case. By 'the growth of the Kingdom' I do not mean the growth or development of the teachings of Jesus, but (1) the growing number of those who claim, whether truly or not, to believe those teachings ; (2) the increasing understanding of the contents of those teachings by those who claim to believe them ; (3) the increasing obedience to the spirit taught by Christ ; and (4) the increasing influence of those teachings and that spirit, even on those who make no claim to believe or follow them.

In our study of religious growth we shall confine our attention chiefly to its manifestation in Christian lands, and especially in Protestant lands, for it will be readily granted by all that religion has here risen to its highest forms and purest type, with the least admixture of superstition. It is in these favoured lands that personal purity, holiness, gentleness, and love have been most fully identified with religion, and considered essential elements of true worship. Did the time and space allow, it would be exceedingly profitable to make a careful examination of the doctrines and practices of the non-Christian religions, and of the character and degree of the civilisations which accompany them. But such an elaborate study, however profitable, is manifestly impossible in such a small work as this. It is, moreover, unnecessary in the attainment of our main purpose, which is to show that in the Christian Church the Kingdom of God is actually growing.

CHAPTER II

THE NUMERICAL GROWTH OF CHRISTIAN ADHERENTS AND OF THE CHRISTIAN NATIONS

'At the present time no intelligent person, standing in the light of the last four centuries, and beholding the great religious movements of this age, can doubt that Christianity is advancing. Every year it is robing itself with new effulgence, and pouring its blessed illumination upon new millions of earth's population.'[1]

'The Christian religion possessed from the outset two characteristics destined to render it an evolutionary force of the first magnitude. The first was the extraordinary strength of the ultra-rational sanction which it provided. . . . The second was the nature of the ethical system associated with it, which, as we shall see, was at a later stage, in suitable conditions, calculated to raise the peoples under its influence to the highest state of social efficiency ever attained, and to equip them with the most exceptional advantages in the struggle for existence with other peoples.'[2]

---

[1] Dorchester's *Problem of Religious Progress*, p. 510.
[2] *Social Evolution*, by Benjamin Kidd, p. 140.

CHAPTER II

CHRIST announced the purpose of His life and teachings in a double form — the establishment of the Kingdom of Heaven, and the saving of the lost. Though different in form, these statements are identical in fact. The prime and only condition of becoming members of the Kingdom is salvation from sin. No sinful heart, however correct an exterior it may carry, can enter the Kingdom. The Kingdom of Heaven consists in a converted heart, a heart in which love to God and man is the supreme law. This shows itself in moral living, in self-sacrifice, in the embodiment of the Christ-life. The Kingdom of God, therefore, is no mere external organisation with ceremonial and officials. It is not the visible Church. This has arisen from the needs of human nature, to give expression and efficacy and expansion and permanence to the life bestowed by Christ. Those who receive that life, spontaneously, as well as in obedience to Christ's command, associate for mutual strength and culture; for the spreading of the life; for the preservation of its purity by mutual watchfulness, by the condemnation of error, and by excluding from the Church those who profess to be Christ's, but who do not have His spirit. This is the origin of the organised, the visible churches. It is easy to confuse things which differ, and to think of the temporal organism as the

2

Kingdom of God. It was especially easy in the early centuries. But no nineteenth-century Christian should make this mistake.

In trying to measure, however, the growth of the Kingdom of God on earth, we are compelled by the nature of the case to measure in various ways the growth of the Church and of the Christian countries. There is no other method open to us. Let it therefore be clearly understood that, though I give national and church statistics, I do not for a moment suppose that all members of so-called Christian nations, or even of churches, are necessarily real Christians; I well know that there are many members of the churches who are not members of the Kingdom of Heaven. But, after all, it is the Church that is trying more or less faithfully to realise the Kingdom ; it is the Church, defective though it is, that is trying, oftentimes with mistaken methods, to increase the power and extend the rule of the King of Righteousness. The best measure, therefore, of the growth and the power of the teachings of that King, in other words, of Christ, is the growth and the power of the churches, and of the nations most thoroughly Christianised.

As we can best estimate both the nature and the amount of the physical forces by observing their effect in organising, and on organised matter; as we can likewise best estimate the nature and the amount of the force of vegetable or animal life by observing the plant and animal organisms which they produce and in which they manifest themselves ; so we can best estimate the nature and the amount of the forces of Christianity, by observing the organised forms which it has produced, namely, the Christian churches, and also by observing the effects of the Christian beliefs on the moral and religious life of the nations in which they have worked out a part of their legitimate fruits.

The science of statistics, like most sciences, is a modern one. Statistics, therefore, of the early centuries are only approximate estimates, yet they are not random guesses. The historians of Europe have repeatedly gone over the material, and have arrived at considerable agreement. In modern times and in civilised countries there has arisen a statistical science. Modern statistics of Christian lands are, therefore, approximately exact. When we consider how few there are of the millions of contemporaneous men and events of which a single individual has personal knowledge, it becomes manifest that if one wishes to know, with some degree of accuracy, the movements of the times, whether commercial, social, or moral, a careful study of the statistics on the respective subjects is all-important. Although statistics are proverbially dull, it is nevertheless important to know what they teach us.

In taking the testimony of statistics, I make three main divisions. We shall consider, first, the statistics of the Ecumenical Church and of Christian nations; then, confining our attention to two nations, we shall study separately the growth of Christianity in England and Wales, and in the United States. We shall first take a broad look in this general chapter, including statistics, not only as to the growing number of professed Christians, but also as to the growth of populations, of political power, of commerce, of wealth, of education, etc.; for all these have a more or less immediate relation to religion. We shall compare nation with nation, in order to study the effect of the different religions, and also of the different branches of Christianity. We shall conclude our statistical study with a brief summary of the facts we have learned; but we shall reserve our remarks on their significance for the last chapter, where, combining these statistical facts with those of a more general nature, to be presented in the intervening chapters, we may take a broad and comprehensive review and survey of the whole. I would here call particular attention to the remark, that I make no claim to have compiled error-less statistics—such statistics are not in existence. It is not asserted that the statistics in this and subsequent chapters are absolutely correct and exact; but I do believe them to be substantially so, and fully to support the argument that is built upon them.

I. The Growth of Nominal Adherents of Christianity throughout the World, from its Beginning to the Present Time.

The growth of the number of Christian believers during the centuries has been a study frequently made by statisticians. The table on p. 21 represents the results that are generally accepted.[1]

1. The accompanying statistical table and chart (No. I.) indicate in a general way the numerical growth of Christianity. The figures for the early centuries are of course only estimates. This table does not give the number of professed Christians, of church members, but only the number of those who may be fairly said to have accepted the Christian standards of moral life,

[1] *The Problem of Religious Progress*, pp. 649, 650.

whether attempting and professing to live up to them
or not.   In this section the word 'Christianity' is used
in its broadest, loosest sense.

Century.	Number.	Century.	Number.
End of 1st century	5 millions	End of 15th century	100 millions
,, 2nd ,,	2 ,,	,, 16th ,,	125 ,,
,, 3rd ,,	5 ,,	,, 17th ,,	155 ,,
,, 4th ,,	10 ,,	,, 18th ,,	200 ,,
,, 8th ,,	30 ,,	1880 . . .	410 ,,
,, 9th ,,	40 ,,	1890 . . .	493 ,,
,, 10th ,,	50 ,,	1896 . . .	500 ,,

2. During the first three centuries Christian believers
suffered many bloody persecutions.   The growth of the
Church was, therefore, comparatively slow.   In 313 the
Roman Emperor, Constantine the Great, proclaimed
religious freedom, having himself accepted the Christian
faith, though it is clear that he was a very imperfect
Christian.   From that time persecutions ceased, and
Christianity became increasingly popular.   It is agreed
by the best statisticians that all the adherents of Christianity (European, Asiatic, and African) did not exceed
fifty millions by the end of the tenth century; but that

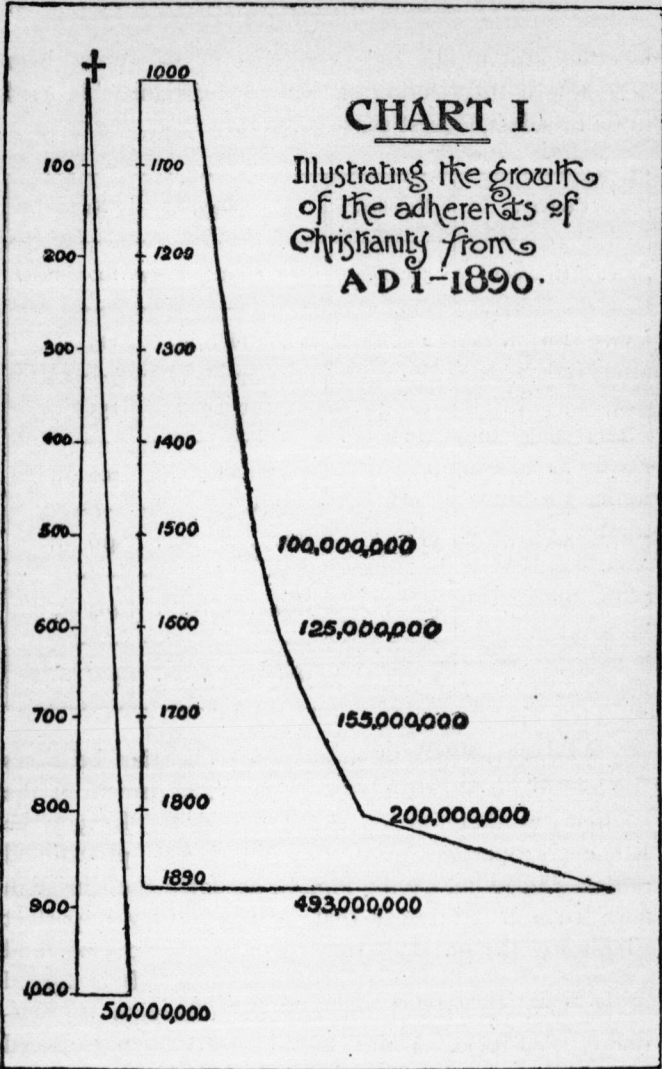

CHART I.

Illustrating the Growth
of the adherents of
Christianity from
A D 1-1890.

1000
1100
1200
1300
1400
1500   100,000,000
1600   125,000,000
1700   155,000,000
1800   200,000,000
1890   493,000,000

100
200
300
400
500
600
700
800
900
1000

50,000,000

22

they doubled in the next five hundred years. From 1500 and onward the growth has been more rapid. During the two hundred years between 1500 and 1700, Christianity added more to its numbers than during the first thousand years. And during the hundred years from 1700 to 1800 it gained nearly as many as during the first thousand years. Since the beginning of the present century, Christianity has much more than doubled; in other words, Christianity has gained nearly three times as many adherents during the past ninety years as it did during the first fifteen hundred years.

The thing most noticeable in this chart is the constantly increasing rate of growth. Never was Christianity growing so rapidly in numbers as now. The number of those who to-day may properly be called Christian, that is to say, the number of those who are living under Christian standards and ideals of moral life and conduct, whether professedly followers of Christ or not, is about 492,865,000.[1]

II. THE GROWTH OF THE POPULATION OF THE WORLD, SHOWING THE RELIGION OF THE GOVERNING RACES.

The population of the world is estimated to have increased from 954,000,000 in 1786 to 1,460,000,000 in 1886. The following table and chart (No. II.) indicate the growth of the populations governed by the various religions of the world:[2]—

[1] Dorchester's *Problem of Religious Progress*, p. 653.
[2] *A Century of Christian Progress*, by James Johnston, chap. iii. The figures for 1890 are derived by compilation from *The Statesman's Year Book* for 1894, and the *Problem of Religious Progress*, p. 749.

		1786. Millions.	1886. Millions.	1890. Millions.
Populations governed by Christians	Protestant . Roman Catholic Greek	157 154 }341 30	468 217 }805 120	520 243 }891 128
By Non-Christians	Polytheist . Confucian . Mohammedan .	245 279 }613 89	130 436 }655 89	}555 }608 53
		954	1460	1499

From this it appears that, out of a total estimated population in the world in 1786 of 954,000,000, about 36 per cent. (*i.e.* 341,000,000) were governed by Christian races, and 64 per cent. (*i.e.* 613,000,000) by non-Christian races; while, at the end of a century, about 55 per cent. (*i.e.* 805,000,000) were governed by Christian races, and only about 45 per cent. (*i.e.* 655,000,000) by non-Christian races. The increase during 104 years of those governed by Christian races is 550,000,000, while the populations governed by non-Christian races have suffered an actual loss of 5,000,000. This is partly, though not wholly, due to the fact that the Christian races have overthrown the governments of some non-Christian peoples and have established their own in their places. The prodigious natural growth of the Christian nations during the past two centuries also has much to do with these astonishing figures. A comparison of this table with the foregoing shows that though there are at present 493,000,000 of nominal Christians, being about one-third of the world's population, yet they govern 891,000,000 of people, *i.e.* about two-thirds of the world. This is a significant fact. It

CHART. II

Illustrating the growth of populations under
the various governments, classified by their religion,
for the one hundred years between 1786 · 1886

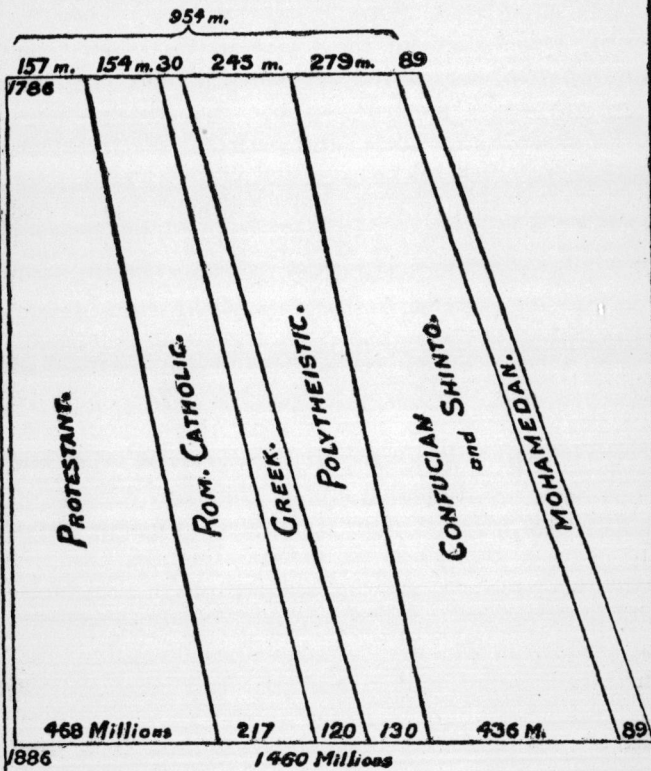

954 m.

157 m.   154 m. 30   245 m.   279 m.   89

1786

PROTESTANT.

ROM. CATHOLIC.

GREEK.

POLYTHEISTIC.

CONFUCIAN and SHINTO.

MOHAMEDAN.

468 Millions   217   120   130   436 M.   89

1886   1460 Millions

25

shows that, however we may explain the cause, those races which have adopted Christianity either had or have come to have the talent of government. Were we to examine not only the statistics, but also the methods of government, and the condition of the peoples under those governments, the vast superiority of the governments of the Christian to those of the non-Christian races would become still more manifest. I do not for a moment suppose that the Christian governments or officials are perfect. Far from it. There is still great wickedness and crime carried on by so-called Christian officials and Christian governments. But for all that, by comparison, the governments of Christian races far exceed those of non-Christian races in ideals, in impartiality, in completeness, and in regularity of execution.

This table does not include the recent partition of Africa among the European nations. Were it to be brought down to the present year, these 130,000,000 of Polytheists would have to be divided between the Protestant and Roman Catholic countries, leaving no polytheistic self-governing country of any importance anywhere on the face of the globe.

In this table and chart Buddhism receives no recognition, for it is the dominant religion of no self-governing people. There are no Buddhists in India. Though there are many Buddhist believers in China and Japan, its teachings are not the inspiring source of the civilisation of these nations. The foundation of the civilisation of China is Confucianism; and of that of Japan a combination of Shinto and Confucianism. Siam most nearly approaches being an independent Buddhist country, but its real dependence on France and England, which countries actually govern large parts of its territory, leaving an estimated population of barely 5,000,000, renders it hardly worthy of being counted as a truly independent Buddhist country.

That none may fall into error, I call special attention to the apparent discrepancy between these statistics and those presented in the first table. In that, the number of Christian adherents is given as having been 200,000,000 in 1800, whereas, in this table, the number of those *under Christian governments* in 1786 is given as 341,000,000. The difference is due to the different methods of counting; the former table has reference only to those who may be supposed to have Christian ideals; the latter figure includes about 150,000,000 pagans who, in 1786, are estimated to have been under Christian governments.

III. The Area of the World, showing the Religion of the Governing Race, for the Two Periods, 1600 and 1893.

In few ways can the marvellous growth of the political power of Christendom be more conspicuously shown than by comparing the geographical areas under Christian and non-Christian rule. The following table and chart (No. III.) exhibit the change which has taken place in the past three hundred years. According to the *Statesman's Year-Book* for 1894, the area under the rule of the various governments of the earth amounts to about 49,100,000 square miles. Of this, about 17,417,900 square miles are under the rule of Protestant nations; 14,147,100 are under Roman Catholic rule; 8,752,700 are under the rule of nations adhering to the Greek

Church, while only 8,782,800 square miles are under the rule of non-Christian nations. The immense growth becomes manifest when the figures for 1600 are placed side by side with those for 1893.

	1600	1893	Per cent. in 1893
Protestant	727,200 sq. miles	17,417,900 sq. miles	36
Roman Catholic	799,700 ,,	14,147,100 ,,	28
Greek	1,954,000 ,,	8,752,700 ,,	18
Christian	3,480,900 ,,	40,317,700 ,,	82
Non-Christian	45,619,100 ,,	8,782,300 ,,	18

In other words, the Christian powers have increased the territory under their rule from about 7 per cent. of the surface of the world in 1600 to 82 per cent. in 1893, while the non-Christian powers have receded from about 93 to about 18 per cent. during the same period. At present the Protestant nations alone rule about twice as much territory as all the non-Christian nations combined. These facts will be made more graphic by the accompanying chart. Their significance we shall consider in a later chapter.

CHART. III.

Illustrating the comparative area
governed by the different religions.

1600   TOTAL INHABITED AREA.   49,100,000 Sq. m.

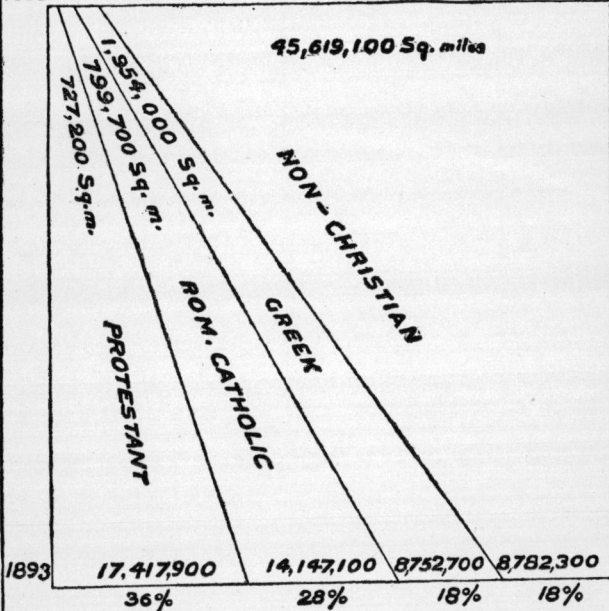

45,619,100 Sq. miles

1,954,000 Sq. m.

799,700 Sq. m.

727,200 Sq. m.

NON-CHRISTIAN

GREEK

ROM. CATHOLIC

PROTESTANT

1893	17,417,900	14,147,100	8,752,700	8,782,300
	36%	28%	18%	18%

IV. THE GROWTH OF POPULATIONS UNDER THE ROMAN CATHOLIC, GREEK, AND PROTESTANT GOVERNMENTS.[1]

From the lack of accurate statistics of the non-Christian nations it is impossible to compare their growth, century by century, with that of the Christian nations. We therefore confine our attention in this section to the growth of the population under the rule of the three great branches of Christendom. Their growth (in millions) is given in the following table:—

	Roman Catholic.	Greek.	Protestant.	Total.
1500	80 millions	20 millions	0 millions	100 millions
1700	90 ,,	33 ,,	32 ,,	155 ,,
1830	134 ,,	60 ,,	193 ,,	387 ,,
1880	192 ,,	110 ,,	445 ,,	747 ,,
1891	242 ,,	128 ,,	520 ,,	890 ,,

The accompanying chart (No. IV.) sets forth the great growth in the numbers of those subject to the rule of Christian governments. The most striking feature is the rapid rise of the Protestant powers during the present century.

[1] The final figures are compiled from the *Statesman's Year Book* for 1894. The earlier figures are taken from Schauffler's *Growth of Christianity*.

CHART. IV.

Growth of Population under Christian Gov'ts

A indicates Growth of Prot. Countries
B   "   "   "   - Rom. Cath. -
C   "   "   "   - Greek -

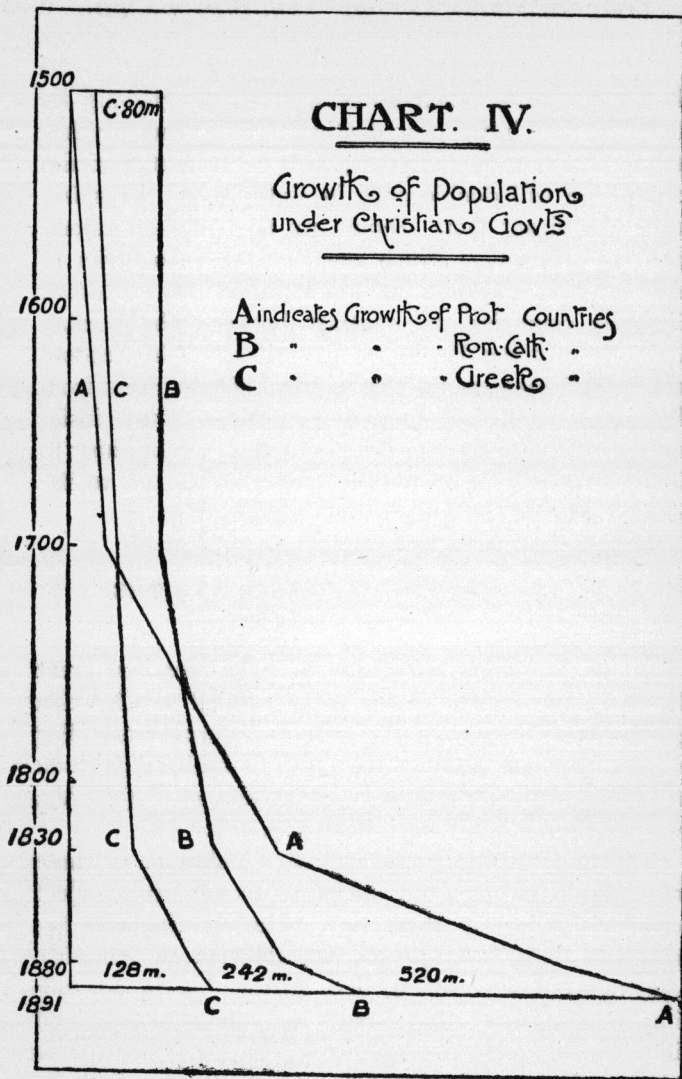

C·80m

A C B

C   B   A

128 m.   242 m.   520 m.

C   B   A

1500
1600
1700
1800
1830
1880
1891

According to a most careful study of statistics, the Roman Catholic countries of Europe are growing by the surplus of births over deaths at a rate whereby they will double once in 138 years, while Protestant countries of Europe will double once in sixty years. This is a most significant fact. Should we take into consideration the advantage which the Protestant countries of America are enjoying by immigration from Roman Catholic countries, the contrast between the Roman Catholic and the Protestant countries of Christendom will be still greater; for the number of emigrants from Protestant to Roman Catholic countries is quite insignificant. Emigrants do not go in any large number to South America or to Mexico, but they do go to the United States and to Canada.

V. The Growth of France and the British Isles.

In the preceding paragraph we have seen how great has been the growth of the peoples ruled by Christian governments, especially Protestant governments. For a more accurate study of the effect of national faith on national growth, the table on p. 33, and chart (No. V.), will give some help (see Johnston, p. 47):—

The figures refer to the actual populations of these countries, and do not include colonies or subject countries. During these two centuries, England has sent out large and prosperous colonies to America, Australia, New Zealand, and Africa. It is not unimportant to note that France was ahead of England in colonising North America. Nor is it amiss to observe in general, that colonies of Roman Catholic

countries have not been conspicuously successful, though
many have been attempted.

Date.	France.	Great Britain.
1700	19 millions	8 millions
1789	26 ,,	12 ,,
1815	29 ,,	19 ,,
1880	37 ,,	35 ,,
1891	38 ,,	38 ,,

We have compared France and England, as countries
typical of the Roman Catholic and Protestant forms of
Christianity. In truth, however, France is not a typical
Roman Catholic country; Spain or Italy would be a
better example. For France has long been more or
less in open revolt against Rome and the pope. The
Jesuits have long been excluded from the country.
Infidelity and Rationalism have found their home in
France. Though the large majority of its people are
nominally members of the Roman Catholic Church, the
characteristic features of Catholicism have had less
sway in France than in almost any other Roman
Catholic country, and the blighting influence of that
faith on civilisation is therefore less visible. Yet the
great contrast between England and France is remarkable. It is no accident, but is the result of some

3

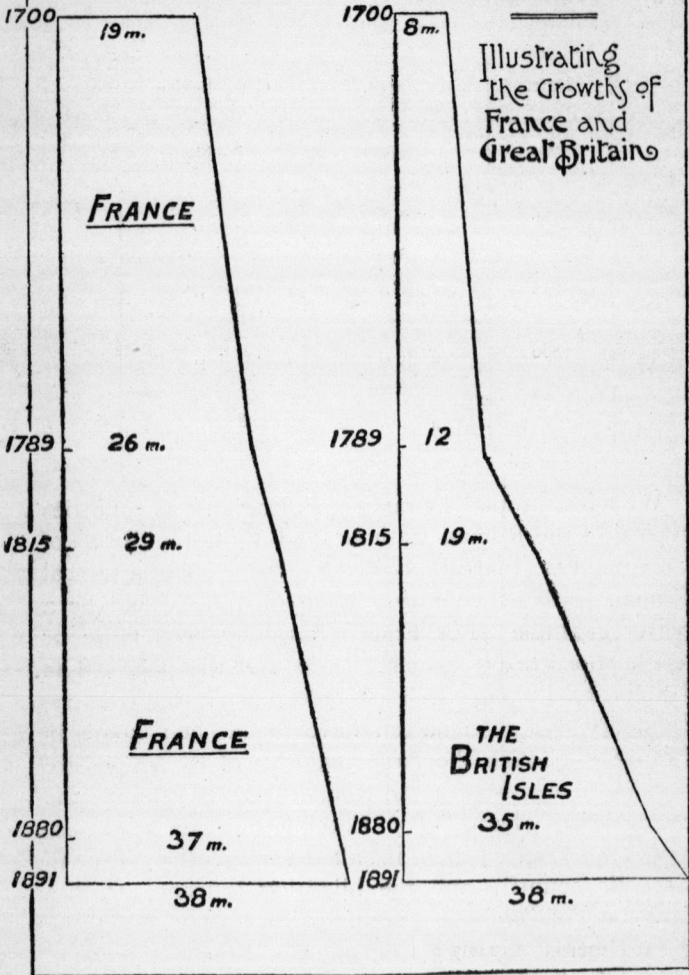

CHART. V

Illustrating the Growths of France and Great Britain

1700   19 m.

FRANCE

1789   26 m.

1815   29 m.

FRANCE

1880   37 m.

1891   38 m.

1700   8 m.

1789   12

1815   19 m.

THE BRITISH ISLES

1880   35 m.

1891   38 m.

profound cause. More typical of Roman Catholic and
Protestant civilisations are Spain and England. When
the 'Invincible Armada' threatened to overthrow Protestant England, she numbered only about 4,000,000
subjects, whereas the former country could boast of
43,000,000. Now she has only 17,000,000, while
England has 38,000,000. What profound causes have
produced this change?

VI. THE GROWTH OF EUROPEAN LANGUAGES.

Another way of learning the present relative size and
recent growth of the various nations is by a comparison
of the numbers of those using the various languages
throughout the world. The *New Era* (p. 62) is my
authority for the following table:—

Date.	French.	Russian.	German.	Spanish.	English.
	(1)	(2)	(3)	(4)	(5)
1800	31 millions	30 millions	30 millions	26 millions	20 millions
1890	51 ,,	75 ,,	75 ,,	42 ,,	111 ,, [1]
	(4)	(3)	(2)	(5)	(1)

From this (see Chart No. VI.) it appears, that while
French was used by the largest number of people
ninety years ago, it is now fourth on the list, and that

[1] This figure is certainly an under-estimate. Now, in 1897, there are
not far from 130,000,000 of English-speaking peoples.

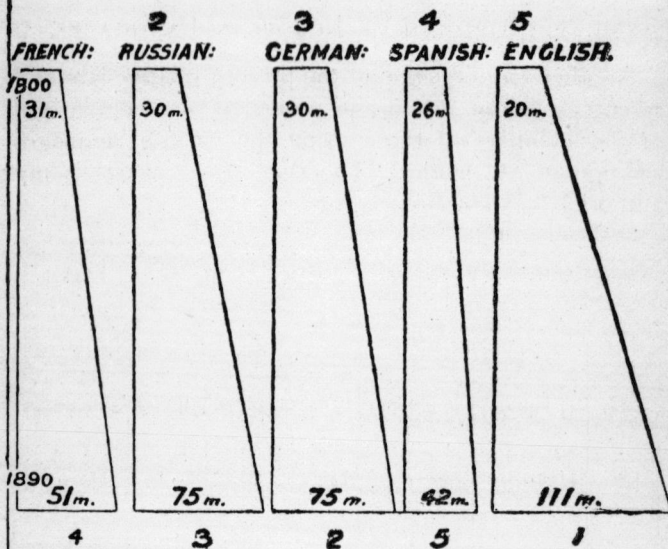

CHART. VI

Illustrating the growth of the number of those using the European languages between 1800 and 1890

	2	3	4	5
FRENCH:	RUSSIAN:	GERMAN:	SPANISH:	ENGLISH.
1800 31m.	30m.	30m.	26m.	20m.
1890 51m.	75m.	75m.	42m.	111m.
4	3	2	5	1

86

English, which was used by the smallest number of people at that same time, is now used by the largest number. There is no other spoken language on the face of the globe which is used by so many and so widely-scattered people as is English, not even Chinese. We should also notice the remarkable fact that the two leading Protestant languages of Europe, English and German, increased in ninety years from 50,000,000 to 186,000,000; whereas the two leading Roman Catholic languages, French and Spanish, increased from 51,000,000 to only 93,000,000.

Not only as a matter of fact is English the dominant language of the world, but it is fitted to be so. The original Anglo-Saxon dialect has been enriched from a great variety of sources—Latin and Greek, Scandinavian and Celtic, Norman French and Latin French, have all contributed important elements ; and finally, in consequence of the spread of English exploration, commerce, conquest, and colonisation, it has come into contact with, and received more or less contribution from, nearly all the great languages of the world. English is to-day 'the most complete language spoken by man.' The dominance of the English and German languages is a fact of momentous interest; for the language and literature of these two Protestant nations are steeped in Christian, in Protestant thought. These two languages have been powerfully influenced by the translations of the Bible into the vernacular of the common people. It is impossible to become familiar with the language and literature of either country without learning much of Christianity and even of the Bible. And this is peculiarly true of English. Yet this is the very language which is spreading over the world, the one which, above all others, bids fair to become the world-language. Several millions of Hindus and Africans, and tens of thousands of Chinese, Japanese, and Siamese, have come to know and speak this language with considerable ease. English is to-day the language of diplomacy. In the recent negotiations for peace between the Japanese and Chinese, the English language was chosen as the best medium of communication. I say these things, not to exult, but only to bring out the truth, the facts. Later, when we have the facts clearly in mind, I shall wish to draw attention to their meaning.

VII. THE FINANCIAL PROSPERITY OF GREEK, ROMAN CATHOLIC, AND PROTESTANT NATIONS.

The comparative truth of the religious beliefs of a man or of a nation cannot be graded by the amount of the wealth possessed. A holy man believing the actual truth does not therefore become wealthy ; nor does the wicked person of necessity become poor. It is the same with nations. Yet it may be affirmed that in the long-run there is a very close connection between national integrity and national prosperity. It needs no argument to prove that national integrity is made up of that of the individuals who compose the nation. In proportion as a nation possesses the truth by living it does it attain freedom and power and prosperity. Modern progress in material civilisation is due to the attainment of much new truth in the physical world. In a general way, it is also true that the attainment of this physical truth has only been in those lands where a considerable degree of both national and individual integrity has been secured, where truth has been loved for its own sake, and where liberty in its search and practice has been quite freely allowed ; in other words, in Christian lands. The connection between Christianity and national wealth, therefore, is not remote, but close.

That the Christian nations are wealthy and powerful is not an accident ; nor is it the result of chance that the non-Christian nations are wretchedly poor.

The Berlin Statistical Bureau estimated that in 1887 the steam-engines of the world were doing the work of a billion men—three times the working population of the world. But these engines are almost wholly in the possession of Christian nations. Because of the fact that (except Japan) no non-Christian nation collects any reliable statistics, to institute a comparison between Christian and non-Christian nations is impossible. Nor, indeed, is it necessary. The immense wealth of the Christian nations, when compared with that of the non-Christian nations, is evident to every observer. For our purpose, therefore, it will be sufficient if we compare the wealth of the countries belonging to the three great divisions of Christendom. The statistics of many of these countries are, however, far from complete. A satisfactory comparison is therefore impossible. Yet for our purpose a comparison of the leading Christian countries will be sufficient.

Mulhall's *Dictionary of Statistics* for 1892 gives what may be considered as nearly an authoritative statement of the wealth of the different nations as can be obtained. Classified according to their religions, we have the following tables :—

(*a*) THE WEALTH OF PROTESTANT COUNTRIES IN 1888.[1]

	Total Wealth.	Population.	Pounds per Inhab.
United States .	£12,824,000,000	62,500,000	£210
United Kingdom .	9,400,000,000	38,200,000	247
Germany . .	6,437,000,000	48,600,000	140
Holland . .	980,000,000	4,600,000	216
Norway . .	243,000,000	2,000,000	122
Sweden . .	637,000,000	4,800,000	125
Denmark .	404,000,000	2,100,000	230
	£30,925,000,000	162,800,000	£190

(*b*) THE WEALTH OF ROMAN CATHOLIC COUNTRIES.

	Total Wealth.	Population.	Pounds per Inhab.
France . .	£8,598,000,000	38,800,000	£224
Austria . .	3,855,000,000	40,100,000	99
Italy . . .	2,963,000,000	30,300,000	100
Spain . . .	2,516,000,000	17,600,000	148
Belgium . .	1,007,000,000	6,100,000	167
Portugal . .	408,000,000	4,700,000	87
	£19,347,000,000	137,600,000	£140

(*c*) THE WEALTH OF GREEK COUNTRIES.

	Total Wealth.	Population.	Pounds per Inhab.
Russia . .	£5,089,000,000	92,000,000	£55
Greece . .	300,000,000	2,200,000	162
Roumania . .	593,000,000	5,500,000	110
Bulgaria . .	205,000,000	3,100,000	70
Servia . .	217,000,000	2,000,000	108
	£6,404,000,000	10,4800,000	£61

[1] Compiled from Mulhall's *Dictionary of Statistics*, 1892, pp. 442, 598.

From these tables it appears that the Roman Catholic countries are more than twice, and the Protestant countries are more than three times as wealthy per individual as the countries holding the Greek type of Christianity.

I would call especial attention to the wealth of France; and would again remark that she is not a typical Roman Catholic country, having long since rejected the Roman Catholic ideal of the relations of the Church and State, of education, and of religious and political liberty. Spain and Italy are better representatives of the effect of Roman Catholic principles. France is, in not a few respects, a Protestant country, and has been reaping the benefits of Protestant principles.

The prosperity and wealth of a country may be also measured by the total import and export trade computed per individual. A careful compilation of the statistics given by Mulhall reveals the following facts :—

(a) THE TOTAL FOREIGN TRADE OF PROTESTANT COUNTRIES IN 1889.[1]

	Total Foreign Trade.	Pounds per Inhab.
United States . .	£320,000,000	£5.0
United Kingdom . .	740,000,000	19.5
Canada	42,000,000	5.9
Germany . . .	367,000,000	7.8
Holland . . .	199,000,000	45.0
Sweden	30,000,000	6.3
Denmark . . .	26,000,000	13.0
	£1,724,000,000	£10.4[2]

[1] Compiled from Mulhall's *Dictionary of Statistics*, 1892, pp. 128, 129.

[2] This figure is secured by dividing the total trade by the total population.

CHART. VII.

Illustrating the comparative wealth of Greek.
Roman Catholic, and Protestant Countries

TOTAL WEALTH

FIVE GREEK COUNTRIES
£ 6,404,000,000

SIX R.C. COUNTRIES
£19,347,000,000

WEALTH OF EIGHT PROT. COUNTRIES
£30,925,000,000

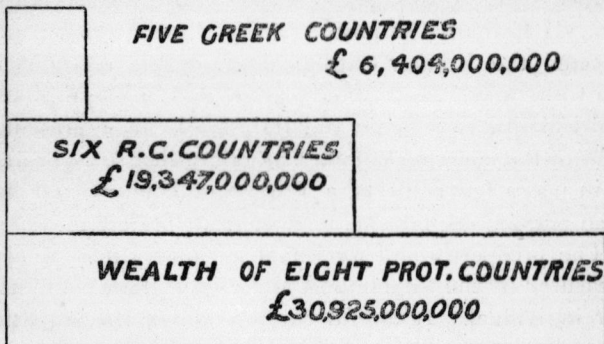

⅕ = $10,000,000,000,00

WEALTH PER INDIVIDUAL

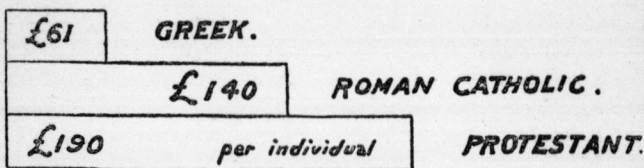

£61   GREEK.

£140   ROMAN CATHOLIC.

£190   per individual   PROTESTANT.

⅕ = $100

(*b*) THE TOTAL FOREIGN TRADE OF ROMAN CATHOLIC
COUNTRIES IN 1889.

	Total Exports and Imports.	Pounds per Inhab.
France	£311,000,000	£8.1
Austria	92,000,000	2.4
Italy	94,000,000	3.1
Spain	59,000,000	3.5
Belgium . . .	111,000,000	18.5
Portugal . . .	18,000,000	4.0
	£685,000,000	£5

(*c*) THE TOTAL FOREIGN TRADE OF GREEK COUNTRIES
IN 1889.[1]

Russia	£118,000,000	£1.3

The striking difference in the commercial activity
of the different groups of countries will become more
manifest by the accompanying chart (No. VIII).

It is in order again to call attention to the degree
in which France surpasses all other Roman Catholic
countries in the extent of her foreign trade. Were
she excluded from the Roman Catholic list, the remaining Roman Catholic countries, amounting to a population of about 91,000,000, would average only about
£108 per individual in wealth, and an average trade
of £3.8 per individual.

Too much must not be made of this argument from
wealth or commercial prosperity. It would be easy to
push it to absurd results. Temporary or local conditions
often have more to do with financial prosperity than re-

[1] The trade of the other Greek countries is too slight to be recorded
by Mulhall.

CHART. VIII.

Illustrating the comparative foreign trade of
Greek, Roman Catholic and Protestant Countries

THE TOTAL FOREIGN TRADE of,

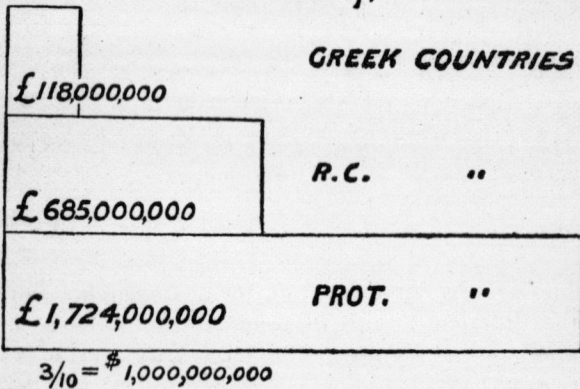

GREEK COUNTRIES

£118,000,000

R.C.   "

£685,000,000

PROT.   "

£1,724,000,000

3/10 = $1,000,000,000

TOTAL FOREIGN TRADE per INDIVIDUAL

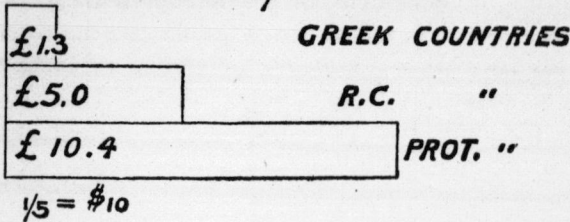

£1.3   GREEK COUNTRIES

£5.0   R.C.   "

£10.4   PROT. "

1/5 = $10

ligious or moral life. Yet the argument has a legitimate place and real force.

VIII. The Condition of Popular Education in the Civilised World.

The relation between popular education, national intelligence, and the religious life, is very close. The following figures have been taken from the Report of the United States Commissioner of Education, for the year 1890-91, vol. i. p. 369. They merit careful study.

(a) POPULAR EDUCATION IN PROTESTANT COUNTRIES.

	Population.	Pupils.	Per Cent.
United States	62,622,000	14,377,536	21.3
Canada	4,832,000	1,022,841	21.0
Germany	42,749,000	9,050,885	21.1
Switzerland	2,917,000	589,794	20.0
Great Britain	37,879,000	6,928,032	18.0
Netherlands	4,621,000	772,021	16.6
Norway and Sweden	6,803,000	920,720	13.5
Denmark	2,185,000	243,870	11.0
	164,608,000	33,905,699	20.6

(*b*) POPULAR EDUCATION IN ROMAN CATHOLIC
COUNTRIES.

	Population.	Pupils.	Per Cent.
France . .	38,343,000	6,492,217	17.0
Austria . .	23,895,000	3,176,147	13.3
Belgium . .	6,069,000	802,175	13.0
Hungary . .	17,463,000	2,187,692	12.5
Italy . . .	30,347,000	3,065,911	10.0
Spain . . .	17,550,000	1,609,800	9.3
Portugal . .	4,708,000	253,342	5.5
South America .	50,334,000	1,826,125	3.8
	188,709,000	19,413,539	10.3

(*c*) POPULAR EDUCATION IN GREEK COUNTRIES.

	Population.	Pupils.	Per Cent.
Greece . .	2,187,000	234,480	10.7
Servia . . .	2,161,000	75,533	3.5
Roumania . .	5,500,000	163,816	3.0
Russia . . .	97,506,000	2,467,454	2.6
	107,354,000	2,941,283	2.7

The accompanying charts (Nos. IX. and X.) render the foregoing facts still more impressive. These figures show how far ahead the Protestant countries are in the matter of popular education, and consequently of popular intelligence, and freedom from superstition. Of the Protestant populations, 20.6 per cent. are attending schools ; of the Roman Catholic populations, 10.3 per cent. are attending schools ; of the Greek populations, 2.7 per cent. are attending schools. Out of every hundred common school pupils in Christendom, 60.3 live in Protestant, 34.5 in Roman Catholic, and 5.2 live in Greek lands. To put the facts in a different way, the Protestant lands have 35.7 per cent. of the population, but 60.3 per cent. of the school children of Christendom. The Roman Catholic lands have 40.9 per cent. of the population, but 34.5 per cent. of the school children. The Greek lands have 23.4 per cent. of the population, but only 5.2 per cent. of the school children. It is not strange, then, that it is the Protestant countries which constitute the energising centre of modern civilisation. The foregoing statistics have reference only to the number of pupils in the lower institutions of learning. It would not be difficult to give the statistics of the universities and colleges ; in this respect, too, the Protestant countries are far ahead of all other countries.

It is not amiss to call attention again to the fact that France is not a typical Roman Catholic nation. The degree of her popular education is one of the results of her revolt from the domination of the Roman Catholic Church. It is an outstanding and also a most significant fact, that the Roman Catholic Church does not favour popular education. Where she possesses a country to

CHART. IX.

Illustrating the percentage of scholars
in each of the three great divisions of Christendom.

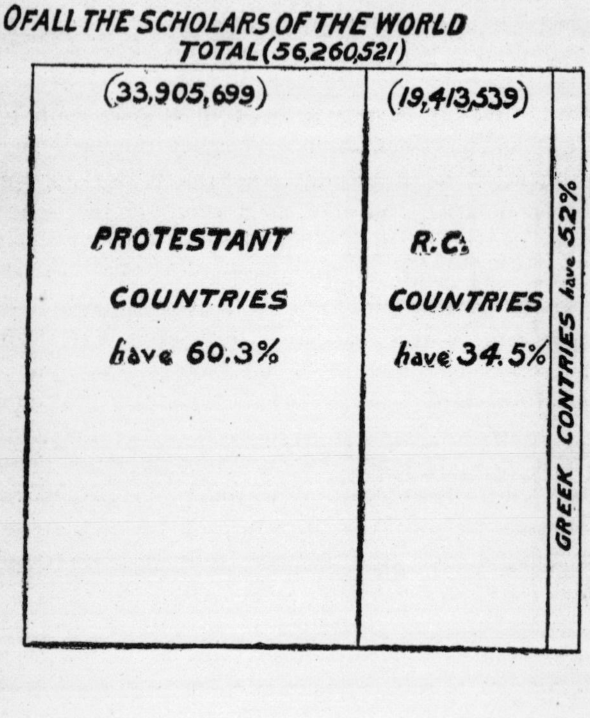

OF ALL THE SCHOLARS OF THE WORLD
TOTAL (56,260,521)

(33,905,699)	(19,413,539)	
PROTESTANT COUNTRIES have 60.3%	R.C. COUNTRIES have 34.5%	GREEK CONTRIES have 5.2%

CHART. X.

Illustrating the proportion of the school attendance to the entire population of the Greek-Roman Catholic and the Protestant nations of the world in 1890.

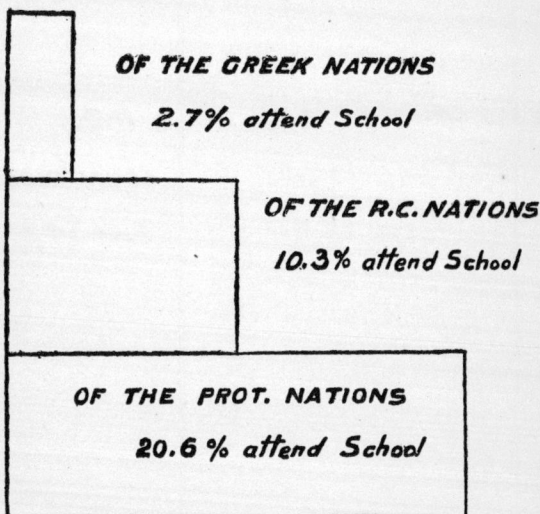

OF THE GREEK NATIONS

2.7% attend School

OF THE R.C. NATIONS

10.3% attend School

OF THE PROT. NATIONS

20.6 % attend School

4

herself, education is at a very low ebb. Witness Italy, Spain, and South America. Only when brought into sharp contrast and conflict with Protestantism does she show any interest in, or put forth any effort for, the education of the common people ; and even then she busies herself with so-called religious, rather than with general or scientific education. It is not strange, therefore, that the Roman Catholic are so far behind the Protestant countries in popular education, in general intelligence, and in national wealth and prosperity. For these of necessity do not keep far apart.

CHAPTER III

STATISTICAL EVIDENCES OF THE
GROWTH OF THE KINGDOM OF GOD IN
ENGLAND AND WALES

3292

'Our inquiry is not merely or mainly concerned with the increase of the material satisfaction of life, with enlarged cities, growing populations, expanding commerce, . . . but with the character and sway of ideas. For ideas are real forces. Ideas are our real world; institutions, laws, events, are the changing garments in which that world appears; so that the progress of a city, of a country, or of a generation, is to be tested by the comparative strength and dominion of true conceptions of the universe and of nature, of life and death, of duty and right, of the individual and of the village, town, city, state, and race in which the individual lives and moves and has his being; of institutions like Marriage and Home, School and University, Pulpit and Press, Church and State.'[1]

---

[1] Dr. John Clifford's *Annual Message to Young Men*, 1897.

CHAPTER III

I N the preceding chapter we have considered some of the more important evidence of the recent growth which has taken place in lands claiming the Christian name. We have seen how, in certain broad aspects of civilisation, the Christian nations have far outstripped the other nations of the earth. We have also compared the three groups of Christian nations in several important respects. If it is clear that the Christian nations are leading the world in every element essential to civilisation, it is no less clear that the Protestant nations are conspicuously in the vanguard of this progress.

This fact, which few will be disposed to dispute, at once raises the question as to the relation of religion to progress. May we legitimately conclude, without further delay, that the Christian countries are making their relatively rapid progress *because* they are Christian, and *in proportion* as they are Christian? or must we maintain that progress does not depend on religion? Shall we believe that religion determines progress? or progress religion? or that they are unrelated? More exactly, is Christianity a causal or an incidental, not to say accidental, factor in national progress in civilisation?

These questions are variously answered. On the one hand, there are many who freely assent, without any careful examination of the facts for themselves, that Christian faith is the most fundamental cause of modern civilisation. Observing that a relatively high degree of civilisation and of Christianity are actually found together, and that where Christianity is not, civilisation is at a low stage of development, they at once conclude that Christianity is the cause of the difference. There are those who go so far as to identify all real progress with the growth of the Church.

On the other hand, there are those who take precisely the opposite point of view. They strongly assert that whatever help Christianity may have been in the past as a factor in the production of our modern Occidental civilisation—and such help in the past is not denied—Christianity as it exists to-day is a positive hindrance to further progress. And, further, in regard to the growth of the organised forms of Christianity, it is maintained by many that the churches are losing their hold on the people, and especially on the peoples of the most progressive lands. Progress, they say, necessarily sets the people free from church control. The masses of the people no longer have any connection with or interest in the churches. And this must go on, say they; for the very essence of progress is the liberation of the mind from superstition, and therefore from church domination.

A complete answer to these various questions, and a full consideration of these many assertions, would demand a very comprehensive study of the facts. Hasty generalisations based on personal experience, or relying chiefly on individual observation, however extensive, are very liable to be wide of the truth. Such a study must cover long periods of time. It must include the millions of individuals that enter into the nation's life. A very essential part of such a study must consist of a statistical investigation of the growths of population, of wealth, of disease, of crime, and also of religious and moral life, of belief, and of church organisations. The statistics should cover periods of time sufficiently great to afford a clear perception of the movements of thought and life, which all these terms imply.

It is often said in disparagement of statistical inquiries, and particularly of religious statistics, that nothing is more deceptive and fallacious,—that figures can be made to prove whatever one wishes. Figures can doubtless be used dishonestly, as can with equal ease any other form of statement. And it may be readily admitted that, in the use of statistics, it is exceedingly easy to fall into error, quite unconsciously. Such errors are due to the lack of a clear perception as to what exactly the figures stand for. Yet, with care to retain this clearly in mind, and with scrupulous care to treat the figures accordingly, they are absolutely indispensable for many kinds of knowledge. Only by their help can we know the actual conditions of the millions of individuals who compose the nation. These millions no single man could ever know, much less their varying states of wealth, health, education, travel, occupation, birth, death, etc. Anything more than the vaguest impressions on these matters can only be given by statistics.

Now, if statistical information is essential to any real and fairly complete knowledge of the present, regarding the actual state of the people to-day, how much more essential is it when we are concerned with the past, and particularly with the relation of the present to the past! Popular movements, covering decades or centuries, can be expressed in no way so completely as by statistics. It is no more possible for an individual to have any adequate idea of the extent or power of a religious movement covering a period of three or four generations of a rapidly growing nation, without any appeal to statistics, than it is for him to have any adequate knowledge, apart from all statistics, of the growth of the population, of foreign trade, or of emigration, for that same period of time. Let us try to realise how vague would be our knowledge of the population of the United Kingdom at the beginning of this century, or even what it is at this present moment, with all our advantages of travel and direct observation, had we no carefully compiled statistics. The growth of England and Wales during the present century (242 per cent.) would be absolutely incredible were there not perfectly reliable statistics to vouch for it. Equally vague would be our knowledge as regards trade, wealth, education, crime, travel, etc. etc.

The need and value of statistics in so-called secular matters is now generally recognised. But, for some reason, their need for accurate knowledge of religious matters is not felt or even admitted by many. Yet they are equally necessary for accurate knowledge. It must be allowed that religious phenomena do not lend themselves to statistical tabulation so readily as the more objective elements of civilisation. No figures can express the heart's deepest experiences of joy, hope, sorrow, despair, conviction of sin, repentance, peace, etc. But statistics can tell something of this story, if rightly prepared. Statistics of starvation, of suicide, of murder, of robbery, of prostitution, of bastards (and their enormous deathrate), of accidents, of poorhouse inmates, etc., all tell a pitiful tale; these are the negative religious statistics.

But no less important, and registering with no less

accuracy the mental and moral experiences of the multitudes, and the heart experiences through which they are passing, are the ordinary religious statistics which deal with the various phases of church organisation and activity. Such statistics, reaching over a period of many decades, giving with accuracy the growth of the churches in number, in membership, in seating capacity, in ordained and lay ministry, in conversions, in baptisms, and in missionary work, give information which is indispensable to any real knowledge of the inner life and experiences of the people, information which they alone can give.

Further remark on this point is surely needless. Personal impressions, whether favourable or otherwise, cannot be allowed to have much force when fairly accurate statistics do not confirm the impressions.

The reply which many a critic will be inclined to make to the statistics about to be presented in this and the following chapters will be simply to disparage or denounce all religious statistics. Such a reply will, however, have little weight with him who seeks to know the facts. The only legitimate answer to the conclusions which are to be drawn from the statistics here brought together is to show, either that the figures themselves are materially in error, or that they have not been correctly used, and that therefore the conclusions are illogical. The statistics invite inspection. If materially in error, none will more cordially welcome their correction than the author, whose primary aim is to get at the actual facts.

The question with which this chapter opened, that, namely, as to whether Christianity is a causal or merely an incidental factor of Occidental civilisation, is one that needs to be divided, if we would seek for a clear answer. It is a problem of immense complexity. We must first settle a question of fact. Are they right who say that Christianity is losing its hold on the people, or are they wrong? This is a question of fact. To its study we shall confine our attention in this and the following chapters. We shall study chiefly the growth of the churches and of those forms of social life which are the direct result of Christian thought and teaching. In this chapter, so far as available statistics show them, we seek to know the facts for England and Wales; in the next, we shall study the religious condition of the United States. It would be interesting to extend our study to other lands as well, but the difficulty of such a study would be enormous, nor would it be likely to reward us with much profit. For our purposes, the study of these two countries will be quite sufficient to furnish us with a pretty sure basis from which to draw a number of important conclusions.

It seems desirable to group the statistics and discussions now to be presented under four main heads. In the first, we shall consider the growth of the population and of the cities of England and Wales, together with the problems briefly stated which this growth has produced. In the second part we shall, after three preliminary discussions as to their sources, character, etc., present such statistics as are accessible, showing the growth of the churches, taken as a whole. In the third part we shall consider some auxiliary methods of religious life and work. And, finally, we shall present some denominational statistics.

It seems desirable again to emphasise the point, that in thus taking up the statistical facts as to the growth of the churches, I do not confuse or identify the visible organised Church with the Kingdom of God, even though condensed phrases here and there may seem to do so. But, since the Church is the most formal and tangible expression of the Kingdom, it is both convenient and valuable to begin our study of its growth in England and Wales, by a careful consideration of the statistics of church growth. This chapter is accordingly chiefly occupied with the statistical evidence, more or less direct, of the relation of the people to the ideas and motives presented by Christ, and disseminated among the people chiefly through churches claiming Him as their Master and Teacher. Other, and in many respects far more important evidence as to the growth of Christ's Kingdom, must be deferred to its proper place in later chapters. This chapter considers simply the statistical side of the question.

PART I. GROWTH OF THE POPULATION OF ENGLAND AND WALES.

If we wish to realise the nature and extent of the problems the churches have had to face during the whole of the present century, it is important that we should realise first of all the immense growth in population which has been taking place, together with the re-location of population through the influence of industrialism. Only when we have fully realised the problem presented to the churches shall we be able to appreciate the extent of that which has been accomplished by them.

It is a remark very frequently heard on the lips of the educated, that England's people have been growing rapidly. But very few seem to have any conception as to what that rate is, or how it compares with the rates of former centuries. The accompanying tables and charts tell the whole story at a glance.

THE GROWTH OF THE POPULATION OF ENGLAND AND WALES.[1]

	Population.	Percentage of Growth.	Total Growth.	Length of Period.
1400 . .	2,750,000	...	...	...
1500 . .	3,500,000	...	750,000	100 years
1600 . .	4,950,000	...	1,450,000	100 ,,
1750 . .	6,400,000	...	1,450,000	150 ,,
1801 . .	8,892,536	...	2,492,000	50 ,,
1811 . .	10,164,256	14.3	...	...
1821 . .	12,000,236	18.0	...	...
1831 . .	13,896,795	15.8	...	...
1841 . .	15,914,148	14.5	...	...
1851 . .	17,927,608	12·6	9,035,673	50 ,,
1861 . .	20,066,224	11.9	...	...
1871 . .	22,712,266	13.1	...	...
1881 . .	25,974,439	13.5	...	...
1891 . .	29,002,528	11.6	...	...
1895 . .	30,394,078	...	12,466,467	45 ,,

No hasty look will suffice to reveal the full significance of these figures and the growth they prove to have taken place. A writer in the *Fortnightly Review* (June 1880), with slightly different figures, presents the same facts in a different form. The following table is based on his statements :[2]—

[1] Cf. *Statesman's Year Book*, 1896 ; *The Encyc. Brit.*, 9th edition, vol. viii. pp. 219, 220; *The Fortnightly Review*, June 1880.
[2] Corrected to date.

	Total Growth.	Percentage of Growth.
1100–1200 . .	233,000	10
1200–1300 . .	233,000	10
1300–1400 . .	233,000	10
1400–1500 . .	700,000	25
1500–1600 . .	1,110,000	30
1600–1700 . .	1,000,000	25
1700–1800 . .	3,750,000	64
1800–1895 . .	21,501,530	242

To appreciate what these figures mean, we need to dwell on them for a few moments. For a period of three hundred years (1100–1400 A.D.) the severity of life was such, with its wars and diseases, accidents and ordinary hardships, that the gains were only 10 per cent. during each hundred years. This is a smaller per cent. in the hundred years than has been gained in each decade of the present century. Then came the times of the Renaissance and the Reformation, when the ratio leaped from 10 per cent. to 25 per cent. in the fifteenth, and to 30 per cent. in the sixteenth century, falling back to 25 per cent. for the next hundred years. These changing figures tell a pathetic story of the severity of the struggle for life during recent centuries. Only in very modern times has there been any conspicuous amelioration of that struggle. The eighteenth century, particularly its latter half, witnessed a great advance, the precursor and promise of what was to take place in our own times. The progress during the past ninety-five years (242 per cent.) has completely overshadowed all previous growth. It tells of a diminution of those hardships and dangers to which

CHART. XI

Illustrating the Growth of the Population of England & Wales.

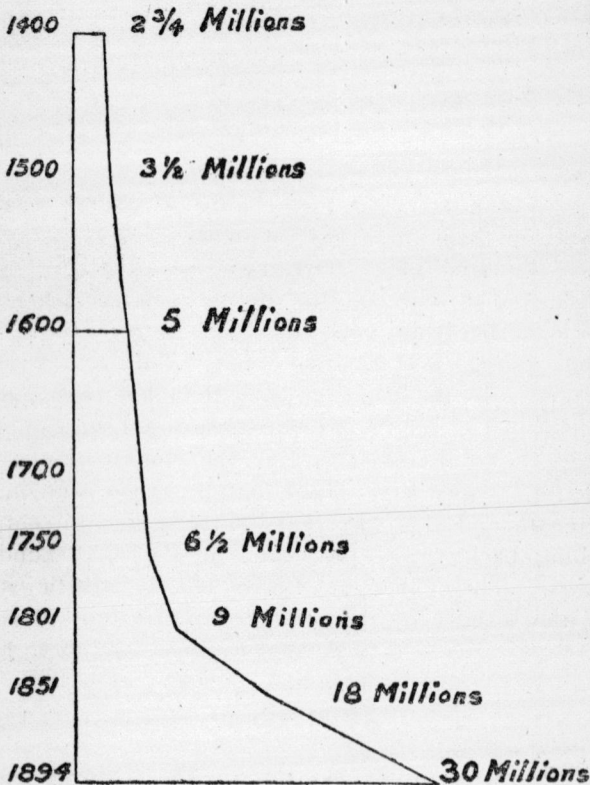

1400	2 ¾ Millions
1500	3 ½ Millions
1600	5 Millions
1700	
1750	6 ½ Millions
1801	9 Millions
1851	18 Millions
1894	30 Millions

CHART. XII.

Illustrating the per cent. of increase of the population of England & Wales, for each 100 years.

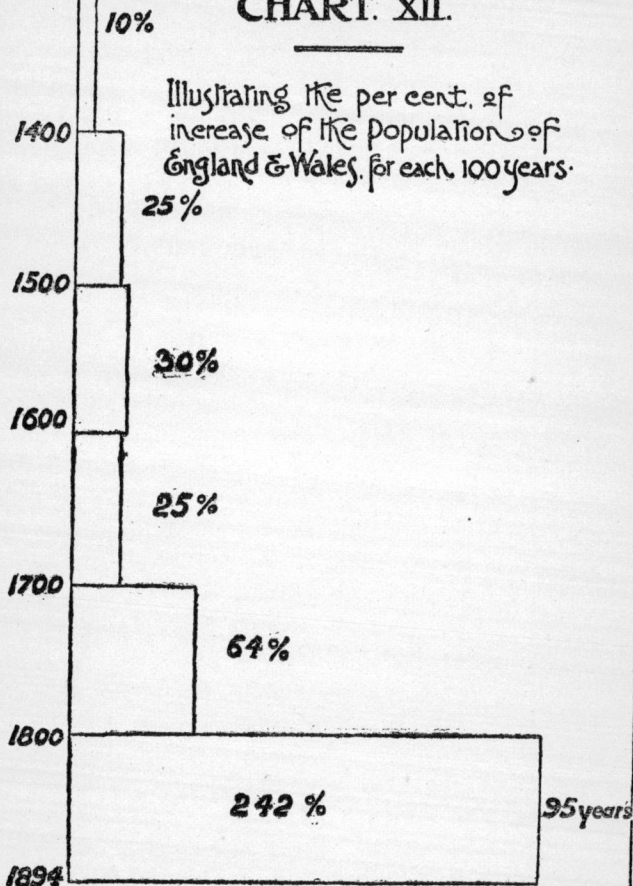

10%

1400

25%

1500

30%

1600

25%

1700

64%

1800

242%   95 years

1894

life was exposed. It tells of relative success in the struggle for personal existence which this new era has brought. It tells of comparative peace and plenty, of good government, of increasing intelligence, of increasing freedom from crime and destructive lust, and raging pestilence and war. There are to-day in the City of London more people than in all England and Wales only three hundred years ago. The increase in population in only four years (1891–1895) was more than that of the entire sixteenth century by about 200,000 persons.

We are concerned now, not with the causes of this marvellous growth, but simply with the fact itself, and with the problem which it raises—the obstacles it interposes to the growth of the churches. Making for the moment the improbable supposition that the nation was sufficiently provided with church buildings at the beginning of this century, many new places of worship would have to be erected, suitably to accommodate the 21,500,000 of people added to the population during the past ninety-five years. How many new churches should there be? If we take Mr. Horace Mann's suggestion [1] that sixty-eight seats should be provided for each hundred of the population, and if we assume that the new churches average three hundred each, there would be needed 46,077 new churches. And if we should further make the very modest estimate of £2500 as the average cost for each (Mr. Mann's estimate for the buildings erected by the Church of England, 1801–1851, is £3000 each), it will be seen that the outlay in providing merely the new churches would be £115,000,000.

[1] Cf. the Census of Great Britain, 1851, 'Religious Worship,' p. xxxix.

This makes no reference to the expenses incurred in repairs, or in the education and support of the thousands of clergymen and others essential to the suitable manning of all these places of religious instruction and worship.

Looking at the problem in this matter-of-fact financial way, and considering how suddenly the demand for this extension work has arisen, due entirely to the extraordinary growth of the population in this century, we begin to realise the nature and extent of the great duty laid on the Christian community. For it is to be borne in mind that whatever has been done has been purely voluntary. With the exception of about £1,500,000, given by parliamentary grants to the Established Church in the early part of the century, whatever has been expended in church erection has been given by private individuals as freewill offerings.

But the financial element of the problem is a relatively minor one. Our conception of the immense difficulty of the problem will be more adequate if we realise the nature of some aggravating factors.

Our supposition has put the matter in its very simplest form. We have assumed that the people of 1800 were sufficiently provided with churches. Such, however, was not the case. According to the religious census for 1851 (p. cxxxi.), there were but fifty-eight seats for each hundred of the population, instead of the sixty-eight thought desirable ; that is to say, there were about 890,000 seats short. This point, however, is of insignificant importance, compared with that which must next engage our attention.

We have thus far taken no notice of that for which this century will ever be memorable—the rise of

5

industrialism and the growth of large cities. A fact so well known hardly needs to be more than referred to here. Yet we do not begin to realise what it means, so accustomed have we become to the general statement. Consider just one fact. With the enormous increase of population, it would have seemed certain that there would have been at least some growth in the number of agricultural labourers. Such, however, does not seem to have been the case to any very appreciable extent. It has been stated that between 1831–1881, during a period of fifty years, in which the population increased from 13,900,000 to 26,000,000, nearly doubling, the number of agricultural labourers actually decreased from 980,000 to 870,000.[1] The increase of the population has, therefore, been gathering in the cities, which have thus been growing at a prodigious rate. The growth of a few of the larger cities will be evident by a brief study of the following table :—

GROWTH OF THE CITIES OF ENGLAND.[2]

	1801.	1841.	1887.
London . . .	959,000	1,948,000	4,215,000
Liverpool . .	82,000	286,000	593,000
Manchester . .	77,000	243,000	328,000
Birmingham . .	71,000	183,000	441,000
Leeds . . .	53,000	152,000	345,000
Bristol . . .	61,000	125,000	224,000
Sheffield. . .	46,000	111,000	316,000

Whereas, in 1801, London contained 9.7 per cent. of the entire population of England, by 1881 it had

[1] Doggett's *History of the Y.M.C.A. Movement*, vol. i. p. 26.
[2] Mulhall's *Dictionary of Statistics*, 1892, p. 445.

advanced so much faster than all the rest of the country that it contained 14.7 per cent. of the entire population. In ninety-one years it grew 341 per cent. In eighty-one years Liverpool gained 611 per cent. But it is hardly necessary to dwell longer on the fact of aggregating populations.

Much more, however, than the casual observer would think, this massing of the populations aggravates the difficulty of the problem laid upon the churches. It does this in two chief ways. First, it creates great congested districts. This means, as related to church accommodation, that the already existing deficiency becomes disproportionately increased. The church buildings and clergy were located and provided for, according to the old distribution of the people. Because of the shifting of the population, whilst the old church accommodation may be, and often is, actually superabundant, new places have arisen in which there is no accommodation whatever. Viewed, then, entirely from the standpoint of church sittings, the shifting of the people into large towns and cities has added not a little to the difficulty which the Christian community has had to face.

But still graver difficulties than those yet mentioned have arisen from the massing of the people in limited areas. I refer now, not so much to the physical deterioration of those who toil in factories and live in contracted, ill-ventilated, crowded quarters, serious though this factor of physical degeneration is,—I refer rather to the intellectual and moral effects of such a life. Among students of the social problems of the day, the fact is well recognised that uncertainty of work and wages, with all the consequences to the home-life these carry, has a most disastrous effect on the manhood and womanhood of the working classes. Moral fibre is weakened, and also intellectual. The high rents inevitable in crowded cities necessitate small quarters for the working man and his family; these are too often crowded and squalid, and admit of no privacy, so important an element in the making of manhood and womanhood. Needless is it at this stage of our history to dwell at length on the various factors which tend to reduce the average city artisan or factory hand to so low a moral and intellectual level. It is surely not necessary to prove that all the conditions that surround him are far more adverse to his upbuilding in moral character and in religious life than are those of the same classes in small towns and villages, and in the country. Too often his relation with his employers, too often his deception and loss at the hands of sharpers in the cities, tend to sour his temper, and render him suspicious of all his fellow-men, and thus to disbelieve even in God. The point of importance for us is the undoubted fact, that the ordinary experiences of city life, for all day labourers and for many other classes as well, exert strong influences adverse to all forms of religious life.

Nor are we to think that these irreligious influences and tendencies are limited to the labouring classes. Among the well-to-do, likewise, varied non-religious interests arise. Opportunities for self-gratification are afforded, such as cannot be had in smaller places or in the country. Social, musical, theatrical, intellectual, and other privileges and interests serve to absorb the attention, and thus help to detach from the Church multitudes who, under other circumstances and in smaller places, would remain relatively faithful to the usual religious duties, and take their part in the ordinary church life. If religious life is to maintain itself in the modern city, it must be much more robust, more aggressive, more vital, more intense, than appears to be needful for a moderate measure of religious activity elsewhere.

If the preceding paragraphs correctly describe the effect of industrialism and of city life in relation to religion, it will not be a matter of surprise to learn, as a matter of fact, that the population, especially in the cities, has far outrun the church accommodation. For the problem in the cities is not merely to provide a sufficient number of seats, difficult though that would be. It is the far more difficult problem of dealing with men and women whose lives have been narrowed and soured and hardened by the vicissitudes of industrialism, or made thoughtless and selfish by social or financial prosperity. It is the problem of dealing with men and women who too often know not whence their daily bread is to come, and who vaguely feel that somehow or other they are living, or rather being crushed, under a system of injustice and oppression, a system that is upheld by the churches themselves. It is likewise the problem of dealing with the moneyed, self-satisfied classes, the most difficult of all to influence ; for it is the task of appealing to their shallow, selfish hearts, worshippers of pleasure, or popularity, or fashion, or the golden calf—the task of showing them at once their own emptiness and the source whence they may be filled with all that is good and true and noble and real. It is an old saying, that one man may lead a horse to the water, but ten men cannot make him drink. Wealth and energy may build the churches, but it takes more than their bare existence to fill them. The real difficulty that confronts the Christian community is, not that of building the churches, but of reaching the godless and of bringing them into the churches. It is in this matter that sceptics and scoffers say the churches have continuously failed. Whether and to what extent this is so, we shall see later on.

Still another point of difficulty demands our attention. We have been speaking as though 'the Church' were a large church erection society, which, after looking over the needs of the field, proceeds to supply the buildings where most needed. It would be well if such were the case, but alas, it is not. For building purposes, 'the Church' is really only those Christians of a district who feel the need of a place of worship, and who exert themselves to secure it. If wealthy, they give the money themselves, assisted perhaps by outside friends; if in only moderate circumstances, they slowly raise the funds by much effort and united labour, seeking help far and wide. But let us suppose a city springs up in a night, all of whose people are common day-labourers, uneducated and unspiritual—the men working hard all the week for the daily bread, so long as there is work, and oppressed with fear and anxiety when work is wanting; the women also, working often for a bare pittance, too busy with work for others to care properly for their own homes and children. Now, in such a community, who is to move toward securing a church? Whence is the money to come from to build it, or to run it? Who can spare the time to canvass for it? Even supposing that some feel the need of a church—and they will be few— who is to take the initiative? Evidently such a community must wait on the missionary activity of other more prosperous and more religious communities.

But what should we expect of missionary activity initiated wholly from without? What will be the natural feelings of those among whom these new buildings are placed? They had no share in their erection, nor voice even in asking for them. To the ordinary working man such places are of necessity distasteful, because emphasising their inferior position in the social scale—places therefore to be shunned, places in which he has neither part nor interest. What is the probability of inducing men with such feelings to attend, or to become active members and upholders of such work? The fact is, missions do not begin with church buildings, but with direct work, the upbuilding of the religious life, the giving of ethical instruction. Only in relatively modern times is it beginning to be seen, and it is not yet seen by very many, that the first step in genuine missionary work is the reconstruction of the social fabric, making it conform to the principles of the Kingdom of God, so that the working classes shall be delivered from the injustice and thraldom to which they are now subject. The churches and the Christian community must ally themselves with the working men in fighting great social evils and oppressions. At the same time, missionary work among them must seek to win their love and confidence, and thus stimulate their moral and religious sense. The organic manifestation of all this new religious life must come later. Missionary activity must seek to work as leaven within, and not simply as an organism from without. Both methods must go hand in hand.

The geographical segregation of the classes renders this kind of work exceedingly difficult. In former times, when all classes of society lived side by side, they had many common ties. In periods of stress and storm, of war or disease, they were drawn together, and instinctively helped each other. It was easy then to see and learn that the welfare of each was important to each and to all. The church buildings too, and the religious life, were shared by all and owned by all. All the members of the community would take interest and pride in that which they felt to be theirs in common. But the times have changed ; geographical distribution as well as education and culture and wealth hold the classes far apart. Mutual knowledge, and with it mutual sympathy, is reduced to a minimum. This is peculiarly disastrous to both moral and religious life.

Such are some of the more conspicuous difficulties organised Christianity has had to face during the present century, due in large measure to the extraordinary social, economic, and industrial changes that have taken place. I have ventured to dwell upon them at this length, though in truth with exceeding brevity, because I feel that the wide condemnation of the churches for their asserted lack of success arises perhaps as much from ignorance, both of the problems they have encountered and of the real success which they have had, as from their failure to accomplish as much as we would like to have seen. For it is usually the case that those who condemn the failures of the Church the most severely are the very ones who least understand its peculiar problems, and least realise how great have been, and still are, its real successes.

It cannot be too clearly stated that the social and industrial reorganisation taking place simultaneously with an amazingly rapid growth of population, though facts well recognised now at the end of this century, were processes operating so silently that very few noticed them in their beginnings, or realised what they meant to State or Church until they had grown to be enormous movements. It is not the churches alone who were overtaken in peaceful slumber, if such an expression is at all justifiable. The whole nation was equally unconscious of the revolutionary character of the changes in progress. Growth, in contrast to convulsive changes, is always silent, and therefore unconscious. Only when growth has in some measure taken place is it possible to perceive it, and to estimate its meaning and direction, its advantages and dangers. It is perhaps safe to say that legislation is as far behind the needs of the modern industrial and commercial world, as is the Church in the performance of its special sphere of work. In estimating, therefore, the growth of the churches in England and Wales, before we condemn it too severely, it is essential that we bear in mind the fact that all these problems and difficulties were sprung upon the Christians, not with blare of trumpets, nor foretold by prophets, but in absolute silence.[1]

PART II. GROWTH OF THE CHURCHES IN ENGLAND AND WALES.

We are now ready to ask what the churches have been doing? How have they met the problems? Have they kept pace with the growth of the population, or have they fallen behind? In view of the difficulties noticed in the previous section, we shall not be particularly surprised if we find that they have not kept up with the population. Indeed, our surprise should be quite on the other side, especially when we remember

[1] Cf. note at the close of this chapter.

how recent is the recognition on the part of the churches that there is a problem for them to face, a recognition which even yet seems to be limited to a minority of the Christians.

Before presenting the statistics of the churches, it is desirable to consider three preliminary matters of importance.

1. *The Character and Extent of the Statistical Sources.*

It will be a cause of surprise to many to learn that there are any religious statistics worthy of the name. It is a common statement that since the census does not include returns on religious matters there are none worthy of credence. It must be admitted at once that there never has been, in the full and proper sense of the term, a religious census of England and Wales. Says the *Encyclopædia Britannica* on this topic: 'There is a singular want of authentic religious statistics in England. While in nearly all the other European countries the number of the population adhering to the various creeds is carefully ascertained at the periodical census takings, or at other times, this has never been done in England, except in a cursory way.'[1] *Whittaker's Almanac*, which annually publishes a tolerable summary of the religious statistics of the United Kingdom, prefaces its first attempt (1872) by the remark, that 'it appears to be almost an impossibility to compile a complete religious directory.' In the face of these statements by those who may be presumed to be authorities (and these statements seem to voice the belief of all intelligent men), it may seem presumptuous to attempt any statistical answer to the questions we have asked. Yet,

---

[1] Ninth edition, vol. iii. p. 246.

as statistics can alone answer our questions—the insufficiency of personal impressions we have already noticed—it may not be amiss to see first of all what statistics there are, and what their nature and extent.

1. It must be admitted at once that previous to 1800 our statistics are of the most fragmentary nature. Such as they are we shall present them in due time. They are very meagre, yet so far as they go they seem fairly trustworthy.

2. The first statistical information of much value is that found in the *Report of the Religious Census of* 1851, published by Mr. Horace Mann, and accompanied by a most valuable and exhaustive introduction. Shortly before the time for taking the census of that year it was found that no penalties could be inflicted on those who might refuse to reply to the questions on religious items. It was decided, however, to proceed on the voluntary basis, it being clearly understood that all replies were to be freely given. On this ground objection has been taken by some to the value of these statistics, urging that they must be in error. The objection, however, does not seem to be well founded. True, the census may not be complete, but it is accurate and of immense value so far as it goes. Its error, if any, is not one of exaggeration, but of deficiency. Whatever the actual facts may have been, the census report of them falls well within them. But did any large number of persons decline to give answers to the questions asked? That seems exceedingly improbable. The returns, Mr. Mann tells us in his introduction, were secured by 40,000 regular collectors, skilled therefore in their duties. Reports were received from 34,467 places of worship. No effort was made in the census to dis-

cover the denominational preferences of individuals. The nearest approach to this was an enumeration of the number of worshippers attending the various services held in each church open on the single Sabbath, March 30, 1851. The nature of the questions, and the fulness of the published report, enable us to gain something of an idea of the growth of the churches during the fifty years preceding. For our study of the growth of the churches during the first half of this century, therefore, we can do no better than rely on the *Religious Census of* 1851.

Whatever may be the reason for it, it is a lamentable fact that the Government has not again attempted to gather statistics of a religious character. It is to be hoped that, in the interests of accurate knowledge of the religious status of the country, it will seem wise to those in authority to provide that the next national census in 1901 shall include, at the very least, such items of a religious nature as do not conflict with the rights of individual religious liberty.

3. In recent decades there have been steadily increasing efforts on the part of leading denominations to secure accurate statistics of their own work and growth. These are published in their year-books. Whoever has studied these year-books cannot fail to be impressed with the marked improvement that has been made in the past ten years. None of them, however, claim more than substantial accuracy. All the editors of the various year-books would doubtless subscribe to the heavily underscored cautionary words placed at the head of the statistical information of the *Official Year-Book of the Church.* They so fitly describe the spirit with which the statistics in this volume are presented,

that I venture to quote them in full. ' In order to guard against the possibility of inaccurate conclusions and statements with regard to the accompanying statistical tables, it is of the utmost importance that very careful attention be paid to the following explanations. Though these records as a whole may be taken as the substantial representation of the truth, in regard to the matters with which they specifically deal, they must not be regarded as exhaustive' (1896, p. xiv.). Attention is then drawn to the fact that only 97 per cent. of the parochial clergy had made reports ; that not all of the organisations are included ; and that the systematic collection of statistics has only recently been attempted, and they are therefore inevitably incomplete. This is also true of all the denominations.

4. Strange to say, and yet not so strange when one stops to think about it, efforts to combine the statistics given by the various year-books have been very seldom made. The most successful as well as the most recent general summary was published in the *Contemporary Review* for Feb. 1897. It shall be our authority for the present status of the churches.

5. On account of the unique character of London and its relation to the rest of England, and because of the great accentuation of the problems there, a little study of its religious condition, past and present, may not be without advantage. There have been, since the census of 1851 was taken, two efforts to discover the church accommodation of London, one in 1866 and the other in 1886. Being in no sense public, but wholly private efforts, the first by *The Nonconformist*, and the second by *The British Weekly*, we may not use their results with the assumption that they are as complete

even as was the voluntary governmental census of 1851. Yet as in that case, so in these, the figures will be under, rather than over, statements, and, as far as they show growth, may be accepted as substantially accurate. Their value to us will be not inconsiderable.

Such are the character and extent of the sources on which we shall rely for our statistical information. To understand the full significance of the statistics, however, we need to understand the situation or environment of the churches to which they relate. We need to know what the statistics were designed in each case to show. Understanding this, they will tell us the truth. Failing it, they will be to us quite valueless, and even positively deceitful. Two points need a little attention.

(*a*) *The two conflicting conceptions of the nature of a Church, as affecting statistical returns, held respectively by the Established and by the Free Churches.* — The view of the former is inclusive; of the latter, exclusive. According to the one, the Church includes all members of the nation, except those who positively refuse to be included. According to the other, only they should be counted as members of the Church who, having had conscious experience of regeneration, make public confession of their repentance of sin and faith in Christ; and having thus formally joined the Church, live in conformity to its rules and their own voluntarily assumed pledges. We are not now concerned with the merits of this long-standing controversy. We are here interested in it only as it bears on the problem of statistics. The theory of the Established Church precludes its publishing, or even its gathering, statistics as to church membership. Records indeed are kept of additions to the Church through baptism and confirmation, but no records are kept of losses through withdrawal, excommunication, or death. It is the custom of many, in trying to estimate the number of those who may properly be regarded as members of the Church, to subtract from the total population the number claimed by the Free Churches, and to count the remainder as churchmen. Statistics gathered in this way, however, throw no light on the problem we are studying, for they assume the very point under discussion, namely, how many millions have no personal or voluntary relation with any form of church organisation. For practical purposes it may be well for the Church to count all as individuals for whose welfare it is responsible. But the question is, how many of them reciprocate the feeling, and are glad to count themselves members of the Church, and show their sense of membership by their daily living and their active attendance on and support of its services? This is what membership in the Free Churches means. If memberships are to be compared and added, they must be comparable. Taking the churchmen's view as to church membership, millions of its members never darken its doors, nor contribute to its support; they have the same feelings toward it as toward any of the Free Churches. Now the question is, how many are these, and are they increasing or not?

It is sometimes said that the ratio of the religious preferences of the population among the various denominations may be discovered by a study of the marriage returns. These, however, give little real light, for the obvious reason that even the most irreligious must get married in some licensed church or chapel.

If only the active supporters of the churches and chapels were married in their respective places of worship, and all others were married elsewhere, then the marriage returns would be most valuable religious statistics. It may be safely assumed, as matters now stand, that those who have no positive religious convictions themselves will be married in the places of worship of the Established Church. Indeed, it is a well-known fact that many Nonconformists prefer to be married in the Established Church. In 1892, 70 per cent. of the marriages took place in churches, and only 30 per cent. in the Nonconformist chapels. But, as we shall see shortly, the number of active Churchmen is probably smaller than that of active Free Churchmen.

It has therefore become clear that the growth of the Established Church, or conversely of the non-church-going element of the people, cannot be measured directly. Nevertheless, as we shall see later on, there are statistical proofs of various kinds in the official year-books, which may guide us to some fairly adequate notion of the immense part the Church plays in the religious development of the nation, and also as to the immense numbers of those who have no church connection.

(*b*) *The incompleteness of the statistics of the Free Churches.*—In view of the principles on which the Free Churches are founded, it would have been natural to suppose that each of them would have made and preserved some statistical records of its growth. And such, indeed, to a certain extent has been the case. The Baptists and Wesleyans, for many decades, have published very careful annual returns of all the reporting churches. Although the Congregational churches publish a full list of the associated churches and their ministers, until recently without an appended summary of their number, yet they purposely omit all statements relative to the size of the church membership. The year-books of all the leading denominations run back into the early decades of this century, and must be the main sources on which to rely for a knowledge of their growth. Although materials doubtless are in existence for a fairly comprehensive summary of the churches, they have not yet been carefully compiled. The labour of it is beyond the strength of any single individual.

Furthermore, since each body has gathered and tabulated its own facts, without regard to the statistics of the other bodies, it follows that many items in one series are not comparable with those of another. Each body has its own peculiarities of organisation and work, and it of necessity gathers its statistics with these alone in view. For instance, the Wesleyan and Baptist churches report large numbers of lay preachers, while the Congregational, the Presbyterian, and the Established churches specify no such class. With reference to these lay preachers the question inevitably arises, whether or not they shall be included in the final summary of all the ministers in the United Kingdom. In either case, whether included or excluded, there is something of a misrepresentation. Likewise with reference to church accommodation. Shall buildings, other than churches, in which religious services are regularly held, year after year, be included or not in the final summary of the total number of churches and church sittings ? In either case, whether excluded or included, the exact facts are not clearly represented. The fact is, that in many items, summary tables, including and combining returns from all the denominations, cannot

6

be prepared, because the basis of computation differs. Any attempt to prepare such summaries must be most carefully explained.

But, once more, the consciousness of the need of statistical information is of very recent origin. As a consequence, many items which are now reported by many churches with considerable fulness have no corresponding figures in earlier years. The item of church membership is such an one.

In view of these varied difficulties, it would perhaps be natural to conclude at once, that any comprehensive view of the growth of the churches is impossible, and that we can judge of the question before us only from the personal impressions of those who have lived long and watched keenly the signs of religious growth and decay. While it must be admitted that these impressions of candid observers merit careful attention, yet, as we have seen, they are contradictory, and in any case, of necessity, limited and more or less conjectural. But in spite of the difficulties of securing such statistics as we would like, I nevertheless venture to think that we have sufficient statistical data to warrant a clear and definite answer to the question engaging our attention in this chapter. The disjointed nature of our statistical evidence, it is readily admitted, prevents its satisfactory tabulation and presentation in a single table, such as we shall see later is possible in the case of the United States. Yet such as it is, it will be seen, I think, to be fairly conclusive.

2. *The Denominational Antagonisms as hindering the growth of the Kingdom of God.*

In Part I. we have noted what may be called the

external obstacles to the growth of the Kingdom arising from the growth of the population, and its massing in large cities under the stimulus of industrialism. Here we must note the internal obstacles to the growth of the Kingdom, those, namely, of denominational differences and antagonisms. It is the fashion of this age to condemn these differences without understanding them, or recognising the truths of profound significance that they reveal. While recognising these, however, we need not close our eyes to the injury they appear to do to the Kingdom. The kernel of these antagonisms, as between the Established and the Free Churches, is in the conflicting ideas regarding the nature of the Church, both in itself and in its proper relation to the State. In a preceding section we have considered one aspect of this conflict, so far as it affects the gathering and tabulation of statistics. Our point here is the conflict itself, and the obstacles it throws in the way of aggressive Christian work. As before, we are not concerned with the pros and cons of either side, but only with the fact.

The conflict has been not merely theoretical, but it has taken concrete form in political and social life. The Church of Christ in England has been and still is divided into two great camps, happily now not engaged in actual war, yet separated by vast differences of thought and belief and practice. To him who looks on from without it is evident that there are great principles of truth involved in the contention of each side. Each in a measure seems to misunderstand the position and contention of the other. Each views the other as insisting on some great wrong, and as striving to carry into operation its own plans and desires, regardless of justice and the rights of others. Each considers its own views right and its own methods wholly just. The present intense discussion of the educational question is but one illustration of what I mean.

This conflict between the two branches of Christ's Kingdom in this land is one of long standing. It has been waged at times with extreme bitterness. The party in power has not failed to use the arm of the Government to upbuild its own interests, and to oppress its opponents. Until recent times those who favoured the Established Church, and believed in a State Church, were largely in the majority. As a consequence, while not suffering from exterminating persecutions, except at rare intervals, now happily long since passed, those whose consciences forbade their remaining in the Established Church were under many serious social and political disadvantages. For nearly two hundred years the Nonconformist Churches were handicapped in many ways. Indeed, it is only within relatively recent times that all political, official, and educational disabilities have been removed from them This long-standing antagonism rested and still rests on a serious divergence of views, conscientiously held by vast multitudes, professedly taking their teaching from the same book and following the same Master. The inevitable consequence has been a great weakening of the Christian forces. Instead of uniting to fight their common foe, sin and wickedness, too often and too long have they been battling against each other.

If all this is true, we may perhaps wonder less that so little has been done to meet the peculiar problems of this age. We may also be led to appreciate the actual noble work that has been done by both, in spite of the difficulties and disabilities peculiar to the work of each.

But the difficulties arising from the differences between the Established and the Free Churches must not be too much emphasised. May it not be that, in the providence of Him who rules not only the winds and the waves, but, we believe, also the Church,—may it not be that each branch of the larger Church was essential in the long-run to the best life and vigour of the whole? May it not be that the deepening of the spiritual life which has been so marked a feature of the present century may have been due, in part at least, to an interplay of influences to which each has contributed? One thing is clear. All history shows that the best growth of a church as well as of a nation, and even of an individual, takes place when there is more or less of struggle, of conflict, of vigorous effort, induced by difficulties and opposition. That, then, which at first sight might seem, and from certain points of view might really be, a serious obstacle to the growth of the Kingdom, may become, in the end and from a higher point of view, a real help. The difficulties which arouse to action and effort are blessings in disguise. The final result of this long conflict is not yet in sight. Only in the light of its ultimate issue, only by the help of the completed history, shall we be able to say whether this struggle may not have been an essential element or condition in bringing in the perfect Kingdom of the Redeemer.

Since I have spoken of the differences dividing the Nonconformist from the Established Churches as an obstacle to the growth of the Kingdom, it may not be amiss to add that the great differences which have developed within both branches have likewise resulted **in disastrous consequences. The denominational con-**

flicts among the Free Churches, and the party conflicts within the Established Church, have been long and serious ; energy which should have been directed to aggressive work has been diverted to interdenominational and interparty discussion and conflict. But here again we must believe that God has been overruling, and that in His providence He is preparing some better and nobler conceptions of the nature of the Church than has been held by any one sect or party.

3. *The Formalism and Moral Degradation of the Churches of the Seventeenth and Eighteenth Centuries.*

The greatest obstacle to the growth of the Churches and the Kingdom has always been the failure of Christians themselves to realise the fulness of the life that might be theirs through Christ. There have always been large numbers of formal, ceremonial, or merely intellectual Christians, who are ever a positive hindrance to the expansion of the Church. Their numbers vary in different ages. With the growth of formalism, moral relaxation and degeneration inevitably take place. The churches of the seventeenth and eighteenth centuries seem to have been peculiarly cursed by these evils.

But one of the most astonishing features of Christianity, wherein it differs from all other religions, is the power it has more than once manifested of mighty spiritual and moral revivals. The growth of the Church in the nineteenth century is out of a period of awful spiritual barrenness and moral degradation. In tracing the statistical evidence of the growth, we are not free to assume that the general moral and religious conditions prevailing to-day existed in the last century. On the contrary, it has been the growth of the Churches, expressing the growth of the Christian ideals and beliefs, that has created the modern moral standards of the whole nation. In trying, therefore, to realise the real significance of the growth which the Churches have made, it is all important to remember how low they were themselves in their moral and religious tone and experience. What these were the modern man can hardly realise. If told, he could not believe.

It would be easy to fill a hundred pages with quotations from trustworthy historians, who have sifted the material and know whereof they affirm. It is beyond dispute that for more than a hundred years there was common in all parts of England a degree of wickedness and immorality, of filthy speech and foul literature, which to us is almost inconceivable. Any reader who wishes details and proofs must go to the historians of the seventeenth and eighteenth centuries, such as Lecky and Macaulay, to name no others. An excellent comprehensive summary of the facts will also be found in Dr. Dorchester's *Problem of Religious Progress,* and in Dr. Doggett's *History of the Y.M.C.A. Movement.*

It would be gratifying to think that the corruption and wickedness and drunkenness of those times was all confined to the world, and that the Church was pure and its office-bearers spotless, filled with Christian spirit and leading exemplary Christian lives. Though, beyond doubt, in every century there have been many most devout and spiritual Christians, laymen and clergy, yet history declares too plainly the painful fact that the English Churches of the last centuries went sadly astray, both

leaders and people. The evils were confined to no one
denomination. Now, that whose growth we are studying in this chapter, that on which was thrown the
problems arising from the growth of cities and of industrialism, was the Church as it actually existed. It
was the Christian community, weakened by its counte-
nance of sin and crime, and more than tainted with the
same itself. As we meditate on these things, as we
compare the Christian community of our own times,
defective though it admittedly is, with the Christian
community of the last two centuries, as made known
to us by authentic history, we can perhaps better appreciate what has been thus far accomplished, and be less
amazed than we are sometimes inclined to be that there
is still so much left undone. It might almost be said
that the Church itself had first to become Christian ere
it could be a fit instrument for the work to which it
was called. Even to this very day this statement is
all too true. We are not yet the Christians we ought
to be.

One more consideration demands our attention ere
we close this section. What, we may ask, was the outward attitude of the people at large to the Church?
Were they regular in their attendance, and active in
their support of the church services? Of the 5,800,000
seats provided by the churches in 1800 what proportion
was occupied from Sabbath to Sabbath? We have no
facts wherewith to answer this question. But if we bear
in mind the extent to which Deism prevailed throughout
the nation, sapping all the springs of vital religion; how
it permeated the churches; how rampant moral evils
were in both the churches and in society at large; how
religion was in the thoughts of vast multitudes merely a

ceremonial, or a semi-magical charm, useful in christenings, in marriages, and in funerals, but without any special relation to daily life, we shall not find it easy to believe that there was a wide and steady attendance from Sabbath to Sabbath at the services in the churches, nor that the worship was very sincere. The magnificent cathedrals and churches existed from previous times. Except among dissenters there was little occasion for additional building. There is no reason for thinking that, as a rule, attendance on religious services was any more general than when the census was taken in 1851. Indeed, the indications point in the other direction. The fact that the Established Church practically made no advance in church accommodation during the first thirty years of this century would indicate that its actual accommodation was far in excess of its needs. We have no means of judging as to the number of churches built in the eighteenth century, but if the period from 1801–1831 may be taken as a basis for judgment, we must conclude that it must have been very slight.

This slight statement of the moral and religious state of the Christian community of the seventeenth and eighteenth centuries must suffice. Out of the barrenness and moral torpor of those times came the great religious revivals, beginning their work in the last century, but showing their power and fruit only in this. It is from that period that we make our start in the statistical study of the growth of the churches.

We pass now to consider the success with which the churches have met the various difficulties, within and without, which lay across their path. We naturally begin with the period of revived emphasis on spiritual religion, commonly known as the Wesleyan Revival. It contained the germ which, widely accepted and more fully developed, was destined to transform so greatly the methods of church organisation and of Christian activity, and render possible the enormous amount of the religious work of our own times. This germ had two forms. It was, first of all, a renewed emphasis on the central principle of the Protestant Reformation—that religion is a personal and vital, not a ceremonial or magical matter; that salvation comes by faith, which results in godly living and spiritual experience, not by formal connection with a visible church, attendance on its services, and performance of its rituals in birth, in marriage, and in death. Genuine religion, it was increasingly felt, could only spring out of a consciousness of the immediate relationship of the individual to God. Religion thus was recovered for the layman; it was no longer the peculiar property of the clergy.

This was the point of transition to the second form of the vitalising germ—this, namely, that the religious activity of the layman was to be exercised, not merely in spiritual experience of his own heart, but also in his actual co-operation in the religious services, even in preaching, and in the management of the church organisation. This second element of the new movement showed itself of necessity chiefly among dissenters, and is in large measure the cause of their great growth during the present century. It was closely connected with a renewed emphasis on the Free Churchman's conception of the nature of the Church and the proper conditions of membership, which insist on a vitalising religious experience as a pre-requisite for entering the Church, and on a continual godly life as a condition of continued membership.

The influence of this new religious movement was not confined, however, to those who severed themselves from the already existing churches in order to join the newly-formed Methodist or Wesleyan Churches. Although showing itself most markedly in them, renewed spiritual life sprang up in due time among other Churches, Established and Dissenting, as well.

The active participation of laymen in religious services and organisations has been described as the salient peculiarity of the Christianity of the nineteenth century. It has made possible the enormous multiplication of religious services and religious societies, which will claim our notice in due time. Unpaid service in the Church has both multiplied the number of workers in an extraordinary way, and it has likewise tended to spiritualise and ennoble it. The admission of tens of thousands of lay preachers into the pulpits, together with the many hundreds of thousands of unpaid Sunday-school teachers, has rendered possible a wide moral and religious instruction of the people, which, it is safe to say, would have been absolutely impossible on any other system. The Established Church has felt and profited by the influence of this movement. Laymen, who till late years were excluded from the pulpits of its consecrated churches, are now in London (and to a certain extent elsewhere) permitted to preach there under conditions ; and this movement shows every sign of spreading. In its countless mission-rooms and unconsecrated churches lay ministry is welcomed by authority, and the 'licensed lay readers' are now numbered by the thousand.

We are now prepared to consider statistical evidences of the growth of the churches in England and Wales.

We begin with a few fragmentary statistics of the churches prior to 1800.

The number of church buildings belonging to the Established Church, and their seating capacity prior to 1800, does not seem to be on record, nor have I found any statement as to the number of the clergy earlier than the beginning of this century. The only indication of that number is the statement that, by the Act of Conformity, passed in 1662, 2000 clergymen of the Established Church left their places. What proportion of the whole number this was we have no means of judging, but there must certainly have been several thousands left.

There seems to be good reason for thinking that in 1716 there were in England and Wales 1107 Presbyterian and Congregational, and 247 Baptist congregations. These figures were increased to 1118 and 391 respectively by 1776.

The Methodists made tolerably rapid gains even during the early decades of their history. Beginning to form congregations before the middle of the last century, by 1770 they had 119 ministers, and a church membership of over 26,000 persons. Their statistics for the eighteenth century are as follows:[1]—

	Ministers.	Members.
1770	119	26,283
1780	170	37,721
1790	278	58,673

We take next the statistics of church growth during the first half of this century.

[1] Census 1851, ' Religious Worship,' p. lxxviii.

GROWTH OF THE NUMBER OF PLACES OF WORSHIP
AND SITTINGS IN ENGLAND AND WALES, 1801–1851.[1]

	Population.	Places of Worship.	Sittings.	Rate of Increase.		No. of Sittings to 100 of Pop.
				Pop.	Sittings.	
1801	8,892,536	15,080	5,171,123	...	...	58.1
1811	10,164,256	16,490	5,524,348	14.3 %	6.8 %	54.4
1821	12,000,236	18,796	6,094,486	18.0 ,,	10.3 ,,	50.8
1831	13,896,797	22,413	7,007,091	15.8 ,,	15.0 ,,	50.4
1841	15,914,148	28,017	8,554,638	14.5 ,,	22.5 ,,	53.8
1851	17,927,609	34,467	10,212,563	12.6 ,,	19.5 ,,	57.0

In the above table we have a summary view of the
growth of all the churches of all the denominations, so
far as the voluntary census was able to reach them.
Since our interest is primarily in the ratios and the
growth, rather than in the aggregate numbers, we may
accept these figures as substantially correct. We see
that during the first two decades the growth of the
population far outran that of the church accommodation.
The number of seats fell from fifty-eight to fifty in
each hundred of the population ; but by the end of the
fifth decade the old ratio was nearly restored, the growth
of churches having exceeded that of the people. Both
of these doubled in fifty years.

Since 1851 no enumeration, even tolerably complete,
has been made of church accommodation. That which
most nearly approaches it is a table compiled from the
denominational year-books of 1896 by Mr. Howard
Evans, and published in the *Contemporary Review* for
February 1897. According to these figures, there are

[1] Census 1851, ' Religious Worship,' p. cxxxi.

to-day 14,388,291 seats, or 47.4 seats for each hundred of the population. This is an apparent loss of about 10 per cent., but it must not be forgotten that these recent figures are for only ten out of the many denominations. We shall not probably be far astray in the conclusion that the ratio does not vary materially from that which existed in 1801 and in 1851.

The keen critic will be likely to object at this point, if not earlier, calling attention to the fact that the amount of church accommodation at any particular time signifies nothing as to the religious life at that time. The mere existence of the churches proves nothing in regard to church attendance and church membership. Churches built from two hundred to five hundred years ago, or even twenty-five years ago, prove nothing as to the spiritual life to-day. For aught we know, they may be standing absolutely closed. The churches needed and built by one generation may be abandoned by the next. There is a truth in this criticism which must not be overlooked. It is certainly true that there are churches existing now which are utterly unused.

But it is a fair answer to the supposed critic that, although we grant the force of his argument, yet it does not affect us, for the simple reason that we are not arguing from the existence of church buildings to the fact of church attendance or of piety. We are arguing from the fact of *growth* of church accommodation to the growth of church attendance, and growth of interest in the church life. No rational man will for a moment suppose that dying religious organisations will go on building churches decade after decade—churches which are decreasingly used, or continuously abandoned, simply to prove to themselves or to the world that they are not dying, or for any other reason! The outlay on the 20,000 new places of worship opened in the course of the fifty years (1801–1851), on the moderate estimate of £2500 each, would amount to £50,000,000. To suppose dying churches able to raise such a sum is rather preposterous. The growth of church accommodation, then, does not point to a waning attachment of the people to the Church, for it is by the gifts of those alone who believe in the churches that the buildings are erected.

An interesting item in the religious census of 1851, is the record of the number of attendants on all the services held in the 34,467 places of worship reported in the census. Mr. Horace Mann also attempted to estimate the number of different persons attending the services on that day. Below are the figures he gives.

ATTENDANCE ON PLACES OF WORSHIP,
MARCH 30, 1851.[1]

	Total Attendance at all Services.	Estimated No. of different Persons.
The Established Church	5,292,551	2,971,258
Protestant Dissenters	5,603,515[2]	3,110,782
Roman Catholic[3] .	...	249,389
Others[3] . . .	.·.	24,793
Total . . .	10,896,066	6,356,222

[1] Census 1851, ' Religious Worship,' pp. clxxxii. and ccc.
[2] This figure includes Roman Catholics and others.
[3] In all tables where these figures are not separately mentioned, they are included among dissenters.

From the table given above we perceive that the total number of attendance at all the services was slightly in excess of the total number of available seats. Comparing the seating capacity with the attendance, we notice that on that particular day the Dissenters had considerably better attendance than the Established Church. The latter had about 25,000 seats that would have been unoccupied, had all the attendants been different persons attending simultaneous services, whereas the Dissenters, under the same conditions, would have been deficient by about 708,000 seats. Since we have no general statistics for attendance at any later or any earlier period, it is impossible to institute any comparisons as to increase or decrease of church attendance. The only conclusion we can draw is that the number of different persons attending was moderately large, being rather more than one-third of the total population. If about one-third of the entire population attended service on one particular Sabbath, will it be unwarrantable to assume that from one-half to two-thirds attend more or less regularly?

As to how many new places of worship have been opened since 1851, we have no direct information. We know that there has been a gain of seats of not less than 4,170,000, which, at an average of 300 seats to a church means nearly 14,000 churches. Taking our former supposition, that the average cost of a church is at least £2500, we may conclude that, roughly speaking, the churches have expended a sum not far short of £40,000,000 in forty-five years for church buildings. Adding this to the £50,000,000, which we have reason to think was spent in the first half of the century, we reach the result that about £90,000,000 have been raised by

Christians in this century for the single item of church erection.

Three observations are natural here. The first is, that with the exception of about £1,500,000, received by the Established Church from parliamentary grants early in the century, all the rest has been raised by voluntary contributions of the nation, probably not more than one-half of whom take any vital interest in the churches. Of this £90,000,000, a table later on will show that the Established Church has raised about £42,550,000. Very roughly, then, we may say that the Free Churches have raised about £50,000,000. The £42,550,000 raised by the Established Church includes amounts expended on repairs, and is therefore not to be taken strictly.

The second observation is, to note that the provision actually made by the churches in this period of ninety-five years falls short of that which we estimated in Part I. should be provided, by about 10,000 buildings, costing about £25,000,000. Our estimate, however, was based on the assumption that there should be sixty-eight seats to a hundred people, a ratio that has never been attained.

Our third observation is, that progress in church building was considerably greater in the first half of the century. But again we need to remind ourselves that our figures for 1896 include the reports of only ten of the larger denominations. Were all the smaller bodies included, as in 1851, we would probably find that the growth had not varied very much. One thing is tolerably clear. The theory of a rapidly dying church is untenable.

The question of the distribution of the church accommodation is not unimportant. In his invaluable *Report*

7

on the Religious Census of 1851 (p. ccxcvii.) Mr. Mann
gives the following figures as the result of his laborious
investigations.

	COUNTIES.		LARGE TOWNS.	
	Sittings to 100 of Population	Ratio of Sittings to Total of Sittings.	Sittings to 100 of Population	Ratio of Sittings to Total of Sittings.
Established Church .	29.6	51.9	17.2	47.8
Free Churches . .	27.6	48.1	18.8	52.2
	57.2	100.0	36.0	100.0

As we had every reason to expect, the counties were
much more fully provided than large towns, the ratio
being as fifty-seven to thirty-six for each hundred of the
population. We have nothing more recent with which
to compare these figures. The Report of the Church
Extension Committee, however, gives a little light which
may be useful at this point. One quotation must suffice.

'Since 1851, and especially during the last two
decades, more frequent services have become the rule.
This tendency has been publicly commented upon in
the case of the Church of England, the Salvation Army,
and other bodies. It is common to all the churches.
Adult Sabbath Morning Schools, the P.S.A. Movement,
now so rapidly advancing, and separate services for
children and young people, which are now very generally
held both morning and evening, must be added in a
just calculation of attendance at public worship. In

most large towns it may be said that buildings which were used twice on the Lord's Day when Mr. Horace Mann took his religious census, are now used thrice, and a similar extension has taken place in week-day services and gatherings. If it could be effected, a re-distribution of religious accommodation throughout the country would meet every existing need.'[1]

As a partial answer to our question concerning the increasing or decreasing hold of organised Christianity on the people, so far as statistics have anything to tell us, we can say, I think, that during the first half of the century there was no material numerical change. Although the population grew at a prodigious rate, and a reconstruction of society and a relocation of the people were taking place amidst grave industrial changes, yet, on the whole, the growth of the churches kept pace with that of the people, though lagging very decidedly behind in the larger cities. This growth, how-ever, was made, as will be seen more clearly a little later on, not by the Established Church, but by the Free Churches. The increase of these voluntary religious associations, in which laymen took such a leading part, was truly phenomenal. What the nation would have been with-out them, it is not hard to see.

With regard to the period since 1851, the facts are not so clear. The recent statistics are very insufficient. It is clear, however, that relatively the Established Church has been growing faster than during the first fifty years, and the Free Churches more slowly. Together, they probably about keep up the average.

One further matter is worthy of notice before we draw this part of our chapter to a close. It is the

[1] *The Congregational Year-Book*, 1894, p. 485.

question of the growth of church accommodation and
attendance in London. We have already noted that
large towns are in a much worse condition than the
counties, the latter having (in 1851) about twenty-one
seats to one hundred of its population more than the
former. Since London may be assumed to be the city
where all the evils are at their worst, it is a matter of
no little interest to inquire what has been the growth,
or lack of it, in London during the last few decades.
While the population has doubled, have the churches
doubled? Since London is the most congested part of
England, the place where poverty seems to be most
grinding, and where the incidental evils of industrialism,
as overcrowding and segregation of classes, appear in
their most virulent forms, if we find grounds for not
utterly despairing about London, we may be allowed to
have some hope for the rest of England, even without
any detailed study of it.

Let us take up first the question of accommodation,
placing side by side the figures for the population and
the sittings given by three successive enumerations,
namely :—

    1. That of 1851 by the Religious Census ;
    2. That of 1865 by the *Nonconformist* ;[1]
    3. That of 1886 by the *British Weekly.*[2]

From these figures we see that although the population of London has gained 91 per cent., the accommodation of the churches has gained 89 per cent. in
thirty-five years. The growth of the Established
Church was 56 per cent. in this period, while that of

[1] *Religion in London: Statistics of Church and Chapel Accommodation in* 1865, Appendix, pp. 3, 22.
[2] *The Religious Census of London*, 1888, pp. 52, 53.

all the Free Churches was 136 per cent, being one-third faster than the population.

GROWTH OF CHURCH SITTINGS IN LONDON.

	1851.	1865.	1886.
Population . . .	2,362,236	3,015,494	4,523,957[1]
Established Church .	409,834	512,067	641,966
Free Churches . .	288,715 [2]	405,828 [2]	624,762
Roman Catholic . .	...	...	56,850
Totals . . .	698,549	917,895	1,323,578
Seats to 100 of Population	29.5	30.4	29.3

We consider next the

GROWTH OF CHURCH ATTENDANCE IN LONDON.

	1851. March 30.	1886. October 24.
The Established Church .	495,227	561,811
The Free Churches . .	313,993	630,518
Roman Catholic, Greek, etc.	65,119	60,115
	874,339	1,252,444

The statistical effort of the *Nonconformist* in 1865 was limited to the single item of church accommodation. It therefore has no place in the above table.

[1] Estimated.　　　　[2] Including Roman Catholics.

Attendance on any particular Sabbath may, for various reasons, vary so much from the average that too much emphasis must not be laid on the result of a single census of attendance. Yet, with this caution, the statistics of attendance give us some help. According to these figures the growth of the attendance at the Free Churches (101 per cent.) slightly exceeded that of the population (91 per cent.), while attendance on the services of the Established Church gained 11 per cent.

On the whole, we may perhaps be not far astray if we conclude, that while there is no marked falling off in the proportion of church accommodation during the thirty-five years covered by the tables, yet there is probably some diminution in church attendance. Remembering that London is undoubtedly the most difficult and the most congested part of all England, that her rate of growth is twice as great as that of the rest of the country, gaining 91 per cent. in thirty-five years, while the rest of England and Wales gained only 47 per cent., I think we should not be unduly cast down by our results; nor yet is there occasion for special elation. It is evident that, if London is to be saved, the churches have got to be more active than they have been in the past. And this is equally true of all other places. But the signs of this increasing activity are not wanting. They will come into view later on, and will help us to feel a new courage and a new hope, which the figures thus far given would not warrant.

PART III. GROWTH OF RELIGIOUS AND BENEFICENT MOVEMENTS AUXILIARY TO THE CHURCHES.

Among the characteristics of nineteenth century Christianity, as seen in England and the United States, that which, perhaps, more than anything else, differentiates it from the Christianity of the seventeenth and eighteenth centuries, is the rise of many auxiliary organisations for Christian work, more or less closely connected with the churches, yet quite distinct from them. All the denominations have felt this movement, but it has naturally found freer scope among the members of the Free Churches. The close of the last century and the early part of this was especially fertile in the beginnings of such movements. From that period date a goodly number of our most important religious societies, such as the great Missionary Societies, the Bible Societies, the Christian Publication Societies, the Sunday-school Movement, etc. etc. If we would measure, or estimate with any degree of accuracy, the growth or decay of religious life in England and Wales, we must not confine our attention to church accommodation or attendance on religious services, important though these items are. We must take a wider view. We must observe the growth of the great religious activities carried on largely by laymen, in some cases closely connected with the churches, and in others quite free from all official connection, yet none the less truly at once expressing and helping onward the growth of the Kingdom of Christ.

Limitations of space forbid more than an outline of what might profitably fill a volume. I begin with the auxiliary movements more closely connected with organised religion and moral instruction, proceeding to those whose relation is not so conspicuous.

1. The Sunday-school Movement is one of the most significant religious growths of the nineteenth century. Like so many other important movements of our own

times, it traces its origin to the revival of spiritual religion, and the introduction of laymen to distinctively religious activity, in the latter part of the last century. ' From the day when Robert Raikes employed his first four teachers to instruct a few dozen neglected children, gathered from the back streets of Gloucester, in or about 1780, the Sunday school has been gradually increasing in numbers and usefulness, until its teachers are reckoned by hundreds of thousands, and its scholars by millions.'[1] The early statistics of this movement do not seem to have been gathered, as is often the case in new movements as yet quite unconscious of their future. The following figures of the later stages of its growth tell a most important story :—

GROWTH OF SUNDAY SCHOOLS IN ENGLAND AND WALES.[2]

	Teachers.	Scholars.	No. of Scholars to 100 of Pop.
1818	...	477,225	4.0
1833	...	1,545,890	11.0
1851	318,135	2,407,642	13.5
1880	...	3,800,000	15.0
1887	616,941	5,733,325	20.0

The facts revealed by this table are of extreme interest and importance. Although no later general

[1] *The Sunday School Army*, p. 4.
[2] Compiled from *The Sunday School Army : its Position and Progress.* A pamphlet by F. J. Hartley, F.S.S., 1889. No later summary for England and Wales has been published. These figures are of course for the enrolment. The actual attendance at the time of the census in 1851, for one particular Sunday (March 30) was 75 per cent. of enrolment for England, and 78.8 per cent. for Wales.

summary of the numbers of teachers and scholars has been made than that for 1887, we have no reason to think that there has been any essential change in the situation. During the period covered by these statistics the gains have been great and regular. The largest advance has been made in recent times. Whereas in 1818, at a time, it will be remembered, when the Free Churches were growing at a phenomenal rate, the number of those in the Sunday schools amounted to but 4 per cent. of the population, by 1887 that number was actually about 20 per cent., with 2 per cent. more acting as teachers. 'When it is remembered that the proportion of the population between five and twenty years of age is 32.19 per cent., and that many of the scholars begin to attend after they are five, and leave before they are twenty, while very few of them attend for the uninterrupted period of fifteen years, the conclusion is irresistible that, deducting the upper classes of society . . . six out of seven of the remainder have been under the instruction and influence of Sunday-school teachers.'[1] And this conclusion is sustained by the fact that 'a large proportion of the occupants of our prisons, penitentiaries, and refuges, during some portion of their early years, have been under Sunday-school instruction.' A comparison of this table with one to be presented shortly, showing the number of children in the day schools, will reveal the fact that the Sunday schools compare very favourably, preceding them in time and exceeding them in number of pupils.

Here is a growth in the instruction of the people, and chiefly of the young, in the moral and religious principles of the Kingdom of God, that has great

[1] *The Sunday School Army,* p. 15.

significance. This does not indicate that the people are growing away from the churches—for the Sunday school has been universally adopted by the churches. It is one of their strongest arms. Surely a people who decreasingly care for Christianity, and who are increasingly opposed to its organic expression in churches, would not increasingly send their children to its Sunday schools, or themselves become active teachers of the principles of the Kingdom they are supposed to ignore or oppose. Never before, in England at least, have so many millions been studying the Bible as in the last few decades. And it needs to be specially emphasised that all this study of the Bible and Sunday-school attendance is wholly additional to the regular services of the churches.

GROWTH OF THE YOUNG MEN'S CHRISTIAN
ASSOCIATION IN THE UNITED KINGDOM.

	Centres of Work.	Members.	Property.
1855 . .	40	6,000	...
1883 . .	292	45,955	£173,637
1890 . .	756	78,694	396,106
1897 . .	1298	98,899	479,525

2. Another movement of no slight significance is the effort of Christian young men to help and strengthen each other, seeking also to reach out and save those who are not yet Christians. It has many forms and names; the Young Men's Christian Association being perhaps the most common name, and the largest organisation of Christian young men. This movement of young men is a relatively recent one, the first society

having been organised in 1844, with a membership of sixteen men belonging to four different denominations. The table on p. 106 tells the story of its growth.

Since the aim of the organisation is specifically 'of young men for young men,' and since the total number of these is, compared with the nation, relatively small, we cannot expect to find very large numbers associated with it as active members. The value of the work of these associations, especially in large cities, in which young men are so liable to be beset with temptations, must be personally known to be properly appreciated. Although the membership is far less than what it might well be, yet its growth has been faster by far than the class for which it exists. But the point of special importance for us is, that the peculiar work of the associations is carried on by laymen, and for men over whom the churches have little or no influence. It is doing a work, therefore, outside and beyond that of the Church, yet in the fullest sympathy and co-operation with it. The fact of growth indicates a growth for the churches and of the Kingdom of God, won from among those least likely to be connected with the churches.

We need not dwell further on this movement among young men, though it may not be amiss to mention the names of two more societies which are doing good work each along its own line—the Church of England's Young Men's Society, and the Brotherhood of St. Andrew.

3. Of much more recent origin than the Y.M.C.A., but perhaps even more significant, is the ' Pleasant Sunday Afternoon Brotherhood.' The single aim being to reach non-church-going workmen, men whom the

ordinary services of the Church not only do not touch, but to whom, in too many cases, such services are positively obnoxious; the success of this movement speaks volumes for the new era in Christian activity which it has inaugurated. Beginning in 1875 with a single 'P.S.A.,' having a membership of about 100, by 1889 there were many such brotherhoods, having nearly 27,000 members; and now, in 1897, Mr. Blackman reports that there are about 2000 P.S.A.s, whose 'membership is upwards of 150,000.' When it is remembered that the membership consists entirely of men—men, the vast majority of whom never otherwise attend any religious service whatever, and that as members of the P.S.A. their attendance is regular; and when we further remember that in connection with this membership they secure regular incentives to live the nobler life, receiving each quarter some elevating book, paid for out of their own fees;—when we consider all these facts, we begin to gain some idea of the meaning and promise of this new advance, which is as yet only in its infancy. Its progress compares well with that of the Sunday school.

4. The Salvation Army is one of the signs of the times fairly conspicuous. It needs only to be mentioned, at once to suggest its varied and energetic activity in striving to save both the bodies and the souls of the downtrodden and outcast individuals and classes of society. The obloquy through which it has passed, and the well-earned position of respect and admiration which it now holds, and the recognition by all good men and women that it is an important factor in evangelising the unchurched masses, are well known to all intelligent men.

Its growth, too, has been very rapid, far in excess of that of the nation. When we consider that its activity is wholly among those elements of the population absolutely untouched by the usual methods of church work and church services, its growth is seen to be most significant. Annual statistics of its work in England and Wales alone are not published, it seems. The single item accessible is the fact, that in 1896 its halls furnished seats for 485,825 persons. In proportion to its seats, it doubtless has more attendance than any of the denominations. From the most recent leaflets published by the Salvation Army, the following statistics have been gathered :—

SALVATION ARMY SOCIAL WORK.

	British.	Foreign.	Total.
Food Depôts and Shelter . .	36	43	79
No. Beds supplied . . .	1,511,071	491,522	2,002,593
No. Meals ,, . . .	3,564,173	1,497,770	5,061,943
Workshops	12	20	32
No. for whom work has been found	11,849	19,829	31,678
Labour Bureaux	20	11	31
No. placed in Situations . .	13,448	1,874	15,322
Prison Gate Homes . . .	1	11	12
No. passed through . . .	463	1,553	2,016
Rescue Homes	16	50	66
No. passed through . . .	1,557	2,464	4,021
Slum posts	40	47	87
No. of Slum Sisters . . .	80	143	223
Farms	1	8	9
Children's Homes	...	13	13
Maternity Homes . . .	3	...	3
Lodging Houses	3	4	7
Midnight Posts	2	...	2

Whereas in 1878 there were fifty corps under eighty-eight officers, by 1896 (July) these 'had increased to 3603 corps under 11,979 officers (not one of whom has any guarantee of salary), who are holding 1,938,040 services every year in forty-five countries and colonies.'

The extent of the social work for the 'past year' (1895 ?) is given in the table on p. 109.

5. Brought into existence doubtless through the example and stimulus of the Salvation Army, and working along the same general lines, is the Church Army, an organisation for religious and social work under the lead of the Established Church. It traces its origin to a consciousness of the need of such work felt by certain bishops in 1882. At that time a 'Church of England working-man evangelist was almost unknown.' In 1888 social work was begun, and several Labour Homes were opened. Of these homes there are now (1896) fifty-two, having accommodation for 1300 inmates. Since the stay of each inmate is limited to three months, there pass through these homes over 5000 persons each year, about one-half of whom obtain work and a fresh start in life. 'A million meals are served annually, with labour test, irrespective of creed.' About sixty men and forty women are annually trained as evangelists and mission nurses for the Church Army and church work. The entire work of the Army is carried on under the direct supervision of the clergy of the various parishes. It is at work at present in 500 parishes. In addition to the regular or local work, the Army has twenty-eight vans with eighty-four evangelists, who continually circulate 'sound church gospel literature,' and hold one week's missions in the villages. For the support of this work, in addition to the sums received from the middle and higher classes, £15,000

are given by the poor themselves, making a total of £81,000 received 'last year' (1896?).

When we recall how recently the Salvation and Church Armies have come into existence, and when we consider the amount and character of the work they are doing, and the classes they reach, there is great reason for hopefulness of a yet larger and more successful work among those vast masses of the people still utterly beyond all religious influences.

We have thus far been considering those auxiliary agencies whose primary aim is the giving of religious instruction, and the exerting of direct religious influences. But these are by no means all the ways in which such instruction is given and such influences imparted. Oftentimes the less direct methods are the more effective. They, at any rate, supplement the more direct method. Continuing, then, our brief enumeration of the various auxiliaries of the churches, we mention next as worthy of no little attention—

6. The University or Social Settlements. Although the first of these was established only so recently as 1885,—the first tentative efforts had been made by Arnold Toynbee some ten years earlier,—yet the results already attained are exceedingly gratifying. These results, however, are not of such a tangible nature as may be made to appear in statistical tables. They consist rather of new ideas and ideals and methods of social work, and the giving of new inspiration for work of this kind. The movement promises great things. Though much has already been accomplished in the direction of creating a new atmosphere, both among the workers and among those who are sought, we believe the attainments thus far are only the prophecies of

a great work ahead. All classes are helped by this University Settlement method of work. It brings together in friendly relations the brain worker and the day labourer, the employer and the employed, the educated and the uneducated ; it helps each to see something of the way in which each views the other. It has been called the clearing - house between the various classes of society. It is the bridge that spans the chasm so threateningly yawning between them. It is perhaps quite as valuable to the upper classes as to any others. It opens their eyes to the wrongs and sufferings of their fellowmen, and to the righteousness of many at least of their complaints. It brings the brains of the cultured and highly-trained classes to consider and seek solutions to the problems which confront the working classes, and to do this from a standpoint of sympathy and fellow-feeling. Through the work of these settlements (and in other ways as well) it is becoming apparent how far the industrial world is from conforming to the principles of righteousness ; how much the whole social organism needs reorganisation along the lines of the Sermon on the Mount.

Already, in a brief experience of but ten years, this movement has accomplished not a little along these various lines. Toynbee Hall, Oxford House, Mansfield House, and many others, each doing quite characteristic work for the elevation of the most destitute and godless parts of the large cities, sometimes directly talking and preaching about the Kingdom of God, sometimes not appearing to do it at all, but none the less really working toward its establishment by practical godliness, living the doctrine of the brotherhood of man, have already more than justified their existence. They now only lack men and money to carry out their plans on a large scale and to do a work for the nation of inestimable value, simply from the sociological point of view. Statistically we note that there are thirty-five of these settlements in the United Kingdom, of which the larger number are in London. Many of these, however, are of very recent establishment, and are only just beginning their work. The seventy-three 'Working Men's Social Clubs,' all of them pledged to temperance principles, having a membership of thousands of men; the P.S.A.s in connection with these settlements, and often conducted by the residents; the part these residents take in the local political life of their respective districts; —these and many similar facts speak with great force of the growing activity for the welfare of the classes of society least open to the ordinary methods of direct Christian work. That these forms of work are really related to the upbuilding of the Kingdom of righteousness, who can doubt? He who would know the full meaning and promise of this new form of Christian activity (it is properly called Christian, even though there are some engaged in it who would spurn the name of Christian for themselves) should study it directly and personally. The point, however, of importance to our argument is, that this recent movement is a most auspicious sign of the growth of the Kingdom among those classes where that growth is by many most vigorously denied.

7. A still more indirect, but none the less truly an agency in upbuilding the Kingdom, is the immense number of charity and benevolent societies and organisations of all sorts and varieties, too innumerable even to be mentioned by classes. The directory to the

8

charities of London names over a thousand such institutions, and their income amounts to several millions of pounds annually. The figures for the growth of these benevolent societies from decade to decade, giving their work and their incomes, would tell a story of profound interest. Their growth during this century would be most significant; but the statistics needful to show it have never been compiled. I am trenching, however, on a line of thought which must be more fully presented in a later chapter. Yet in considering the growth of the Kingdom of God in England and Wales, the immense and growing sums annually spent in direct benevolence must be taken into account. This use of money is a practical execution of the principles of the Kingdom. There is no reason to think that it is diminishing. The Mansion House Indian Famine Relief Fund, after only about two months from the date of its opening, having received nearly £450,000, is a straw that shows how the wind is blowing.

8. Due place must likewise be accorded to the evidence afforded by the growing activity of the great religious publication societies, such as the Bible, Tract, and various denominational societies, and also the many religious weeklies and monthlies. Though largely dependent for their growth on business success attending the publication and sale of their publications, yet the fact that they are able to sell their specifically religious works indicates that there are increasing millions of those who buy and read. The devotional publications of such men as F. B. Meyer, and the sermons of such preachers as Spurgeon, which, as a rule, go into the homes of those who are already spiritually minded, are being sold to-day in quantities that would have seemed incredible a genera-

tion ago. Nor are these religious publications read only by the great middle and church-going classes. Religious literature, suited to the tastes and needs of the very poorest and lowest classes of society, is increasingly plentiful. The publications of the Salvation Army have 'a circulation of over 42,000,000 copies annually.' The *Church Army Gazette* reaches ' over a quarter of a million readers' every week ; and although the price is but a halfpenny the profits to the headquarters were £1522 in 1896. Never before were the lowest classes of society reading so much Christian literature.

GROWTH OF BOARD, BRITISH, NATIONAL, AND ROMAN CATHOLIC EDUCATION IN ENGLAND AND WALES.[1]

	Board Schools.		British.		National.		R. C.		Total.	
	Teachers.	Pupils.	Teachers.	Pupils.	Teachers.	Pupils.	Teachers.	Pupils.	Teachers.	Pupils.
1854	..	..	1,555	63,406	5,930	298,449	506	29,400	7,991	391,255
1861	..	..	3,870	101,573	15,223	530,490	1209	32,877	20,302	664,940
1871	..	..	6,076	245,444	20,440	857,315	1542	66,272	28,060	1,169,021
1881	21,764	769,252	9,191	364,420	39,931	1,471,615	3832	145,629	74,718	2,740,916
1891	41,898	1,491,571	10,587	386,206	47,076	1,677,123	5623	195,056	105,184	3,749,956
1895	54,455	1,879,218	10,107	364,875	52,876	1,850,545	4487	230,392	121,925	4,325,030

9. One of the conspicuous characteristics of the nineteenth century is the growth of popular education. A fuller consideration of its significance and especially of its

[1] Compiled from the Blue Books of the Council of Education. It seems desirable to state, for the information of those who may not know the facts, that the Board School system of public education was established only in 1871 ; that the British schools are chiefly, if not exclusively, voluntary schools, established by Nonconformists ; and the National schools are managed by the Church of England. The Government gives annual grants, upon certain conditions, even to the private or voluntary schools. The ' total' is of the four great classes of schools here enumerated. The next table gives the true total for Great Britain.

relation to Christianity, both as arising from Christian principles and as furthering their supremacy, we must defer to its appropriate place in a later chapter. But as helping to an answer to the question immediately before us, as to whether the Kingdom is growing or not in England and Wales, we need to take some notice of it here. The statistics on p. 115 merit careful study.

The system of making parliamentary grants in aid of private schools submitting to Government inspection, and maintaining a certain degree of efficiency, was established in 1830 by the formation of a Board of Education. It was given the power to expend £30,000. The system has grown. The total national appropriation for education of all kinds in 1895 was £10,032,835, in the United Kingdom. This does not include the millions raised privately by the Board and voluntary or denominational schools. The following table shows the

GROWTH OF EDUCATION IN GREAT BRITAIN
(not including Ireland).[1]

	Sum Voted.	Number of Schools Inspected.	Accommodation for Pupils.	Average Attendance.
1850	£180,000	2,613	...	225,500
1860	724,000	7,272	1,400,000	884,000
1870	912,000	10,949	2,215,000	1,454,000
1880	2,854,000	20,670	4,843,000	3,155,000
1888	4,168,000	22,326	6,043,000	4,111,000
1894 [2]	6,390,232	22,763	6,602,000	4,793,276

By these tables the fact is brought out very clearly that popular education is a relatively very recent thing,

[1] Mulhall's *Dictionary of Statistics*, 1892, p. 232.
[2] *Whittaker's Almanack*, 1896, pp. 160, 377.

and that it has been growing far faster than the population. The number of pupils in the schools has increased from about 1.0 per cent. of the population in 1850 to 15.7 per cent. in 1895. When it is remembered that these schools teach not only facts, but truths; not only how to read and write, but also to think and to obey; together with no small amount of moral and religious truth, we begin to gain some conception of the great increase in recent over past times, of direct instruction of the masses in matters that have a most intimate connection with the Kingdom, although not immediately resulting in the growth of the churches. Taking the church services, the Sunday schools, and the day schools all together, it is safe to say that no previous generation ever had so much direct moral and religious instruction as the present one is receiving.

10. The statistics given above become still more impressive when we set beside them those relating to crime and pauperism. In this section we take the first of these (see p. 118).

In that table we have a most valuable series of progressions. Education, both secular and religious, reaches continuously larger proportions of the youth of the land, while criminal convictions are just as continuously decreasing. It may be said by the critic that economic conditions, efficiency of police organisation, and a change in the strictness of judicial penalties, have more to do with the increase or decrease of criminal convictions than has education, either secular or religious. This is not the place to enter into a discussion of criminology. But it may not be amiss to observe that, even supposing the critic to be correct

EDUCATION AND CRIME IN ENGLAND AND WALES.[1]

	Sunday-School Children to 100,000 of Population.	Day-School Children to 100,000 of Population.	Annual Average of Convictions.	Number of Criminals to 100,000 of Pop.
1841–50	12,000	1,100	24,300	122
1851–60	13,500	2,600	21,200	96
1861–70	14,000	4,700	17,010	68
1871–80	14,500	8,200	13,900	50
1881	15,000	10,500	(?)	(?)
1887	20,000	12,500	12,150	38
1894	(?)	15,900	9,934	31

we still have a remarkable evidence of the growth of the Kingdom in the fact that, whatever be the connection, or lack of it, between the sets of facts, while the population has gained 75 per cent., day school education has gained 2219 per cent., and the number of convicted criminals has apparently diminished 75 per cent., dwindling from 12.2 criminals among 10,000 persons in 1841, to 3.1 in 1894. Surely this great change can hardly be charged entirely to inefficiency of the police or judicial systems. While we may readily admit that economical, police, and judicial conditions do have an important relation to the increase or decrease of crime, it is nevertheless true that they are not the only, nor even the most important factors in crime. Character is far more important. Indeed, it would not be far from the truth to say that character is the vital, because the internal, factor, while economic conditions, etc., because external, are only conditions. What vitally affects

[1] Cf. Mulhall's *Dictionary of Statistics*, 1892, p. 233, and the preceding tables on Sunday and day schools ; from these latter the first two columns have been computed.

CHART XII

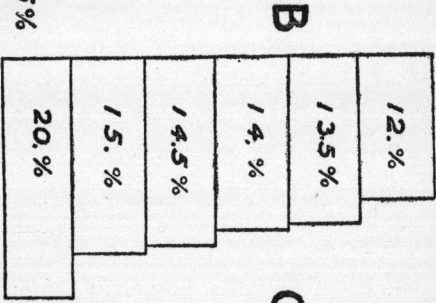

Illustrating the Growth of Sunday and Day School
Education & the Decrease of Criminal Convictions in England & Wales

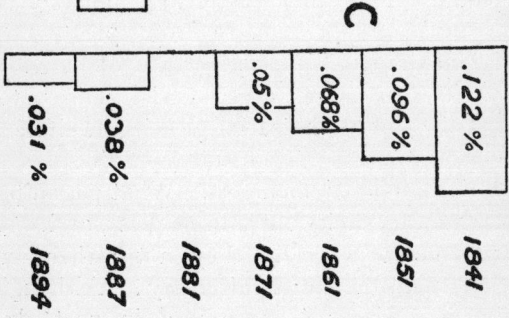

DAY SCHOOL PUPILS	S.S. PUPILS	CRIMINAL CONVICTIONS	
A	**B**	**C**	
1841 1.1%	12.%	.122 %	1841
1851 2.6%	13.5 %	.096 %	1851
1861 4.7%	14.%	.068%	1861
1871 8.2%	14.5 %	.05%	1871
1881 10.5%	15.%	.038 %	1881
1887 12.5%	20.%	.031 %	1887
1894 15.9%			1894

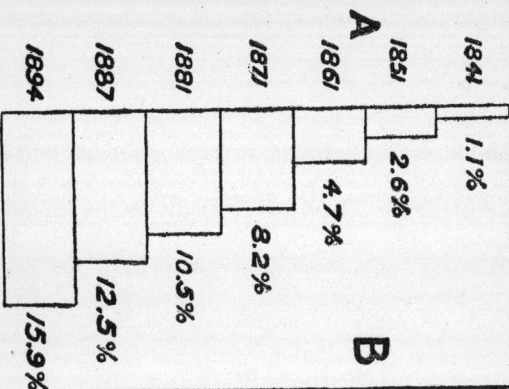

119

character, therefore, as religious and general education do, or ought to, has an important bearing on crime. In order to bring out clearly the full force of this inverse progression of education and criminal convictions, the chart on p. 119 has been prepared.

11. The decrease of paupers, while the population is growing rapidly, is a fact of no little importance. The following figures are given by Mulhall in his invaluable work (p. 439) :—

PAUPERS AND POOR-RELIEF IN ENGLAND AND WALES.

	Total Number of Paupers.	Per 1000 Inhabtnts.	Expenditure.	Pounds per Pauper.	Cost per Inhabtnt.
1850	921,000	51.1	£5,400,000	5.9	72 pence.
1860	851,000	42.6	5,450,000	6.4	66 ,,
1870	1,079,000	46.9	7,650,000	7.1	80 ,,
1880	803,000	30.9	8,020,000	10.0	74 ,,
1888	810,000	28.0	8,440,000	10.4	72 ,,

Little comment on these interesting figures is needful. The decrease of paupers from 51 to 28 per thousand inhabitants, with an increase of expenditure from £5.9 to £10.4, are the special points to be noticed. This surely indicates growing welfare, and also a growing sense of responsibility on the part of the nation for its individual members. What pagan people ever took such care of its old and helpless, of its feeble and insane members? Did they not rather expose them, or let them die most miserably? Although the diminution in paupers is no doubt in part due to economic laws, over which man has no control, yet it is also in part due to wise legislation establishing just trade relations, enforced by honest officials, and in countless ways stimulating manhood and self-respect. Such legislation, while not perhaps consciously, is nevertheless really Christian, and is due to the growing power of the Kingdom of truth and righteousness in this land.

12. Closely connected with the preceding section, and suggested indeed in its closing sentence, is a point which needs peculiar emphasis. It is the growing sense of righteousness and justice. The fact that the interests and welfare of the working classes are increasingly finding recognition, not merely because it is politic—although this motive without doubt is the sole motive that moves many—but because justice demands such recognition, is but one more indication of the growth of the Kingdom of God. This point will come up again for much fuller consideration in a later chapter. I content myself with one single illustration, namely, the progressive widening of the elective franchise during the present century. The relation of the idea of democracy (in its true sense) to Christianity must be deferred to its proper place further on. But no estimate of the growth of Christ's Kingdom in England and Wales would be fair to the facts which made no reference to this most significant sign of the times. For the point of our interest is that this widening of the franchise was not due to violent seizure of it by those who had not possessed it. It has not been wrung from the ruling few by threats or intimidations. On the contrary, it has been granted by the few to the many, on the principles of general righteousness and justice. It indicates a growing confidence in each other as reasonable men ; it indicates an increase of mutual goodwill. Yet what

is this but the growth of the Kingdom of God? **The** following table gives the

GROWTH OF VOTERS IN ENGLAND AND WALES.[1]

1835 . . . 668,000	1881 . . . 2,538,000
1846 . . . 846,000	1889 . . . 4,502,000
1871 . . . 2,066,000	

PART IV.—DENOMINATIONAL STATISTICS.

Although we might at this point bring this interminable chapter to a close, yet, in view of the intrinsic interest of the subject, I venture to present with only the briefest remarks some statistical tables regarding the growth and present size of the leading religious bodies. Should the reader be not interested in such statistics, he will do well to pass at once to the few general conclusions with which this chapter ends. The statistics in this Part (IV.) have no immediate bearing on those conclusions.

1. We begin with the statistics of the *Established Church*—

(a) GROWTH OF THE NUMBER OF PLACES OF WORSHIP AND SITTINGS PROVIDED BY THE ESTABLISHED CHURCH, 1801–1851.

	Places of Worship.	Sittings.	Rate of Increase of Pop.	Rate of Increase of Sittings.	No. of Sittings to 100 of Pop.
1801	11,379	4,289,883	...	...	48.2
1811	11,444	4,314,388	14.3 p. ct.	0.6 p. ct.	42.4
1821	11,558	4,357,366	18.0 ,,	1.0 ,,	36.3
1831	11,883	4,481,891	15.8 ,,	2.9 ,,	32.3
1841	12,668	4,775,836	14.5 ,,	6.6 ,,	30.0
1851	14,077	5,317,915	12.6 ,,	11.3 ,,	29.7

[1] Mulhall's *Dictionary of Statistics*, 1892, p. 244.

CHART. XIV.

Illustrating the proportion
of population to sittings
furnished by the Church
of England.

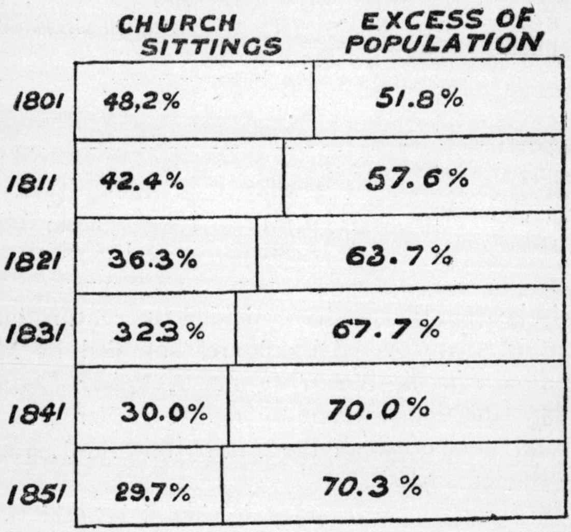

	CHURCH SITTINGS	EXCESS OF POPULATION
1801	48.2%	51.8%
1811	42.4%	57.6%
1821	36.3%	63.7%
1831	32.3%	67.7%
1841	30.0%	70.0%
1851	29.7%	70.3%

(b) GROWTH OF THE ESTABLISHED CHURCH, 1861–1895.

	Clergy.	Sittings.	Confirmations.
1861	c. 17,000	...	...
1871	c. 18,500	5,448,891	117,852[1]
1881	c. 20,800	c. 6,000,000	176,783
1891	c. 21,000	c. 6,465,000	214,730
1895	c. 21,600	6,778,288	217,743

(c) GROWTH OF VOLUNTARY CONTRIBUTIONS FOR THE ERECTION OF NEW AND THE REPAIR OF OLD CHURCHES BELONGING TO THE ESTABLISHED CHURCH.

	Total.	Per Year.
1801–1831[2]	£1,847,956	£51,598
1831–1851[2]	5,575,615	278,780
1840–1874[3]	25,548,703	729,962
1873–1892[3]	20,531,402	1,026,570

It will be seen that we have divided the century into two periods, that covered by figures supplied by Mr. Horace Mann in his *Report on the Religious Census*, 1801–1851, and that covered by figures gathered from the Official Year-Books of the Church and the London Diocese Books (annual).

In the interests of accuracy it should be said that the sums given in the above tables do not include estimates for churches not reporting, nor any sums under £500. Were these included, the sum totals would be much larger. The overlappings of dates are also to be noted. In the last two lines, I have estimated

[1] 1872.   [2] *Religious Census*, 1851, p. xli.
[3] *Official Year-Book of the Church*, 1896, pp. 566, 567.

the yearly average, on the assumption that 1840–1874
covers a period of 35 years, and 1873–1892 a period of
20 years. The total for the whole period from 1801–
1892, would seem to be about £42,550,000.

2. *The Free Churches.*

(*d*) GROWTH OF THE NUMBER OF PLACES OF WORSHIP
AND SITTINGS PROVIDED BY THE FREE CHURCHES,
1801–1851.

	Places of Worship.	Sittings.	Rate of Increase of Population.	Rate of Increase of Sittings.	No. of Sittings to 100 of Pop.
1801	3,698	881,240	...	...	9.9
1811	5,046	1,209,960	14.3 p. ct.	37.2 p. ct.	12.0
1821	7,238	1,737,120	18.0 ,,	43.0 ,,	14.5
1831	10,530	2,525,200	15.8 ,,	45.3 ,,	18.1
1841	15,349	3,778,802	14.5 ,,	49.6 ,,	23.8
1851	20,390	4,894,648	12.6 ,,	29.5 ,,	26.3

The figures of this table are compiled from preceding
tables, partly by rearrangement, and partly by new
computations.

The chief point of interest is the extraordinary growth,
far surpassing the growth of the population. In this
connection the following quotation from the *Encyclopædia Britannica*[1] may not be without interest: 'A
careful analysis of the marriage returns for forty years
from 1837 to the end of 1876 makes it apparent that

[1] Vol. viii. p. 246.

the number of Nonconformists is steadily increasing, and that although the great majority of the population still adhere to the Church of England, the probability seems that it will be otherwise in the course of one or two generations.'

(*e*) THE FREE CHURCHES IN 1896.[1]

	Sittings.	Communi-cants.	Sunday-Schl. Teachers.	Sunday-Schl Scholars.
Baptists [2] .	1,231,024	316,569	47,283	483,073
Congrega-tionalists .	1,626,865	406,716	59,103	603,841
Presbyterians .	156,815	69,632	7,452	80,969
Wesleyans .	2,165,657	529,786	130,286	955,962
Prim. Meth. .	909,823	196,628	61,899	466,052
Calvin. ,,	420,000	147,297	25,118	194,798
United ,,	368,242	79,657	24,391	193,826
Meth. New Connexion .	135,728	33,932	10,857	83,377
Bible Christns.	110,024	27,506	7,296	41,387
Salva. Army .	485,825	...	...	...
	7,600,003	1,807,732	373,685	3,103,285
Estab. Church	6,776,288	1,778,361	200,596	2,329,813

[1] Cf. *Contemporary Review*, Feb. 1897, where Mr. Evans explains the origin of this table in detail. Enough here to say that the figures are taken from the year-books, with a few exceptions.

[2] It is a taunt frequently flung at the Free Churches that there are over 250 denominations, and new ones forming each year. This assertion rests on the list of registered places in which marriages may be legally per-formed. The latest number is 293. Any cursory examination of the list shows at once that many of these places are denominations in no sense whatever. Here are a few of the names :—

Bible Defence Association.
Blackburn Psychological Society.
Halifax Psychological Society.
Hope Mission.

Describing the two preceding tables, the following quotation finds its place :—

'With regard to Mr. Horace Mann's calculation as to the number of sittings in 1801, it was founded on the Census Returns of 1851 ; when, as far as possible, information was obtained as to the date of erection of all places of worship. It can only be regarded as approximately correct ; but there is no reason to doubt Mr. Mann's impartiality. The figures are all the more astonishing, when we consider the vast wealth of the Established Church, and its almost

---

Lodging-House Mission Association.
Society for Visiting the Sick.
Young Men's Christian Association.
Young Women's Christian Association.
Woman's Mission.
British and Foreign Sailors' Society.
Children's Special Service Association.
Moslems !
Eastern Orthodox Greek Church !
Church of England !
Presbyterian Church of England.
Presbyterian Church of Scotland.
Presbyterian Church of Wales.
Roman Catholic Church.
Salvation Army.
Salvation Navy.
Rescue and Evangelisation Mission.
Christian Soldiers.
Gospel Lifeboat Missioners.
Gospel Army Mission.
Mormons !
Latter-Day Saints !
Spiritualist Investigation Society.
People's Gospel Mission.
Working Men's Evangelistic Mission Chapels.

This is a motley array of denominations! The truth is, most of the names here given are not denominations at all. How many more of the 293 'denominations' are of this variety, missions, union evangelistic efforts, Mormons, etc., it would be interesting to know. An authoritative list of genuine denominations, or *groups* of *associated churches*, is a desideratum.

exclusive hold on the aristocracy and upper middle class. Until the passing of the Toleration Act (1689) Nonconformity hardly had any fixed local habitation. Its adherents had to meet, when they were allowed to meet at all, in the halls of city guilds, in private houses, barns, and temporary buildings. Practically Nonconformity started in 1689 with no sittings at all. In the first hundred and ten years it provided nine hundred thousand sittings. In the fifty years succeeding it provided four millions more. In the forty-five years that followed it provided two and three-quarter millions more. Yet never, from first to last, has Nonconformity received a single penny from the State for the erection of places of worship, and it has always supported its own ministers.

' Now let us take the Established Church, which at the beginning of the period started with possession of all the ancient parish churches and cathedrals, and national endowments of the value of £6,000,000 a year. Between the passing of the Toleration Act (1689) and the year 1801 there was hardly any church building, save in London; when the ' Queen Anne Churches ' were built by means of local taxation. At the beginning of the century the Established Church started with rather more than four and a quarter million seats. Although Parliament voted £1,370,000 for church building, and relieved church building materials from taxation, and although very large sums were also borrowed on the security of church rates, by 1851 only about one million more seats had been provided. In the last forty-five years, when the Established Church has had to rely almost entirely upon voluntary effort for church building, nearly one and a half millions of additional seats have been provided.'

3. *The Roman Catholic Church.*

The question as to the growth of the Roman Catholic Church in England is one of considerable interest. It might appear from the first table below that the Roman Catholic Church has been making great gains. If, however, we recall the fact that multitudes of emigrants from Ireland have come to England, especially during the time of the great famine, we are led to look a little further. The second table corrects the impression made by the first.

(*f*) THE GROWTH OF ROMAN CATHOLICISM IN ENGLAND AND WALES.[1]

	Total Number.	Number to 100 of Population.
1699 . .	27,696	0.50 per cent.
1767 . .	68,000	1.00 ,,
1780 . .	69,400	0.90 ,,
1845 . .	284,300	1.70 ,,
1851 . .	758.800	4.22 ,,
1861 . .	927,500	4.61 ,,
1891 . .	1,500,000	5.01 ,,

(*g*) THE GROWTH OF ROMAN CATHOLICISM IN ENGLAND, WALES, AND IRELAND.[1]

	Total Number.	Number to 100 of Population.
1841 . .	6,958,737	28.8 per cent.
1851 . .	6,137,749	25.1 ,,
1871 . .	5,141,933	18.2 ,,
1891 . .	5,047,307	14.9 ,,

[1] Dorchester's *Problem of Religious Progress*, Appendix.

9

Part V. Conclusions.

It is to be hoped that the reader has judiciously skipped all that has failed to interest him in this extended chapter. Yet, long as it is, I do not flatter myself by thinking that I have done the subject justice. Because of the lack of sufficient statistical information from which to draw an immediate conclusion, it seemed desirable to allow ourselves considerable liberty in the study, first of the problem itself, and then of the various direct and side lights that would help us to an accurate conclusion. Some of the points touched on will come up again. Others which might have been brought in here have been entirely ignored for the present. In this chapter we have been primarily studying the statistical evidences for the growth or decay of the Kingdom. In later chapters we shall consider other evidences. The conclusions which I venture to think we may legitimately draw from the facts are—

1. In spite of the rapid growth of the population, and its aggregation in cities and large towns, the churches as a whole are fairly holding their own. In some districts there may be loss, and in others gain.

2. Direct moral and religious instruction is far more general than ever before.

3. The principles of righteousness and justice, which are essential elements of the Kingdom of God, are more widely recognised and practised by all classes to-day than in any previous generation.

4. The recent movements of aggressive Christians, in such forms of work as the Y.M.C.A., the P.S.A., the Salvation and Church Armies, the University Settlements, etc., give ground for hope that the great working

class, which seems the most alienated from the Church and from religion, may be reclaimed at least for the Kingdom of God, even if not formally connected with the various existing church organisations.

6. The religious life of the churches as a whole is far more spiritual and real than it has been for at least two hundred years. There has been a marked growth in recent decades in this respect. From the nature of the case statistical evidence of this is impossible. It has therefore not received much notice in this chapter; yet, after all, this is the most important of all the facts that have been presented.

The Outlook (April 1897) published a most enlightening description of 'The Higher Life of London,' by Sir Walter Besant. He who would become acquainted with the nobler side of London could make no better beginning than by giving this paper a careful reading. As bearing witness to what has been said in the preceding pages regarding various difficulties and problems, the following paragraphs are most pertinent :—

'What is included in the higher life of London? Surely everything which advances its people—the agencies, societies, institutions, churches, colleges, schools, libraries, which act incessantly and unweariedly upon this huge mass of five million souls, most of whom, but for these agencies, would be continually choosing the easier way, and sinking lower and lower. There is the work of keeping alive the religion of the people—a task of enormous difficulty ; there is the work of rescue ; there is the work of education ; there is the work of restoration—most difficult of all ; there is the work of temperance ; there is the capture of waifs and strays ; there is the work of relief ; there is the care of the sick ; there is the work of admonishing the easy class of their duties and their responsibilities ;—on all these subjects one could write volumes, and yet the result would be but a tale half told.

'The note of that larger charity which feeds the mind and purifies the soul ; which, like the nobler kind of medical science, ascertains causes and destroys microbes ; which especially characterises the charity of the present day—is personal service. It is not too much to say that until very recently personal service was a thing unknown. Five hundred years ago, however, it was known ; then the world enjoyed the personal service of the Franciscans, not yet crystallised into a mere form. In the eighteenth century there was no personal service at all, save that of the hospitals, in which physicians and surgeons and nurses were paid. The century was not, on the whole, lacking in charity ; almshouses and "charity" schools were founded, though not in such numbers as in preceding ages. Nor was it by any means an irreligious age, seeing that in London nearly every church had its two daily services, its week-day and its Sunday lectures; there was, it is true, atheism in certain circles, and there was paganism in the lower strata; but the great middle class, throughout the century, was profoundly religious. In every church a learned divine preached sermons on doctrine; there were free seats for those poor who choose to come; the "means of grace" were freely offered. But, if they did not come, nobody asked why they stayed away or what sect they followed. The common people, as a fact, went neither to church nor to chapel; they lived chiefly in the suburbs—at Clerkenwell or Whitechapel, outside church influence; they were wholly illiterate; if they could read, there was nothing for them to read; there were no cheap newspapers, no cheap books, no free libraries; after their day's work they went home and drank; in the intervals of drink they fought—with cocks, with dogs, with fists. In the Hogarth pictures you will find something of the working man's life of that time. Never, I am sure, was there a time when our people were more thoroughly besotten and debased with drink. They were inarticulate; if they had grievances, they could not put them into words.

'The craftsman's greatest pleasure was in a hanging, conducted, as it was, with the pomp and ceremony of a triumphant procession all the way from Newgate to Tyburn. There was generally a "batch"—half a dozen men and women—taken out to die together; they rode in carts, sitting on their own coffins. The Ordinary went from one cart to another praying for them. They scoffed and jeered at him; the crowd, which was enormous, lining the whole road, cheered them as they passed. The young men ran beside the carts, shaking hands with these high-spirited martyrs who went out to die as cheerfully as St. Lawrence. Stalls were erected all along the line for the sale of gin. The friends of the sufferers, when they were turned off, pulled them by the feet to shorten their agonies. Realise, if you can, that procession, and think what lessons in civilisation and humanity were thus offered to the London mob!

'I say that the people were left to themselves; their hangings and their floggings were administered in public as a deterrent; pillory and stocks were served out with the same benevolent intention. But we cannot elevate a people by hanging them or by flogging them. Nor is it enough to open a church door and offer admission free to all the world. Charity schools there were, but they received no more than one in a hundred. Almshouses there were, but not enough for more than a fraction. Things grew daily worse. The lowest strata increased in numbers and in brutality until the Gordon Riots opened the eyes of London to the dangers in which they lived. Out of the experiments, tried one after the other—the church schools, the charity schools, the Sunday schools, the alms and doles and benefactions, the heavy duties on spirits, the cheap newspapers, the cheap books—we have come at last to personal service. "How shall I do my part in helping the poor?" asks the young man of the present day. Money, he has learned corrupts them; doles pauperise them. There is, in fact, nothing in the world that does the poor folk any real good except personal service among them.'

CHAPTER IV

STATISTICAL EVIDENCES OF THE
GROWTH OF THE KINGDOM OF GOD IN THE
UNITED STATES.

'I am not undertaking an exhaustive description, but only a brief characterisation of Evangelical Christianity, as it is manifested in the United States. It was never more powerful or prosperous.'[1]

'It would seem that no mind could fail to be impressed with the wonderful facts of American Protestantism, so transcending in magnitude and significance anything ever before seen in the history of Christianity.'[2]

---

[1] H. K. Carroll, LL.D., *The Religious Forces of the United States*, 1893, p. lx.

[2] Daniel Dorchester, D.D., *The Problem of Religious Progress*, revised edition, 1894, p. 605.

CHAPTER IV

IN studying the question of the growth of the
Kingdom in the United States, we shall find our
problem much more easy of solution. And this for two
reasons : partly because the State and the Churches
are wholly distinct—neither has any direct control of
the other ; partly because in the United States the
statistics have been carefully gathered and elaborately
tabulated for a considerable period of time.

Remembering, then, that the United States has no
Established Church or State religion, that every person
is free to join a church or not, just as he pleases, and
that no one is counted a Christian unless he is actually
a member of some church, we readily see that our
problem is much simplified. It is the custom of the
Protestant denominations in the United States to admit
to membership only those who make special application,
and who do so on the basis of repentance from sin, and
for the purpose of living a Christian life. As a result,
the church membership is limited to adults of intelligence and of moral life ; for, even though one has
become a church member, it is customary to excom-
municate those who do not obey the rules of the Church,
and those whose lives are not moral. It is thus possible
to measure with great accuracy the religious condition
of the people of the United States. By comparing the
denominational statistics for various decades, it is also

possible to measure with great accuracy the increase or decrease of the number of those who, in profession at least, are Christians.

The following statistics and charts are worthy of careful study by all who wish to be informed of the actual increase of professed Christians in the United States of America.

The authorities for these figures are the United States Census; *The Problem of Religious Progress*, pp. 555–606; and *The Religious Forces of the United States*, by Dr. Carroll.

THE RELIGIOUS STATISTICS OF THE UNITED STATES.

	Population.	Protestant Christians.	Adherents.[1]	Total Protestants.	Non-Christians.	Roman Catholics.
1800	5,308,000	364,872	912,180	1,277,052	3,931,436	100,000
1810	7,239,000	...	...	...	...	...
1820	9,658,000	...	...	...	...	...
1830	12,886,000	...	...	...	...	...
1840	17,069,000	...	...	...	...	...
1850	23,191,000	3,529,988	8,824,970	12,354,958	9,222,918	1,614,000
1860	31,443,000	...	...	...	...	...
1870	38,558,000	6,673,391	16,683,470	23,356,866	10,601,515	4,600,000
1880	50,152,000	10,065,963	25,164,907	35,230,870	8,554,996	6,367,000
1890	62,622,000	14,180,000	35,450,000	49,630,000	5,794,000	7,198,000

[1] In order to preclude a misunderstanding, I would call special attention to this column; it is secured, not by count, but by computation. This element of the population is largely composed of the children of Christian parents, of non-Christian husbands, and brothers and sisters of those who are church members. It is from among this number that new recruits are won for the Church by the regular and special services of the Church. The church-going population, aside from church members, belongs to this number. The justification of the ratio, $2\frac{1}{2}$, will not be attempted here. I would refer those who question it to the full discussion of the proper ratio of church members to the total number under religious influence, *i.e.* to

These same facts are seen to be still more striking when represented in percentages.

	National Population.	Church Members.	Protestant Adherents.	Total Protestants.	Total Roman Catholics.	Non-Christian.	Rate of Growth of		
							Nation.	Prot.	R.C.
1800	100	6.8	17.0	24.0	1.9	74.5	...	...	...
							In fifty years.		
1850	100	15.2	38.0	53.2	6.9	39.9	4.37	9.67	16.14
							In twenty years.		
1870	100	17.3	41.8	59.1	12.0	28.9	1.62	1.88	2.83
							In ten years.		
1880	100	20.0	50.1	70.0	12.7	17.3	1.30	1.51	1.38
							In ten years.		
1890	100	22.6	56.5	79.1	11.5	9.3	1.24	1.41	1.13

The accompanying charts (Numbers XV. and XVI.) will render these facts appreciable to the eye.

REMARKS ON THE RELIGIOUS CONDITION OF THE UNITED STATES.

1. *The Protestant Churches.*—To understand the condition of the Protestant churches, we should recall how the great wave of infidelity swept, not only over France, Germany, and England, but was equally disas-

those who can be best described as adherents, to *The Religious Forces of the United States*, by Dr. Carroll, p. xxxv. It seems to me probable that the ratio has changed considerably during the century, and that we should add several hundred thousand to the adherents in 1800, and very likely subtract several hundred thousand, and possibly a few millions, from the estimated number of the adherents to-day. But remembering that this column stands, not for professed Christians, but only of those who may be called under more or less direct Christian influence, it is a column of considerable interest.

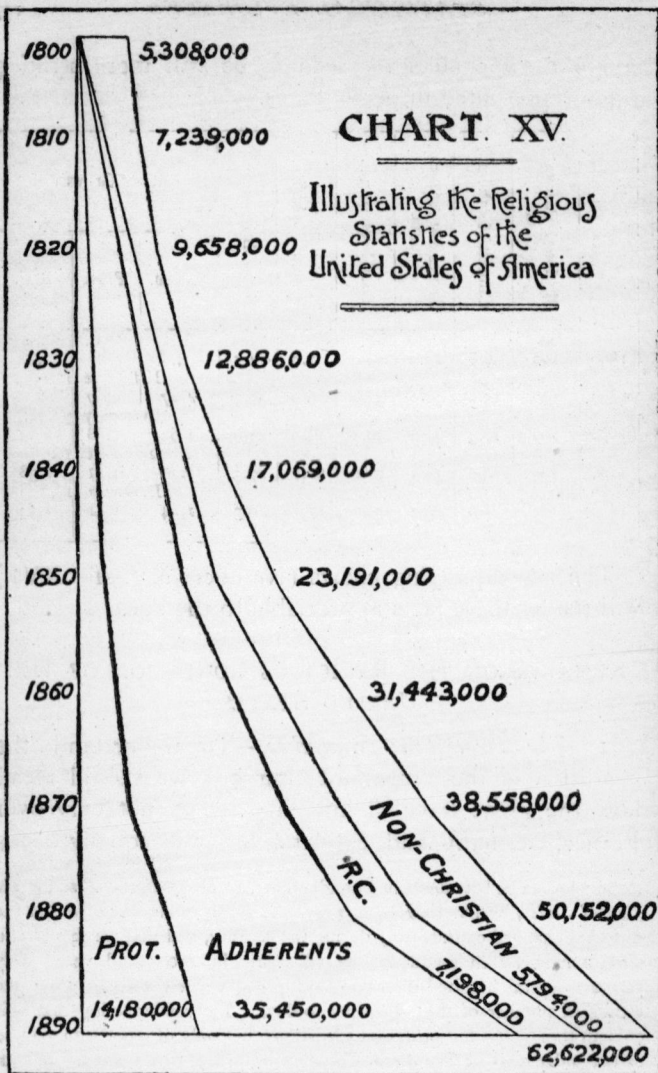

CHART. XV.

Illustrating the Religious
Statistics of the
United States of America

1800	5,308,000
1810	7,239,000
1820	9,658,000
1830	12,886,000
1840	17,069,000
1850	23,191,000
1860	31,443,000
1870	38,558,000
1880	50,152,000
1890	62,622,000

PROT. ADHERENTS R.C. NON-CHRISTIAN

14,180,000 35,450,000 7,198,000 5,794,000

trous in the United States. It reached its highest point
in the States in the middle and toward the close of the
last century, and left the churches not only weak in
numbers but lax in discipline. Much immorality went
unrebuked, even in the churches. If there has ever
been a time when the Protestant churches seemed
doomed to failure, it was toward the close of the last
century. At the beginning of the present century, out
of 5,300,000 inhabitants, the church members numbered
only 364,000, *i.e.* about seven out of each hundred. The
growth, however, during the present century is astonishing. In 1850 the church membership had reached the
sum of 3,529,000, being 15 per cent. of the population ;
and after forty years more (1890) it has reached the sum
of 14,180,000, being 22½ per cent. of the population.
The percentages show how much faster the Church has
grown than the whole population. During the ninety
years the total population increased twelve times, while
the church membership increased thirty-nine times. So
that the evangelical church membership has grown
more than three times as fast as the population. The
New York Independent for January 3, 1895, has brought
down these statistics to a later date, and finds that the
Protestant church membership in December 1893
amounts to 15,023,000, a gain for the three years of
1,342,000, or about 450,000 each year. A remarkable
series of articles in the *Independent* for January and
February 1895, on 'Men and the Church,' concludes,
after a careful examination of the facts, that 'there is
to-day a larger proportion of men in the membership of
the Protestant Churches of America than at any previous
time during the present century.'

2. *The Protestant Population.*—The foregoing para-

graph was confined to the consideration of church membership. To estimate, however, the actual number of those who are in close contact with, and so under the influence of, the churches, it is necessary to count the children and other members of Christian families who for one reason or another are not admitted to the membership of the churches. After repeated investigations, statisticians have agreed that for every 100 Protestant church members there are about 250 other persons who should be counted as belonging to the Protestant system of belief and worship. In other words, a town that has 1000 church members would have a Protestant population of about 3500 persons. By calculating for each period, we find that the Protestant population of the United States, including church members and adherents, has grown from 1,277,000 in 1800 to 12,354,000 in 1850, and to 49,630,000 in 1890. Stated in another way, the Protestant population has grown from 24 per cent. of the total population in 1800 to 53 per cent. in 1850, and to 79 per cent. in 1890. This shows how rapidly the Protestant community has been gaining on the people as a whole.

It is, of course, a legitimate question whether this population is or is not growing away from the Church. Is their church attendance, for instance, increasing or diminishing? To this question I have found no direct statistical answer. There has been no census of church attendance. Something, however, may be judged from the rapidly growing number of church members, who are recruited wholly from this class. The fact that church members increased from 17.3 per cent. of the entire population of the nation in 1870 to 22.6 per cent. in 1890, shows a gain of 5.3 per cent. This surely could

CHART. XVI.

Illustrating the growth of Christianity
in the U·S· by per cent of population

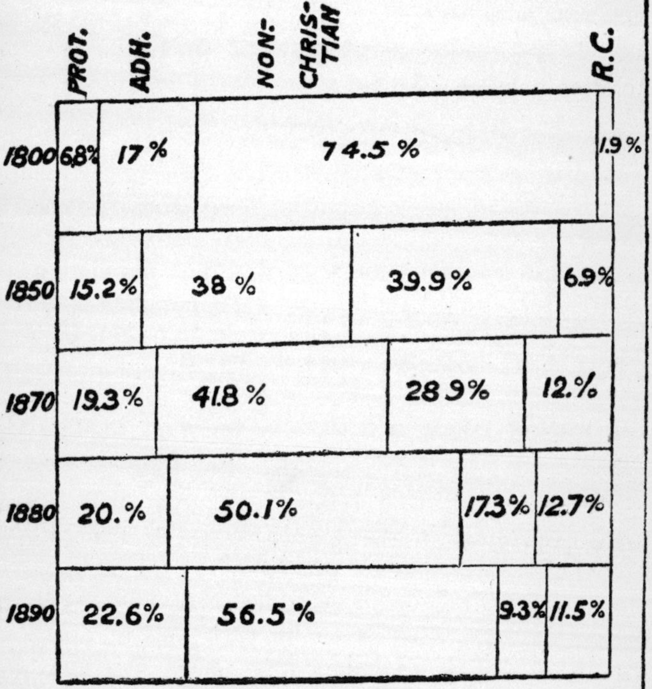

	PROT.	ADH.	NON-CHRISTIAN		R.C.
1800	6.8%	17 %	74.5 %		1.9 %
1850	15.2%	38 %	39.9%		6.9%
1870	19.3%	41.8 %	28.9%	12.%
1880	20.%	50.1%		17.3%	12.7%
1890	22.6%	56.5 %		9.3%	11.5%

not have taken place had the average tendency of the
adherents been to draw more and more apart from the
church life.

But a more significant measure of the interest and
tendency of the non-professing members of the Protestant population may be found in the rapid increase
in recent years of church accommodation. If we
consider that no body of Christians would go on,
decade after decade, building churches for which there
is no need, the following statistics become very significant of a growing tendency among the people at large
to attend church:—

GROWTH OF CHURCH SITTINGS, 1850–1890.[1]

	1850.	1860.	1870.	1880.	1890.
Evangelicals .	13,173,179	17,276,103	19,112,515	...	39,414,250
Roman Catholic	667,863	1,404,437	1,990,514	...	3,365,754
Others . .	391,782	448,214	562,033	...	841,837
Aggregate .	14,234,824	19,128,754	21,665,062	...	43,621,841

By a comparison of these figures with those of the
total population of the United States, it will be discovered, that whereas for every hundred of the population in 1850 there were seats for sixty-one persons, in
1890 there were $69\frac{6}{10}$ seats for each hundred persons.
Surely, if church accommodation proves anything, we
may conclude that the people, *as a whole*, are not
drifting away from the Church, whatever may be true

[1] *Problem of Religious Progress*, p. 567.

in certain congested centres of population. It is noticeable that the greatest gains have been made in recent
times, the sittings having doubled in the twenty years
between 1870 and 1890.

3. But the Roman Catholic Church has likewise
been making enormous gains. In 1800 there were
about 100,000 Roman Catholic Christians in the States,
i.e. nearly 2 per cent. of the entire population. By 1850
they had reached the sum of 1,614,000, being about 7
per cent. of the entire population; and by 1870,
4,600,000, being 12 per cent. of the nation. This
enormous growth was largely due to immigrants into
the United States from Roman Catholic countries. By
this means, in parts of the United States which were
wholly Protestant, the Roman Catholics are now in the
majority. Such is the condition of parts of New
England. This is not due to conversion, but to migra-
tion. Since 1870, although the Roman Catholic Church
has increased greatly in actual numbers, it has not
gained on the nation; during the two last decades there
has actually been something of a falling off, it having
dropped, from 12 per cent. of the total population in
1870 to 11.5 per cent. in 1890. Compared with the
79 per cent. of the Protestant Churches, the Roman
Catholic Church seems quite small.

It should be added that the Roman Catholic statistics
are exceedingly unsatisfactory. Except for 1890, which
ere derived from the United States census, they are
.nerely estimates. After pages of careful examination,and
showing how different authors differ by millions for the
same year, Dr. Dorchester well says : 'Such staggering
statistics show how wild and unreliable are the claims
to large numbers made by the Church of Rome.' Dr.

CHART. XVII.

Illustrating the comparative rates
of growth per decade of the nation
and of Prot. and R. C. Churches.

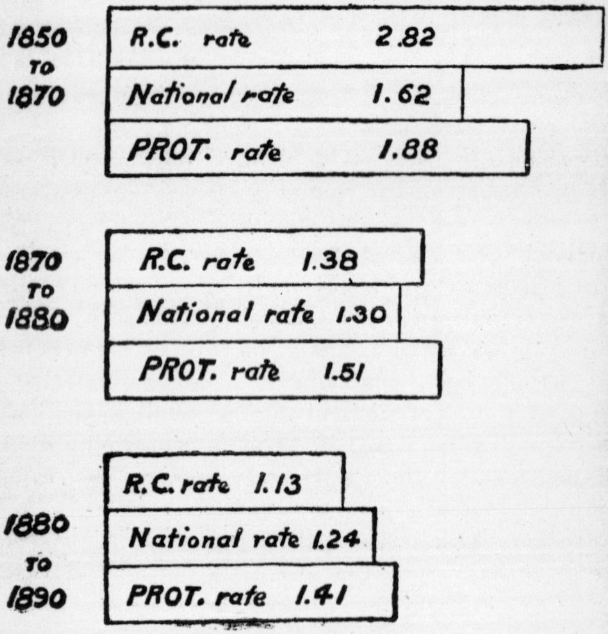

1850 TO 1870		
	R.C. rate	2.82
	National rate	1.62
	PROT. rate	1.88

1870 TO 1880		
	R.C. rate	1.38
	National rate	1.30
	PROT. rate	1.51

1880 TO 1890		
	R.C. rate	1.13
	National rate	1.24
	PROT. rate	1.41

Dorchester also says, that if the original Catholic stock migrating to America, and their descendants, had remained true to the Roman Catholic Church, they would now (1895) number over 40,000,000. As we have seen, however, they actually number but little over 7,000,000. The Roman Catholic Church is therefore suffering a great defeat in the United States. She has grown by immigration, not by propagation; but she has not grown as much as she should. 'An intelligent Roman Catholic layman in Boston, not many years ago, said—"We shall hold our ground for a while, but we understand that in the fight of a hundred years we shall be whipped." '[1]

4. *The Non-Christian Population.*—The numbers of non-Christians are determined not by count but by calculation. Adding together the Protestant and Roman Catholic population, and subtracting their sum from the entire population of the nation, we find the number of those outside of all religious connection or influence. By this operation it appears, that while in 1800 the non-Christian population numbered about 3,931,000, or $74\frac{1}{2}$ per cent. of the entire population, in 1850 it numbered 9,222,000, or 40 per cent., and in 1890, 5,794,000, or only $9\frac{1}{2}$ per cent. of the population. This shows a remarkable state of things. Although the nation has been making phenomenal progress, the religious forces have been growing so much faster, that the non-Christian population is not only diminishing in its proportion to the nation, but seems to be diminishing even in actual numbers. In 1870 the non-Christian population reached its largest sum, about 10,600,000, or $27\frac{1}{2}$ per cent. of the nation; in 1880

[1] *Problem of Religious Progress,* p. 603.

this was reduced to 8,554,000, or $17\frac{1}{2}$ per cent.; and in 1890 to 5,794,000, or $9\frac{1}{2}$ per cent. This way of looking at the facts brings out as clearly as any other the great vitality of the religious forces of the United States.

It may help to give some idea of the preparation of the religious forces of the United States to furnish the masses of the nation with Christian instruction, to give a brief summary of the last religious census of the United States. The number of religious organisations is 165,177, with 20,610,806 communicants; the church buildings, worth $697,930,139.00, number 142,521, and have a seating capacity of 43,564,863 persons, being more than 22,000,000 more than all the communicants; the non-religious classes could be accommodated more than three times over in the spare room. The number of regularly-employed ordained ministers is 111,036.

It should, perhaps, be said that in the non-Christian class are included Theosophists (695), Jews (130,496), Chinese (70,000 (?)), Spiritualists (45,000), Mormons (166,000), Christian Scientists (8700), and some others, numbering all together about 356,000, who profess to have some religious life and belief. The Unitarians (67,700), Universalists (49,194), and a few other small bodies, are included under the Protestant denominations.

To preclude all possibility of a misunderstanding, I again draw attention to the fact, that the number of the adherents, as well as of the non-Christian class, is secured not by count but by calculation. They are not to be considered, therefore, as in any sense exact, but only rough approximations, yet the best which can be made from the available material. The non-Christian population are those who may be said to be wholly outside of, and even antagonistic to, any kind of religious organisation. It is possible that they may number even one or two millions more than the estimate here given. But even so, it is clear, I think, that their ranks are being diminished by the vitality of the Christian churches—diminished not only relatively to the whole population, but in actual number from decade to decade.

5. *Religion and Education.*—It is not infrequently said that religion, being but a form of superstition, is most prosperous among the ignorant; that in proportion as a people become educated they give up their adherence even to Christianity; and that, in Protestant lands, they either join the Unitarians or reject all forms of religion. It is also stated as a proof of the antagonism of religion and education, that the common schools of the United States give no religious instruction. To understand, therefore, the real and growingly religious life of the people of the United States, a few words on this topic are necessary. But before we consider the relation of education to religion, we should first consider the fact of popular education; and we should observe how the Protestant idea of popular education has been gaining ground, so that the number of those enrolled in all kinds of schools has been growing much faster than the population. The figures on p. 148 have been compiled from the *Eleventh Census Report of the United States on Education.* The accompanying charts (Nos. XVIII., XIX., and XX.) will render their significance more conspicuous.

It is true there is no religious instruction, as such, given in the public schools. It by no means, however, follows, as some are inclined to think, that the children receive no moral or religious instruction. This instruction is provided for in three ways.

(*a*) *The Home Instruction.*—The United States are the product of Protestant ideas. In the Protestant system

STATISTICS OF EDUCATION IN THE UNITED STATES, COMPILED FROM THE ELEVENTH CENSUS OF THE UNITED STATES.

	Population.	Pupils.	Per Cent.	Gain in Population.	Rate of Gain in Pop.	Gain in Pupils.	Rate of Gain in Pupils.
1840	17,069,000	2,026,000	11.3	...	...	...	...
1850	23,191,000	3,634,000	15.7	6,122,000	1.359	1,517,000	1.797
1860	31,443,000	5,477,000	17.4	7,953,000	1.356	1,834,000	1.50
1870	38,558,000	7,210,000	18.7	7,414,000	1.226	1,733,000	1.32
1880	50,152,000	9,952,000	19.8	11,594,000	1.300	2,742,000	1.38
1890	62,622,000	14,374,000	22.9	12,466,000	1.248	4,422,000	1.44

each family is a religious community, having its own daily religious life. This frequently shows itself in family worship, in which there is reading of the Scripture, religious singing, and prayer. In addition to this, each child is taught by the mother, from its youngest days, to pray to the unseen God, to confess to Him all his sins, to ask His daily help to live aright. These religious and moral instructions are enforced by punishment in the more flagrant cases of disregard. The main part of the religious and moral instruction of children is expected to be given at home, around the family altar.

CHART. XVIII.

Illustrating the Growth of the School
Attendance in the United States ❀

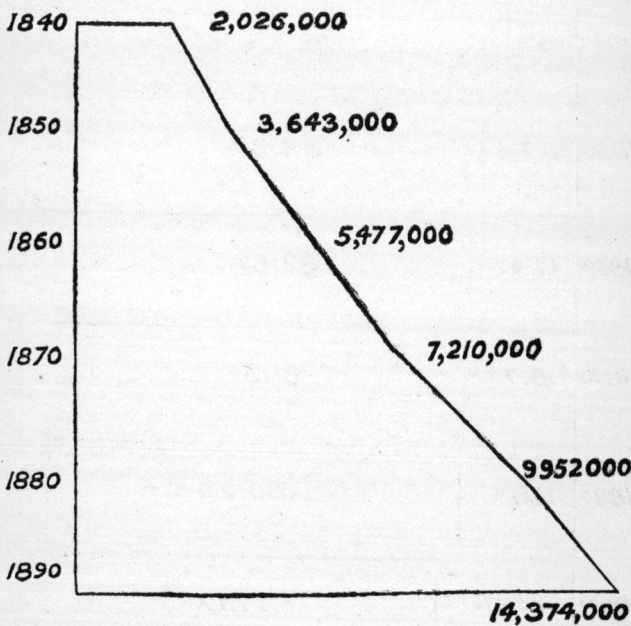

1840   2,026,000

1850   3,643,000

1860   5,477,000

1870   7,210,000

         9952000

1880

1890

         14,374,000

149

CHART. XIX

Illustrating the Growth of School
Attendance in the U.S. by per.
cent of population.

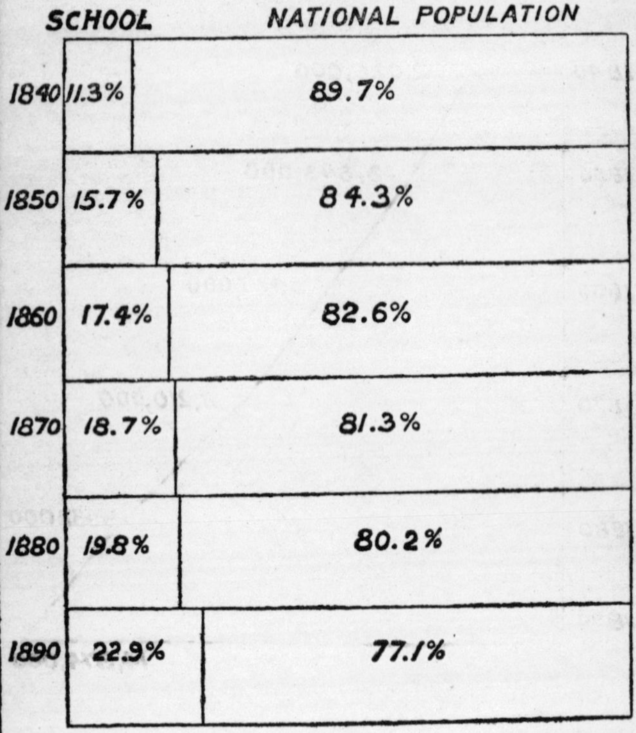

	SCHOOL	NATIONAL POPULATION
1840	11.3%	89.7%
1850	15.7%	84.3%
1860	17.4%	82.6%
1870	18.7%	81.3%
1880	19.8%	80.2%
1890	22.9%	77.1%

CHART XX.

Illustrating the comparative ratio of growth per decade of the national population & School Attendance in the U·S

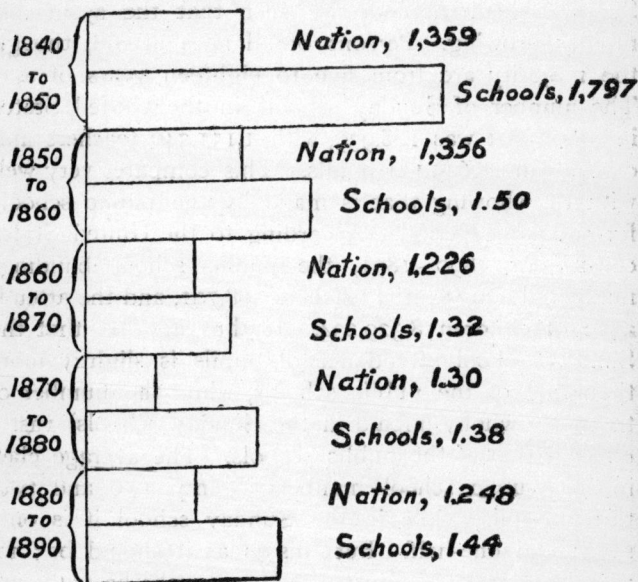

1840 TO 1850	Nation, 1,359
	Schools, 1,797
1850 TO 1860	Nation, 1,356
	Schools, 1.50
1860 TO 1870	Nation, 1,226
	Schools, 1.32
1870 TO 1880	Nation, 1.30
	Schools, 1.38
1880 TO 1890	Nation, 1.2 48
	Schools, 1.44

(*b*) This, however, is supplemented by the *Sunday school.*—The Sunday-school system is a comparatively modern movement, being designed (1) to give the children a more systematic knowledge of the Bible and its teachings than can well be done at home; (2) to provide for children whose parents are lax in the home religious life; and (3) to instruct the children of those who are not Christian, who, nevertheless, wish to have their children receive moral instruction. Attendance on the Sunday school is entirely voluntary; yet the Sunday-school methods are such that the system is rapidly growing. Persons of all ages attend, though the majority are from five to eighteen years of age. The number of Sunday schools in the United States in 1890–1891 was 108,939, with 1,151,340 teachers and officers, and 8,649,131 pupils. This compares very well with the showing that is made by the public schools for the same period. According to the United States census for 1890–1891, the public school buildings numbered 226,884, the teachers 368,791, and the attendance of children 8,329,234. It thus appears that the Sunday-school attendance of pupils is slightly more than that of the public schools, while the number of teachers (wholly unpaid in the Sunday schools) vastly exceeds that of the public schools. The average class in the public school numbers twenty-two and two-thirds pupils, while in the Sunday school it is only seven and one-half. But this is as it should be; for moral and religious instruction can only be truly imparted by direct personal character. Furthermore, in connection with all Sunday schools are to be found circulating libraries of religious books, suited to the tastes and capacities of the children. These are made use of by the great majority of the children, and constitute the largest amount of reading matter in the hands of the children. The influence and religious instruction of the Sunday school extends, therefore, throughout the seven days of the week. The foregoing facts reveal the immense and growing place occupied by the Sunday school. These Sunday schools are carried on only by Christians; the teachers are church members. The children of the Sunday schools are not of necessity members of the churches; indeed, a large majority of the children, even though baptized, are not church members, and do not become so till they seek for it on the ground of conversion. The Sunday-school statistics, as reported at the last Sunday-school Convention, held in Boston in June 1896, are—schools, 132,639; officers and teachers, 1,396,508; scholars, 10,890,092; being a total of 12,286,600 persons who, Sabbath after Sabbath, are engaged in the study of the Bible and in direct religious worship, the most of them children.

(*c*) A sharp distinction should be drawn between religious and moral instruction. Although the public schools do not give the former, they *do* give the *latter*. It usually takes the form of readings from the Bible, with prayer or a hymn, or both. The teachers also keep a strict watch over the conduct of the pupils, requiring proper deportment, and making this one of the factors in determining the rank of the pupil.

When we consider the rapid growth of church membership, and, at the same time, the wide reach of popular education, it must be clear that the assertions of an inherent antagonism between education and religion are false in regard to the United States at least. If this antagonism were real, it should be particularly manifest in the higher institutions of learning, in the colleges and universities. It is instructive, therefore, to study their religious condition, not by general impressions, but in the light of statistics.

In 441 higher institutions of learning (not including professional schools) there were enrolled in 1892–1893, 70,419 students ; of these, 38,327 were church members.[1] Taking the United States as a whole, only five young men out of a hundred are church members, while in the highest institutions of learning, fifty-four out of a hundred are members; this shows how much stronger a hold the religious life has on the highly educated than on the masses of the young men.

A study of the growth of the religious life in the colleges and universities shows that it has been more remarkable than the growth among the people as a whole. When infidelity swept over England and America, it showed itself most powerfully in the higher institutions of learning. A hundred years ago there were only three professed Christians in Yale College, and in Princeton College, as late as 1813, only one. Now, their Young Men's Christian Associations are large and flourishing, and more than half of the students are church members. Inquiries among the graduates of Harvard, which is supposed to be one of the most liberal of all the universities, show that out of 1400 recent graduates only two declared themselves to be unbelievers. Never before were there so many evangelical church members among the students of that institution. 'The Inter-Collegiate Young Men's Christian Association is the largest college organisation

[1] See *The Congregationalist*, January 1894.

in the world. No fraternity, no athletic organisation, compares with it in size.'

These facts make it apparent that in the United States, at least, education is not a foe to, but rather a friend of, religious life.

In non-Christian countries, and even in non-Protestant countries, it is doubtless true that religion has a more powerful hold on the uneducated and ignorant masses than on the educated ; but it is not so in the United States. Rather, it is clearly the reverse. In the United States, it is the ignorant and uneducated who are most irreligious.

The effect of the Protestant type of Christianity is to remove ignorance and superstition. It insists on education. Every believer must read and study and understand the Bible for himself. Either the religion makes a man fairly educated and drives out the superstition, or the ignorance and superstition drives out his religion. The two cannot long go on together.

6. *Religious Societies in addition to the Churches.*— No comprehensive view of the growth of the religious life of the United States can overlook the auxiliary religious societies, organised in the interest of Christianity, yet quite distinct from the churches. Of these there are several kinds.

(a) *The Young Men's Christian Associations.*—Their purpose is to band together Christian young men, stimulate their spiritual life, strengthen them to meet the temptations of city life, and set them to doing Christian work for their comrades who are not Christian. They are not ' missions' *to* young men, but Christian organisations *of* young men. The membership is not limited to those who are church members, though only these latter are organisers and managers. All who wish to avail themselves of the social, literary, educational, recreational, and other advantages of the associations are welcomed. In brief, the aim of the association is to provide a wholesome environment for young men. In addition to the regular associations, there are many special branches, such as the College Young Men's Christian Associations, the Railroad Young Men's Christian Associations, the Coloured Young Men's Christian Associations, the Indian Young Men's Christian Associations, etc.

The whole number of associations in the United States in 1893 was 1286, with 232,653 members, owning buildings valued at over $15,000,000.00, and employing 1282 general secretaries and other officers. In addition to these paid and trained workers there were 36,000 who gave time and labour for the Christian work of the associations. The recent rapid growth of the movement will be apparent by a comparison of these figures with those for 1883, at which time there were 868 associations, with 108,000 members, owning buildings valued at $3,900,000.00, and employing 388 paid officers. For the training of Young Men's Christian Association workers there are now two training schools.[1]

(*b*) *The Young People's Societies of Christian Endeavour and kindred Societies.*—These have for their aim the strict observance of the teachings of Jesus, not by compulsion, but by the voluntary pledges of the young people who are its members. It has many members who have not yet joined the churches, although all look forward to doing so. The upbuilding of the church organisation, however, is not the main aim of the

---

[1] *Young Men's Era,* June 7, 1894.

society. Their motto is, 'For Christ and the Church.'
Not the extension of the Church as such, but of the
Kingdom of God is its sole aim, the helping of young
men and women to be noble, pure, Christ-like. The
growth of this form of Christian organisation is one of
the wonders of modern times. Originating in 1881, in
the United States, it has spread to every land. The
statistics of its growth are given below. Its annual

YOUNG PEOPLE'S SOCIETIES OF CHRISTIAN ENDEAVOUR.
STATISTICS FOR THE WORLD.

	Number of Societies.	Number of Members.
1881 . . .	2	68
1882 . . .	7	481
1883 . . .	56	2,870
1884 . . .	156	8,905
1885 . . .	253	10,964
1886 . . .	850	50,000
1887 . . .	2,314	140,000
1888 . . .	4,874	310,000
1889 . . .	7,672	485,000
1890 . . .	11,013	660,000
1891 . . .	16,274	1,008,980
1892 . . .	21,080	1,370,200
1893 . . .	26,284	1,577,040
1894 . . .	33,679	2,023,800
1896 . . .	43,112	2,568,000

conventions are not only the largest religious meetings
the world has ever known, but exceed in size even the
largest political conventions of the United States. The
delegates at the convention in New York, in 1894, were
about 40,000 persons; and in Boston, in 1895, about
60,000, with more than 10,000 visitors in addition. The
various committees of arrangement numbered more than

5000 persons, and the choir, which trained for several months previously, numbered 3000 persons. The enthusiasm for the Christian life which these societies and general conventions arouse is contagious. This modern religious movement of the young people is the promise of a new period in church history. Not having the statistics for the United States alone, we give those for the entire world. But it is safe to say that three-fourths, if not four-fifths of the whole number, are in the United States.

(*c*) *The Sunday Schools.*—These have already been somewhat considered under a previous head. For a full understanding, however, of their relation to the religious life of the nation, it is important to observe that they do not only arise in connection with some local church. There is a society whose object is the founding of Sunday schools in regions destitute of churches and Sunday schools. These new Sunday schools develop rapidly into churches. On a previous page, such statistics of Sunday schools were given as to make them comparable with the most recent public school statistics. Sunday schools are, however, in the process of rapid increase. In 1893, there were 123,173 schools, an increase of 14,264 in three years, or an average of 13 schools for every day during the three years; the teachers numbered 1,305,939, an increase of 154,599, or an average of 141 for each day; and the pupils numbered 9,718,432, an increase of about 1,069,301, being an average daily gain of about 986 pupils. Still later figures I have given on a previous page, and also below. They show that during the past three years an average of 1070 new scholars have been brought into the schools for each day of the three years.

CHART. XXI.

Illustrating the Growth of the Y.P.S.C.E. in the World.

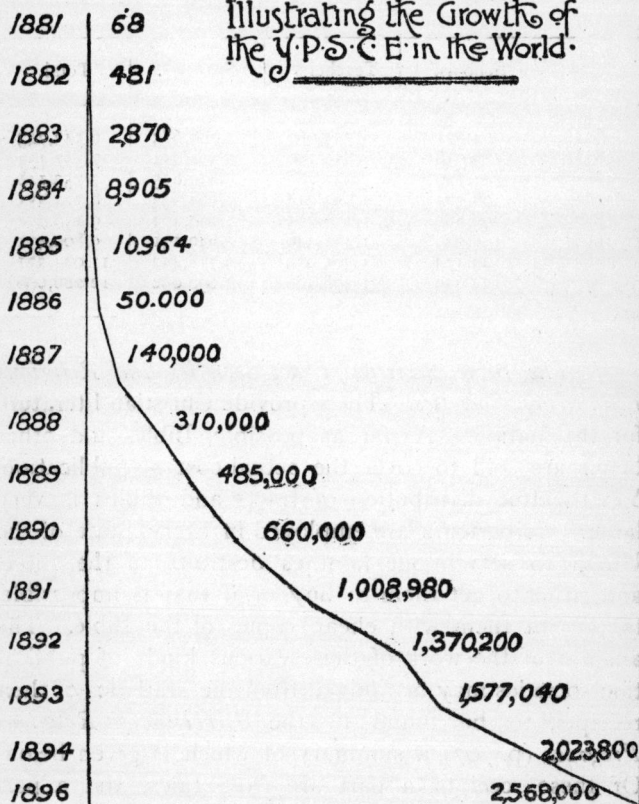

1881	68
1882	481
1883	2.870
1884	8,905
1885	10,964
1886	50.000
1887	140,000
1888	310,000
1889	485,000
1890	660,000
1891	1,008,980
1892	1,370,200
1893	1,577,040
1894	2,023,800
1896	2,568,000

Throughout the world there are 223,186 schools, 2,237,043 teachers, and 20,239,007 pupils.

Below are the statistics of the growth of Sunday schools in the United States :—

Date.	Schools.	Teachers.	Scholars.	Total.
1875	64,871	753,060	5,790,683	6,543,743
1878	78,046	853,100	6,504,054	7,357,154
1881	84,730	932,283	6,820,835	7,753,118
1884	98,303	1,043,718	7,668,833	8,712,551
1887	99,860	1,108,265	8,048,462	9,156,727
1890	108,939	1,151,340	8,649,131	9,800,471
1893	123,173	1,305,939	9,718,432	11,024,371
1896	132,639	1,396,508	10,890,092	12,286,600

(*d*) *The Bible Societies, Tract Societies, and Religious Publication Societies.*—These provide Christian literature for the nation. As far as possible, Bibles and other books are sold to cover the actual cost of publication. Yet the free distribution of tracts and Bibles is very large. Colporteurs are employed in every State of the Union to search out families destitute of the Bible, and either to get them to buy, or, if that is impossible, to present them with cheap copies of the Bible. The amount of the work of these various kinds of publication societies may be judged from the statistics of their receipts, to be found in the *Problem of Religious Progress* (p. 707), a summary of which is given below. Of these receipts, a part are from sales, and a part are from the contributions of Christians; but the total represents correctly the growing work of these societies.

CHART. XXII.

Illustrating the Growth of
the S·S in the U·S·

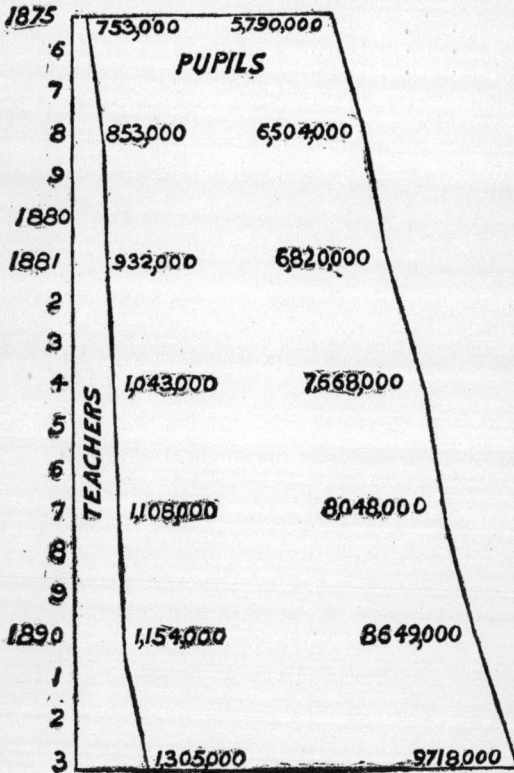

1875	759,000	PUPILS	5,790,000
6			
7			
8	853,000		6,504,000
9			
1880			
1881	932,000		6,820,000
2			
3			
4	1,043,000		7,568,000
5			
6			
7	1,108,000		8,048,000
8			
9			
1890	1,154,000		8,649,000
1			
2			
3	1,305,000		9,718,000

TEACHERS

II

			Total.	Yearly Average.
1790-1829	. .	40 years.	$2,385,162.00	$59,629.00
1830-1839	. .	10 ,,	4,539,096.00	453,909.00
1840-1849	. .	10 ,,	7,187,403.00	718,740.00
1850-1859	. .	10 ,,	18,382,312.00	1,838,231.00
1860-1869	. .	10 ,,	30,119,595.00	3,011,959.00
1870-1880	. .	11 ,,	42,169,863.00	3,833,624.00
1881-1894	. .	13 ,,	55,475,277.00	4,267,329.00

(*e*) Mention should also be made of the denominational missionary societies. These have a great deal
to do with the rapid extension of the religious life
among the non-Christian part of the population. They
will receive fuller consideration in Chapter V., where
their statistics may be found.

(*f*) The multitude of 'reform homes,' charity organisations, etc., which also will receive fuller notice
later, likewise merit consideration in this connection.
Their modern growth has contributed not a little
to the growth of religious life in the United States.

(*g*) This completes our study of the religious
statistics of the United States. We have seen how
much more rapidly the church membership is growing
than the population; how the non-religious population
is ever decreasing; how the religious and moral instruction of the children is being more and more fully
provided for; how education is a friend, not a foe, to
the religious life. These are facts that cannot be
disputed. If we compare the growth of Christianity
in the United States with its growth in the early
centuries, we shall learn that during the ninety years
of the religious history of the United States more
persons have come under the direct influence of the

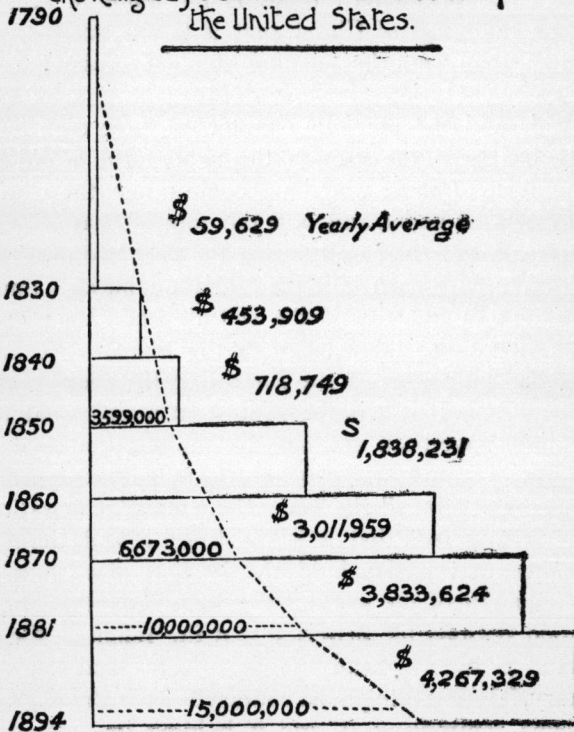

CHART. XXIII.

Illustrating the Growth of the Receipts of
the Religious Publication Societies of
the United States.

1790

$ 59,629   Yearly Average

1830 $ 453,909

1840 $ 718,749

1850   3,599,000   S 1,838,231

1860 $ 3,011,959

1870   6,673,000 $ 3,833,624

1881   --------10,000,000 $ 4,267,329

1894   --------15,000,000--------

------- This dotted line shows growth of
                              Church Members

Christian Church than during the first thousand years of Christianity in all lands combined. In later chapters we shall come to see that the Christian belief and practice of modern times is far more in accord with the teachings of Christ, that is to say, more truly Christian, than were the common practice and belief of those early centuries.

In this and the previous chapter we have seen how steady has been the growth throughout the world of the numbers of those who have come under the Christian system of belief, and how the rate of that growth has marvellously increased during the past two hundred years. We have seen how the Christian nations, numbering only a quarter of the world's population, rule considerably more than a half of the human race, and more than four-fifths of the surface of the globe. We have seen, too, that it is the Protestant nations that for some time have been and still are making the greatest comparative gains in national growth, and that they lead the world in all the main elements of civilisation. We have also seen that it is the English and German languages that to-day hold the leading place among the languages of the world. We have seen that there are good reasons for believing that the religious life of England is by no means on the wane; that, on the contrary, it is grappling most courageously with the great problems confronting it, and is holding its own even numerically. And, finally, we have seen how great has been the growth of the religious life in the United States; great though the growth of its population has been, that of the Church has been greater, reducing not only the proportion of the non-Christians, but even, in recent decades, reducing their actual numbers.

We have not yet considered whether the growths here proven are merely numerical or real ; whether it is genuine or nominal Christianity that is making the wonderful gains in modern times. In the succeeding chapters we shall study this aspect of the problem. We shall then be in a position to estimate, with some degree of accuracy and assurance, the significance of the numerical growth here proven. We shall then be in a position to judge whether the growth of Christianity is intensive as well as extensive.

CHAPTER V

GROWTH IN COMPREHENSION

'The supreme Person of history has left the mark of His hand on every generation of civilised men that has lived since He lived ; and it would not be science to find Him everywhere, and never to ask what He was and what He did. Persons are the most potent factors of progress and change in history, and the greatest person known to it is the one who has been the most powerful factor of ordered progress. Who this is, is not open to dispute. Jesus Christ is the name that represents the most wonderful story, and the profoundest problem. Can He, who of all persons is the most necessary to the orderly and progressive course of history, be but the fortuitous results of a chapter of accidents ? ' [1]

'So long as there is a radical difference between truth and falsehood, and so long as truth sustains relation to life, it will make a difference whether men believe true or false doctrine. Doctrines are the roots of life. Great lives do not grow out of false beliefs. Yes, doctrine is immensely important, but not all-important.' [2]

'Each of several ages of the Christian era has been characterised by a germinal idea, which has been more or less central to the thinking of that age. These germinal ideas have followed each other in logical sequence, and have sprung naturally from Christ's revelation of God. When, therefore, Christ gave to the world a new and higher conception of God, there was sure to result in due time a new and higher conception of man.' [3]

---

[1] A. M. Fairbairn, M.A., D.D., *The Place of Christ in Modern Theology*, p. 6.

[2] Josiah Strong, D.D., *The New Era*, p. 125.

[3] *Ibid.*, p. 131.

CHAPTER V

IN the previous chapters we have considered the numerical increase of Christianity, both in general and in two of the most important nations of Christendom. Though this study brought to light many interesting facts and important lessons, yet it has also revealed many unpleasant facts. The counting as Christian of so many who are only nominally Christ's, and the admission which every Christian must make of the un-Christian use of power by so-called Christian men and nations, brings with it many sad reflections. It is therefore with a feeling of relief, even of joy, that I turn to a new and more pleasant subject of consideration, namely, the growing understanding of the teaching of Christ. By this, I mean the development within the Christian Church itself of a keener appreciation of and insight into the essence of the teachings of Jesus.

Though, strictly speaking, comprehension and practice of Christian truth are inseparable, yet, for the purpose of clearly perceiving the progress that the Church has made, it seems desirable to distinguish between these two elements of the same act, between the inner comprehension and the outer manifestation of the Christ-given life. As I study the history of the Church, it seems to me that I can clearly see the evidence of a constantly growing understanding of the will of God.

The present generation seems to have the advantage

over every preceding one, not only in its national, but also in its spiritual civilisation in understanding the great problems of life, in comprehending the nature of religious truth, in recognising God's actual presence in the world, and in doing His will.

There are those who look back to the Reformation as the time when the Protestant churches were at their best, as the time when men walked with God, understanding His purpose, and doing His will. Others look still further back for such a period, beyond the Middle Ages, to the time of the Church fathers, and fancy that, though the world was full of vice and corruption, yet the Church was pure and unspotted; that the Christians were so filled with the spirit of Christ, that the one and constant thought of their lives was service to Him; that His presence was so real to them that temptation had little power; and that the Holy Spirit so guided them, that they, better than any succeeding generation, could understand the full meaning of the gospel of Christ. It cannot be doubted that the earliest Christians were filled with burning zeal for Christ, and that they did have no little comprehension of the essentials of the truths He taught. The most of the Christians of the early centuries, however, even of the first century, knew less, I think, of the actual teachings and life of Christ than is known to-day by the ordinary Protestant. Not only so, with the exception of the apostles themselves and a few of the earliest disciples, I am confident that the average Protestant Christian of to-day has a better appreciation, both of what Christ came to do, and of the nature of the salvation He offers, than had the mass of the Christians of any previous century. Though this is not the place in which to discuss the causes for this condition of things, it is not amiss to state that its chief reason is the general education now prevalent in Protestant lands, together with the universal possession of the Bible, both of which have been rendered possible, among other things, by the steam printing-press.

In the present chapter, it is my desire, in a very brief way, to present the leading features of the interpretations given to Christianity, in its successive periods or stages of development. Those who wish fuller information should consult recent historical and theological works.

All truth takes its form of statement, its colour, from the mind that perceives it and states it. A clear mind will see a truth clearly; a confused mind will see confusedly; a philosophical mind will see the philosophical relations; an organising mind will construct an organism to give effect to the truth it sees. Now, it is a fact, well known to students of history, that there are national types of mind. Though closely related in ancestry and history, the Greeks and Romans were very different in national endowment, in their mental temperament and make-up. If people so closely related in language have clearly marked mental variations, much more would we expect to find marked differences in the mental characteristics of races so different as the Hebrew and the Teuton. As Christianity therefore passed from the Hebrew sources to other nations, we should expect to find the national characteristic moulding what it received into new forms. Such in fact was what happened to Christianity when it passed to the Grecian, to the Roman, and to the Teutonic nations. Already, each had its characteristic methods of thought and life; each therefore understood ànd interpreted Christianity in its own way, and made its own characteristic contribution to Christianity. Now, the point in this chapter to be brought clearly into view is, that by these successive steps the Christian world has come more and more to understand itself, more and more fully to comprehend the innermost principles of the teachings of Jesus.

The growth of Christianity may be divided into five periods—Hebrew, Greek, Roman, Teutonic, and Anglo-American. Or, to name them by their leading characteristics—first, the simple facts; second, speculation; third, organisation; fourth, reformation; fifth, application. Or, again, naming them by the peculiar sphere of thought in which they were chiefly active—first, foundations; second, theology (the nature of God; the doctrine of the Trinity, and so the nature of Christ); third, anthropology (the nature of man); fourth, soteriology (the nature and method of individual salvation); fifth, sociology (the nature and method of social, national salvation).

Josiah Strong's words in the *New Era* on this matter are specially appropriate. 'Each of the several ages of the Christian era has been characterised by a germinal idea, which has been more or less central to the thinking of that age. These germinal ideas have followed each other in logical sequence, and have sprung naturally from Christ's revelation of God. Man's conception of his God and his conception of himself are closely related; each influences the other. Without a revelation, man's idea of his God is little else than his own image enlarged and projected on the sky. Give him a new idea of the character of God, and there will follow a new and corresponding idea of human nature, . . . new conceptions of man's personal relation to God, and of his social relations to fellow-men. . . . This, then, is the natural, and, as history shows, the actual order in the development of human thought. First, theology; second, anthropology; third, soteriology; fourth, sociology.'[1]

PERIOD I. HEBREW: APOSTOLIC, SIMPLE (35–75 A.D.).

This period was very brief, not covering the lifetime of the apostles. It is the period in which the Hebrew mind, with its prevailing tendencies, held supreme control.

Christianity originated in the experience of a few plain fishermen and tradesmen of Palestine. A young man appeared among them, who, though unlearned in the schools and ignorant of the philosophies of the day, taught such simple, yet grand moral truth, had such high ideas of life, of God, of the future, and lived a life so in conformity with His teachings, that though He was crucified by His enemies after only three years of teaching, yet those who heard and loved Him were ever after different men—different, not only in their callings and trades, but in their personal characters and ambitions for this life, in their hopes and aspirations for the next, and in their disregard of persecution, and fearlessness in the face of death. They gave their lives to the propagation of the teachings and spirit of their young Teacher, regardless of the ridicule and scorn and persecuting opposition of the educated and of the rulers. They preached not doctrine, not philosophy,

[1] *The New Era*, p. 131.

not a theory of the universe, but simply the facts of their experience; what this young man had said and done; how He had lived and died; and how, though dead, He yet was able to help and guide and strengthen those who trust Him. They doubtless thought deeply on these facts. But, being Hebrews, they did not speculate on what these facts implied, or arrange them in scientific form. The facts were wonderful, but true. Their explanation of the facts was simple, *i.e.*, God fulfilling ancient prophecies in an unexpected way, by sending His own Son to earth. The intellectual, metaphysical difficulties attending such a view received little thought. The facts alone received their serious attention.

It is not meant by this that the early or Apostolic Christians had no theories as to God, Christ, and men; or as to their mutual relation; nor that Christ's teachings did not contain profound philosophical and metaphysical assumptions. By no means. Even the Sermon on the Mount, the most clearly and simply ethical part of Christ's teachings, implies and upholds the essential parts of subsequent theologies. As Canon Gore has well expressed it, early Christianity, the teaching of Christ Himself, and the preaching of the first disciples,—in other words, the revelation,— 'was not in the form of ordered knowledge; its meaning, its coherence, its limits, were very imperfectly recognised; its terminology was not exact. The faith of the Church as it expressed itself in life, in worship, in fervent statement, in martyrdom, was vigorous and unmistakable in meaning, . . . but it was a faith, not a science.' [1]

[1] *The Incarnation of the Son of God*, p. 93.

This first period of Christian history is recorded for us chiefly in the first three Gospels and the Acts.

It is a matter for great gratitude that this was the first stage of Christianity and the first attitude of the believers. The facts involved many profound truths and valid inferences, but it was not important that the first disciples should give us these in logical scientific form; each successive generation must draw these inferences for itself, or at least on its own account estimate those of previous generations. The facts themselves are of the utmost importance; we must have them for the foundation of all our thinking and speculation.

In proportion as they have been ignored or forgotten, the truth has been lost. For this reason it is right and important for each age to look back, not only to the immediately preceding ages, but especially to the first age; not because the development of the Church during the intervening ages is useless or necessarily defective, but in order that the foundation on which that development stands may be clearly seen. ' In the discussion of its own problems, Christianity cannot avoid coming into contact with questions which are in their nature philosophical, and to which, unless it is to abdicate thought, it must take some attitude and attempt some solution.' I hold that theological thought and metaphysical speculation is a necessity of the human mind, because man is a thinking as well as a feeling and an active being. The organic development of the Church is necessitated by the evolution of society. Both of these movements, the philosophising and the organising, are not evils, but blessings. But I also hold that both intellectual speculation and organic evolution need to be constantly checked and guided by comparison with the actual teachings of Christ's life. It is providential, therefore, that the first period was simple and straightforward, and that it laid its emphasis, in all its thinking and preaching, on the actual facts.

PERIOD II. GREEK: SPECULATIVE, THEOLOGICAL, AND CHRISTOLOGICAL (75–500 A.D.).

Since Christianity was by its nature suited, not simply to the Jews, but also to the whole human race, it naturally soon spread beyond the limits of the Hebrew people—first in Palestine, and later in Asia Minor, in Greece, in Egypt, and in Rome, with all its colonies. For centuries previous to the birth of Christ the Greek mind had been meditating profoundly on the nature of the universe, and from its nature had been inferring its cause, that is, God. Socrates and Plato and Aristotle, and all the host of Grecian thinkers, had attacked the problems, as to the origin of the world, the nature and origin of good, of knowledge, and of cause and effect. Various systems of thought had been developed, but each was found seriously defective. It is unnecessary here even to name these systems. It is enough to observe that the Greek mind was absorbingly interested in the metaphysical problems, as well as skilled in the use of logical definition and dialectic. This metaphysical interest and habit of mind was influencing all who came in contact with Greek civilisation and education, among whom were not a few Jews, the Apostles Paul and John being doubtless among them.

As a consequence, when the facts of Christ's life and teachings became known to the Greeks, it was most natural for them to attack the old metaphysical problems with the help of the new materials; to reconstruct their old theories in such a way as to admit and explain the new facts. The New Testament itself gives the beginning of this movement in the writings of Paul, and especially of John. Greek Christians, less familiar with, and so less controlled by, the facts of Christ's life and works, originated many strange theories, which, carried out to their logical end, not only could not explain the Christian facts, but, if widely believed, would have even destroyed the Christian faith.

Such one-sided theories became known as heresies. They clustered chiefly around the question as to the nature of Christ, around the dogmas of theology and Christology. The effort of the Greek mind to give the Christian facts and teachings a philosophical explanation, and a metaphysical foundation, produced a tremendous intellectual tumult, attended by the rapid intellectual growth of the Church. Sect after sect arose, teaching peculiar, one-sided views. To deny the errors of those sects, offset their evil tendencies, and distinguish the true from false beliefs, creed after creed was formulated by the Church. Some modern critics are inclined to attribute these creeds to the mere speculative bent of the Church, to its loss of interest in the vital truths of Christianity, and to cite them as evidences of its deterioration. All philosophical and metaphysical thought they consider not only useless and unnecessary, but positively injurious to Christianity. Others, with better appreciation of those times, affirm that the speculative effort was forced on the Church by its mistaken friends within, and its keen enemies

12

without. Not to have entered on the intellectual
conflict would have been sure death to the struggling
Church, because it would have been virtually a
surrender to error. It was essential to its acceptance
by the most cultured, intellectual race the world had
yet produced, that Christianity, using the best science
and philosophy of the times, should think through, and
hold for itself, as well as present to the world, a
thoroughly self-consistent, balanced, scientific view of
the universe, paying special attention to the essential
natures of God and Christ, and to their mutual
relations. As subsequent history has proved, that was
a life-and-death struggle through which the Church
passed. Thomas Carlyle, who at one time had spoken
contemptuously of the theological disputes of the early
centuries, later came to have a very different view; he
admitted that ' Christianity itself was at stake. If the
Arians had won, it (Christianity) would have dwindled
away to a legend.' 'Man is in the long-run logical;
either his theories must justify his actions, or his
actions will settle down to the level of his theories.
By their metaphysics Christians sought to justify their
worship of Christ; had they not done so, their worship
would have ceased.'[1] Those sects which by their
philosophical explanations practically surrendered the
reality of Christ's divine Sonship, were unable to
sustain for many decades a vital Christian life. The
heresies once clearly perceived and condemned, died a
natural death. Thus arose the creeds of Christendom.
They record the efforts of the Church to preserve its
life-giving truths; they were due, not so much to the
desire to speculate, as to the desire to reject one-sided

[1] Canon Gore, *The Incarnation*, p. 100.

views—views which, in one way or another, denied the reality of Christ's divinity, and thus lacked the essential life-giving element of Christianity.

These creeds and the movements of thought they represent were not accidental or useless. On the contrary, they were of vital importance. If Christianity was what Christ pronounced it, a seed, it needed to grow. Its growth must be in human minds. Since man is a thinking being, it was inevitable, it was essential, that the religion of Jesus should grow beyond the first stage in which Christ left it, a religion chiefly of facts; it must develop also a philosophy of the universe, and particularly of God and of Christ, a philosophy which was already involved; it must state in scientific, orderly fashion both the facts and their underlying metaphysical presuppositions. Before it could claim to be fitted for world-wide propagation, it was essential that it should meet, and prove itself able to satisfy, the philosophical demands of the most philosophical race the world had yet seen. Though beginning as the religion of the lowest, illiterate, despised classes of society, of slaves, yet, by the mere force of the character of the Christians, and the coherence of its philosophical views, it won the two most illustrious people of antiquity, Greeks and Romans. It conquered them, not by force of arms, but by superior living and logic, by having manifestly truer views of God, of man, and of the world.

In its historical facts, Christianity furnished to the brilliant Greek mind just those profound metaphysical elements for which it had long been waiting, by which it was enabled to take the great forward step of the third century. Looked at as a philosophy, says Prof. Fairbairn, speaking of the philosophy of the Trinitarian creeds, it 'is a bold and splendid piece of constructive meta-physics, the completion of the ancient Greek quest after a scientific conception of God and His relation to man. It combines elements that had before been held to be incompatible in thought. It endeavours to translate God from an abstract into a concrete, related, living Absolute; to conceive Him as a Godhead, which has within Himself all the constituents and conditions of a real, intellectual, moral, and social existence, as if He were a universe while God. This is the meaning of the heroic struggle to affirm at once the unity of the Divine Essence and the distinction of the Divine Person.'[1]

That the elaborated doctrine of the Trinity is the product of Greek metaphysical philosophy none will deny; but the doctrine is not therefore false, nor of necessity alien to Christianity. On the contrary, as has been already clearly indicated, it was a vital step in the development of Christianity. Though a Greek structure it stands on the solid foundations of Jewish history, religion, and revelation, and, above all, on the self-consciousness of Jesus Christ. Dr. Hatch sums up the influence of the Greek mind on Christian faith by saying that 'it furnished a reasoned basis for Hebrew Monotheism. It helped the Christian communities to believe as an intellectual conviction that which they had first accepted as a spiritual revelation.'[2]

We may say therefore, without fear of successful contradiction, that the Greek period of the Christian Church saw a great advance; that the Greek mind

---

[1] *Christ in Modern Theology*, p. 90.
[2] *Hibbert Lecture*, p. 207.

gained an insight into the system of Christian thought which the Christian Jews did not have, and probably never would have attained unaided. Yet we should add that, important as was the contribution which the Greek mind made to Christian thought, it still did not grasp the deepest and most essential part of Christianity. The scholars and theologians became interested primarily in the scientific and philosophical aspects of Christian truth. That these are less important than the practical and vital, none will deny. This intellectual struggle of the Church gradually transferred the prime attention from life to logic, from conduct to belief, and gave rise to the pernicious habit, which more or less exists to this day, of laying more emphasis on correct belief than on correct life. Highly as Professor Fairbairn estimates the metaphysical contribution of the Greeks, he does not hesitate to say later, 'Metaphysics had triumphed over ethics, scholastic terms over moral realities.' [1]

Yet we need also to beware of falling into the opposite error of minimising the importance of the doctrinal truth. Some critics would banish all doctrines from modern Christianity. But, as Josiah Strong pointedly puts it, 'So long as there is a radical difference between truth and falsehood, and so long as truth sustains relations to life, it will make a difference whether men believe true or false doctrine. Doctrines are the roots of life. Great lives do not grow out of false beliefs. . . . The root does not exist for itself; it is a means to the tree, and the fruit as an end.' [2]

[1] *Christ in Modern Theology*, p. 91.   [2] *New Era*, p. 125.

Period III. Roman : Organising, Anthropological (500–1400 a.d.).

Speaking exactly, the Greek and Roman periods of the Church development started together ; the philosophical the sooner rising into prominence, reaching its culmination, then largely passing away ; while the organising activity proceeded more slowly and lasted much longer.

To comprehend the contribution of the Roman mind we need to notice the native endowment and characteristics, as shown by the national history. The Roman race, above all the ancient nations, had the faculty of government, of organisation, of creating laws and enforcing them. It was the possession of this faculty that made it possible for the City of Rome, first to conquer the separate tribes of Italy one by one, and impose on them her iron laws, and later to dominate all Europe, Western Asia, and Northern Africa. The system of laws which the Roman race worked out has become the foundation of all civilised government since their time. Not only Europe, but America, and even Japan, owe Rome a debt of gratitude for her legacy of laws.

When, therefore, Christianity came to the Romans, they naturally interpreted it in the terms with which they were familiar ; or, to put it in another way, they naturally seized on those elements which were in special accord with their own customs of thought, their national traits. The ‘ Kingdom of God ’ was most easily grasped in its literal sense, as a universal, temporal kingdom, having rule, not only over the bodies, but also over the souls of men. In this Kingdom, which was only a larger, more powerful Roman empire, God was dictator; His will constituted law; to administer that law were rank on rank of officials, a completely organised executive, a perfect government. This Kingdom on earth is the Church, with its one supreme commander, the vice-gerent of God (the pope), and archbishops, bishops, priests, etc., as its various under-officials. This idea did not attain full development at once, nor indeed for several hundred years. It was elaborated by degrees, under the stress of much external pressure. The severe persecution rapidly helped on the union of the local churches: they needed each other's help and protection. The intense intellectual struggle also greatly aided the movement; for it was natural that the more powerful intellects should be placed at the head of churches and of the local unions, to battle for, as well as to ead, the weak and the ignorant. The exclusion of the heretical sects, too, stimulated the union and broad organisation of the churches holding a common faith.

The continuous external and internal pressures, together with the natural tendencies of the Roman race, building on not a few figures of speech and expressions in the New Testament, finally produced the Roman Catholic Church. It was a grand idea, that of a universal, holy, all - powerful, fully - organised, visible Church, the Kingdom of God on earth. To this day tens of thousands of Christians outside of the Roman Church have this as their ideal of visible organic Christianity. Under the lead of this ideal, the ancient Church developed to a wonderful extent, practically ruling Europe for some hundreds of years. That this powerful Roman Church was a great blessing to Europe, few, I think, will deny. But for it, the preservation to

modern Europe of Christianity, and even of the ancient
Greek and Roman civilisations and literatures, might
not have been accomplished.

Yet its blessings were attended with serious evils.
The completed organisation of the Church reacted on
the popular conceptions of God and Christ ; legalism
gained great prominence. When Christianity became
the established religion of the Roman empire, great
multitudes of ignorant non-Christian men and women
flocked into the Church, without caring for its spirit and
teaching ; later, the hordes of barbarians from the North
swept over Europe, destroying not only the Roman
empire, but even its civilisation. The Church alone
survived the general ruin, taking into its membership
vast multitudes of the conquerors. These two incur-
sions of heathen multitudes brought into the Church
many strange, even pagan, doctrines and practices,
some of which still have their influence on modern
Christianity. But the points to which I wish to draw
special attention are two—(1) But for the united action
of the Christians, *i.e.* the organic Church, it is doubtful
if Christianity would have been able to endure the
persecutions and overcome the heresies of the earlier
period, or to retain its very existence during the later
period, when the Roman empire fell. (2) In theology,
likewise, the Roman mind made a very important
contribution to the development of the Christian
system of thought, namely, the doctrine of man, his
sin and inherent nature.

As truly as the doctrine of God (including Christ)
is the first step in the intellectual comprehension of
Christianity, so is the doctrine of man the necessary
second step. This step the Roman mind took. Their

centuries of experience in law, in the rule of sinful men, fitted them, as perhaps no other race has been fitted, to perceive the necessity for and the fixity of law, and the sinfulness of sin. Here was genuine progress. This second theological step was as essential to the millennial progress of Christianity as was the first.

But, though an essential step, it was not the essential of Christianity. Like the Greek, the Roman interpretation of Christianity failed to grasp the inner meaning. The Greek and Roman types of Christianity were 'the result of a failure to apprehend Paul's profoundly evangelical ideas, and of the intrusion of the conception of Christianity as a "new law," which conception had for its counterpart the legalising of the outward framework and institutions of the Church, the growth of the hierarchy and of sacerdotalism.' Indeed, so powerful became the church organisation in the later ages, that multitudes of wicked men sought and secured its high offices. The whole organisation seemed rotten to the core; to many, Christian truth seemed almost to have perished under the Roman legalistic interpretation and executive organisation. The reason for the failure is apparent.

Each national interpretation proceeded on principles not furnished by Christianity itself. In their interpretation each race took those dominant principles which had made themselves to be what they were. This, however, was inevitable. Not until Christianity had become sufficiently assimilated by the common people to produce an essentially Christian civilisation, was it possible to see the principles furnished by Christianity itself, and seeing, to apply them to the intellectual understanding of Christianity. Interpretation by life of necessity precedes interpretation by the understanding. As Charles Gore well puts it: 'All right theory emerges out of experience, and is the analysis of experience,' *i.e.* is inductive. Christianity needs to be experienced by a nation, needs to so permeate the nation as to produce a Christian civilisation, before its real nature can be fully appreciated intellectually.

PERIOD IV. TEUTONIC: SOTERIOLOGICAL (1400–1750 A.D.).

That great moral upheaval that took place in Europe during the thirteenth, fourteenth, and fifteenth centuries, the 'Reformation,' was the beginning of the truer and deeper comprehension of Christianity, and became the beginning of the interpretation of Christianity through the principles which it itself furnishes. 'Salvation by faith' was a great step forward. The increased emphasis laid on a moral life, as evidence of that faith, was also a matter of no little significance. Yet, while making this forward movement, the Protestant churches by no means shook themselves clear of many mistaken traditional views. For our present purpose it is not necessary even to mention these. We willingly grant that there were many such. That to which we wish to call attention is the fact of real growth, a genuine development. This we find in the emphasis laid on faith. That it was the Teutonic race that made this contribution will not seem strange, when we recall the Teutonic emphasis on and love for personal freedom. It was natural that they should lay emphasis on the personal relation between God and man, and that they should thus be led to realise the importance of faith for every individual.

These elements were already in the gospel, and those who had eyes to see, and hearts to feel, easily saw and felt them.

PERIOD V. ANGLO-AMERICAN—MODERN : PRACTICAL, SOCIOLOGICAL (1750).

The modern period is the most complex as well as the most interesting. In no previous age has there been anything like the number of educated believers in, or scholarly students of, Christianity. This is at once a product and a cause of the peculiarity of the modern period. Tradition, as such, has lost much of its power. Every belief and custom must be justified both by reason and by history. Popular education banishes superstition, and with it, more and more, all those forms of Christianity that cannot prove themselves to be more than mere superstition. Careful scholarly and searching investigations into the origins of Christianity have done and are doing much to bring modern Christians to understand their faith, as in no previous period. The modern press has put the Bible into the hands of every Protestant Christian. Never before was the Bible in the hands of such a large proportion of the people. The Church and the Sunday school are securing the careful study of the Scriptures, not only by professional scholars and learned men, but by laymen, and by millions of young men and women, a thing which never was before.

This alone is a significant sign of growth, and warrants the statement made on a previous page that 'the average Protestant Christian of to-day has a better appreciation both of what Christ came to do, and of the nature of the salvation He offers, than did the mass of the Christians of any previous century.' A brilliant negro, at a recent session of the Inter-Seminary Missionary Alliance, in summing up the contributions of the different races to Christianity, said : ' The Jew has given us ethics ; the Greek, philosophy ; the Roman, law ; the Teuton, liberty—these the Saxon combines into one.'

We are only on the threshold of this period in the growth of the Christian Church. I have ventured to call it ' Sociological,' not so much because of what it has already accomplished, as because of its promises. Never before in the history of the world has there been such systematic study of social problems and forces ; never before has there been such insistence on the right of all men to an honest living ; never before has there been so much consecrated energy bestowed on the uplifting of the working masses in many ways, and especially by means of education, both technical and theoretical and ethical ; and, finally, never before has there been such movements toward the reconstruction of the social order on the principles laid down by Christ. The signs of the times point to a great advance in the coming century all along the line.

The main facts presented in the preceding paragraphs on the five periods of church history are graphically represented in the accompanying chart (No. XXIV.). It will be observed that though each age is characterised by the prominence of some particular element or movement, yet that the movement is not limited to that one period, but is also to be found more or less plainly in all the other periods.

In the remainder of this chapter we shall consider briefly some of the leading features of the progress

CHART. XXIV.

A Graphic Representation of the Periods
of the Growth of the Kingdom of God.

Emphasis on Reform: Social & National Salvation.
Anglo American Period 1750-1900 A.D.

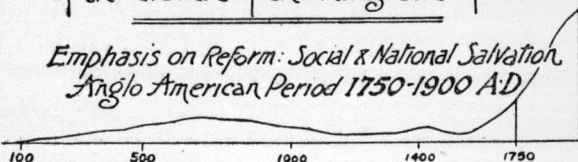

| 100 | 500 | 1000 | 1400 | 1750 |

Comparative Emphasis on Reform: Individual Salvation
Teutonic Period 1400-1750 A.D.

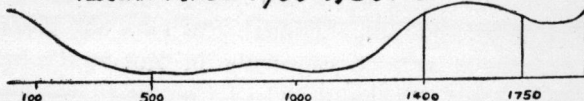

| 100 | 500 | 1000 | 1400 | 1750 |

Comparative Emphasis on & Development of Organization.
Roman Period   500-1400 A.D.

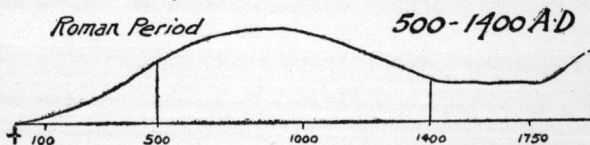

| + | 100 | 500 | 1000 | 1400 | 1750 |

Comparative Emphasis on Philosophical Theology
Greek Period. 100-500 A.D.

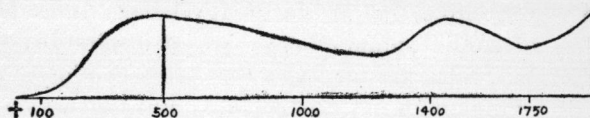

| + | 100 | 500 | 1000 | 1400 | 1750 |

Comparative Emphasis on the Facts
Jewish Period 50-100 A.D.

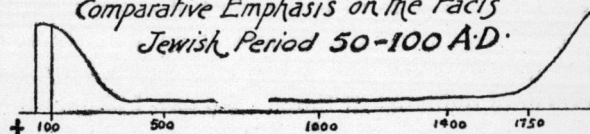

| + | 100 | 500 | 1000 | 1400 | 1750 |

made by the Protestant Church in its comprehension of Christ's teaching and of Christianity in general.

1. Within the present century a great change has come over the Protestant churches in regard to their view concerning the salvation of those who have heard nothing about Christ, *i.e.* concerning the salvation of the heathen. In former times, it was the common thought of Christendom, that all other religions were wholly false, the products of scheming priests, or even of the devil; and that all adherents of the non-Christian religions are doomed to everlasting punishment, even those who, dying in infancy or being idiots, have committed no personal sin. Though this view has become by no means extinct, especially in Roman Catholic countries, there are multitudes of Christians who have grown beyond it. The view is seen to be no part of Christ's own teaching, nor in accord with His spirit; God, being a loving Father, can do nothing unjust. None shall eternally perish except for his own eternal sin. A man's sin cannot be measured by an absolute standard, but by the light he has had, and by the circumstances, the environment, and the heredity which have helped to make him what he is. It is increasingly admitted, and even asserted, that all the great religions have more or less of truth, contain more or less of inspiration and revelation. Such are the views that are becoming more and more dominant in Christendom. But that which is of special interest to us is the spirit of charity and the freedom from dogmatic assertions about the fate of all the heathen, a spirit and a liberality which have been so rare until quite recent times. No one, I think, will be disposed to doubt that this is a great advance, a true growth in the comprehension of the real spirit of Christ.

2. This century is peculiarly the missionary age of the Church. Not that there has not been great missionary activity in previous ages. No age, indeed, has been wholly without it. But by comparison with previous ages, in the world-wide nature of the movement, in the systematic work, in the numbers of missionaries engaged, in the amount of money expended, and in the number of organisations at work, no age compares with this. But the point to which in this section I would call special attention is, the new views that prompt it, and the new ideas that control and regulate it. It is true that the missionary movement of to-day springs from the desire to save the lost; but although this desire does not of necessity imply the belief that all heathen are damned, and that all non-Christian religions are wholly false, yet it does imply the belief that none equal Christianity in the amount and self-consistence of the truth attained, in the fulness of the revelation of God, and in the nature and extent of the salvation given. The modern missionary movement among the majority of Protestant Christians springs from the desire to obey Christ's command, and to publish abroad the gospel of love, the gospel of a loving Father in heaven, the gospel of the Fatherhood of God and the brotherhood of man. It does not rest on the ancient belief that baptism and church membership are essential to salvation, nor does it spring from the desire to propagate merely a church organisation or a sect as such. This is a most important forward movement, a growth in the intellectual comprehension of Christian truth. Sad to say, there are many critics of the missionary movement who still attribute to it the motives held by former generations. They are evidently behind the times.

3. We are coming to see in modern times that asceticism, especially for its own sake and in all extreme forms, is no true part of Christianity, but may be even a hindrance to the most useful Christian life. Separation from the world in caves or convents, makes neither the subject nor the world any the better. We see, as never before, the meaning of Christ's prayer, that His disciples be not taken out of the world, but rather saved from the sin of the world.

4. Charity, too, has come to have a new significance in modern times. True charity is not the lavish scattering of money among the poor and needy, but rather the helping of the helpless to help themselves. The difference in these two conceptions is world-wide. It has been found by long experience that the first really degrades, actually pauperises its recipients, while the second really elevates them. And in carrying out this newer form of charity, the ideal is not simply to provide ways and means of work ; that is only the first, and the easiest, step in the process. The more essential part is personal intercourse, giving oneself, day by day ; the contact of character with character, by which alone is secured the development of the ideas and ideals ; the teaching of little ways of economy and prudence ; suggestions as to cooking and eating and general health ; teaching the mothers how to care for the children, the clothes, the home, and the earnings ; and with it all instilling self-respect and self-reliance. How infinitely higher is this conception of charity than that which would lead to the giving of even an abundance of money, but not to the gift of self ! But the point to which I call attention is, that it is a modern movement, a modern development in the understanding of the principles given by Christ. It is more nearly like the work of

Christ Himself in giving Himself for others than most forms of Christian activity.

5. The great change that has come over the Christian pulpit, in the subject-matter of the sermons, is another remarkable evidence of the modern development of the comprehension of Christianity. It is no longer common to dwell at length on the wrath of God against the sinner, and the awful doom that awaits the unrepentant unbeliever who dies in his sin. Rather is it common to dwell on the love and the mercy of the Father, and on the matchless sympathy of Jesus. The sinner is to be attracted to the home by love, rather than driven into the fold by fear. This change in the general style of preaching indicates the new conception of God, of Christ, and of the gospel, which we must surely pronounce a growth, a better comprehension of the real nature of Christ's teaching.

6. The modern growth in the comprehension of real Christianity may also be perceived in the great change that has come over the nature of the arguments used for proving the truth of Christianity and in answering the attacks of its critics. The emphasis of the argument has passed from the external and miraculous nature of the Christian religion to its internal and essential character. Though the miracles are by no means disbelieved, yet they are seen to be not the strongest proofs of the gospel. Prophecies and miracles have their place, but it is a subordinate one. Moral character, and that alone, is seen to have supreme religious worth. The moral majesty of Christ, and the moral truth of the gospel, are seen in no way to depend on the accompanying miracles. Even though the miracles recorded in the New Testament should have to be wholly given up as historical

13

verities—which I by no means believe—Christ's claim
to be the Son of God would not be one whit abated.

7. One further characteristic of the new movement is
the modern reconstructions of theology, giving Christ a
more conspicuous place, if not always the pivotal position. The very progress of dogmatic and speculative
theology has seemed to depend on this. Not infrequently do we hear now of 'Christocentric theology.'
One of the most widely read of recent theological works
is that entitled *The Place of Christ in Modern Theology*,
already referred to more than once, while another vigorous work of still more recent date bears the title of
Christ in the Faith of To-day, by Dr. George A.
Gordon. In truth, the past fifty to seventy-five years
have witnessed a profound though silent revolution in
the attitude of the Protestant churches towards theology
and formal systematic statements of belief. The old
creeds and theologies are being studied and criticised
from the standpoint of the place they give to Christ
and His teaching. Taking the place of the more
elaborate and systematic statements of belief, are simple
expressions of belief in Christ and of loyalty and
devotion to Him. Some are inclined to interpret this
movement as a rejection of all creeds and all theology,
as an assertion that creeds are useless and needless, and
theologies positive hindrances to the spiritual life. Such,
however, is not, I think, the real character of this movement. Those who hold such views are relatively few,
and belong rather to an eddy in the stream than to the
general current. Its real character is, as I have already
said, a renewed emphasis on Christ as the supreme
factor in every creed, as the real centre of every systematic statement of Christian truth. The movement is

due to a recovery of Christ, and a relegation of formal creeds to an inferior place.

8. And this movement shows itself even more conspicuously in the worship of Christians. The prayers offered in Christian pulpits and the hymns sung in Christian churches have far more of Christ in them than formerly.

9. With regard also to the questions of fitness for church membership, far more is made now than formerly of a daily life of devotion and loyalty to Christ. Not that creeds and beliefs are thought to be needless. It is still well recognised that so long as man is an intelligent being, and is guided by his beliefs and his reason, so long are creeds and individual statements of belief both useful and needful. But it is also well recognised, and this is the point for us to note, that mere beliefs and creeds are not all, nor even the most vital part of a Christian life. Nothing can be a substitute for the life itself. And this life is found to flow out of knowledge of and love for Christ. Hence comes this renewed emphasis on Christ; hence comes this exaltation of Christ into the forefront both of theology and of worship—of Christ as at once a historical person and an ever-living, ever-present, and powerful factor in the life of the humble disciple. One has but to call to mind the nature of the instruction in Christian truth now given the young and comparatively ignorant, together with the character of such institutions as the Sunday school, the Young Men's Christian Association, the Young People's Society of Christian Endeavour, and similar societies, to see what a change has come over the conception of what it is to be a Christian.

10. Another sign of the time is the rapid laying aside of denominational, sectarian strifes and jealousies. The

prayer of Christ that His followers should be one, is being realised to-day as in no previous age. Though there are more separate church organisations than in any previous period, yet there is also more mutual good-will, more mutual respect, and even cordiality, and far more co-operation. The continuous discussions and efforts to secure organic church union, and the success in many cases, reveal how great is the heart union which has already taken place, and which, after all, was the main thing for which Christ prayed. Those who point to the many divisions of Protestant Christianity, as evidence of its weakness and disintegration, seem to forget that greater internal differences may be and are included under a single organisation, as in the Roman Catholic or Episcopalian Churches, than exist in separate organisations, such as the Presbyterian and Congregational Churches. The degree of the real union cannot be judged simply from the unity of the external organisation. In this paragraph I refer, not to the external but to the internal, to the heart union of Christendom, which is growing apace. We see it not only in the Evangelical Alliance, but in the Bible and Tract Societies, Young Men's Christian Associations, in the Young Women's Christian Associations, in the Young People's Societies of Christian Endeavour, and in the many similar undenominational and inter-denominational societies, in all of which the various denominations work together in the most cordial relations. These inter-denominational movements would hardly have been possible a century or two ago.[1]

11. One more evidence of modern progress must be

[1] *Note on Church Union.*—Not only have there been many discussions regarding the desirability and conditions of union between different de-

mentioned, namely, new zeal in and new methods of studying the Bible. No longer is the meaning of critical passages to be settled beforehand, according to the theological needs of the interpreter. Each book and each text must be interpreted in its natural, original, historical meaning, and in no other. To determine this, vast learning and profound scholarship have been bestowed on the study of the Bible, which are giving the Christian and especially the Protestant world new insight into the real meaning of Christ's teachings, and the significance of the religious life. This modern growth is a matter of no slight importance.

12. The final evidence of the modern development in the comprehension of Christ's teachings which I shall mention, is the growing realisation of the meaning of Christ's words, 'Thou shalt love thy neighbour as thyself.' It is this growing comprehension, accompanied by obedience, that has produced such a vast number of philanthropic and evangelistic organisations as have arisen in recent times. The new social sciences receive their noblest foundation and greatest impulse from the

nominations, but in both England and America several such unions have already been effected. That which is perhaps the most promising of large results in the near future is the Federation of the Free Churches of England and Wales. Its last annual meeting, held in London, March 9–11, was one of great enthusiasm. The leaders of the thought and life of the Free Churches of England were present, and spoke with great freedom and unity. All the leading denominations sent delegates to the 'National Council.' The meeting this year was the first under the new organisation, which secures permanent federation, with definite aims and methods of work. The cordial sympathy with this forward union movement of the Free Churches expressed by many of the leaders of the Established Church, was but one more sign of the growing harmony and unity of spirit that is springing up between Christians of different folds, representing most diverse principles and tendencies.

teachings of Jesus. Never before was the doctrine of the brotherhood of man so loudly proclaimed or so fully accepted. Obedience to this teaching of Christ manifests itself chiefly in action, and will thus receive more particular attention in the following chapter. Yet it is important to observe that the increasing obedience implies increasing comprehension, both of the nature and of the importance of the teaching. It is full comprehension of and obedience to this ' law of love' that is making the modern age the most noble, because the most Christian. But the chief point for us to notice is that this is a modern movement. The social sciences are only in their infancy, but their tap-root is in the teaching of Christ, ' Thou shalt love thy neighbour as thyself.'

In the preceding paragraphs I have very briefly indicated the leading features of the five periods into which it seemed fitting to divide the history of the Church. I have attempted to show that in each period there was a real growth in the intellectual apprehension of some part of Christian truth. I close this chapter with three general remarks.

1. A great deal of criticism directed against Christianity is the result of a serious misapprehension. Modern Christianity, as organised into churches, customs, and systems of belief, is the product of the centuries of growth; in other words, is the result of natural development. Like every growing organism, it has been subjected to laws of growth. The fact that there remain to this day old fixed types of Christianity, traditional beliefs, views and customs, which took form a thousand or more years ago, and now have no moral power or significance, by no means proves absence of life in the whole body; for the signs of the life we must

look to those parts that are growing, to the budding branches, not to the dead bark, or decaying stumps.

2. Many of the tirades against Christianity and affirmations of its rapid decay may be traced to false definitions of Christianity, as was pointed out in the first chapter. If, for instance, one conceives the peculiar philosophy, the theological system, and the ceremonials of the churches of the eighteenth century to be Christianity, then Christianity is certainly rapidly passing away, is being rejected. But if the teachings and life and spirit of Christ are conceived to be the essence of true Christianity, then few, I think, will dispute its growing power.

3. In speaking of the growth of Christianity, I would not for a moment conceal the defects and deficiencies of each period of Christianity. These have been many and serious. They exist, however, not as fruits of Christ's teachings, but in spite of them. No nation, no government, and few individuals have become wholly Christian. Much of paganism still lives in Christendom, and even in the Church. These defects, these sins, these superstitions, deserve all the criticism and scorn and castigations they have received. It is neither my purpose nor my desire to cover them up. But neither is it my purpose to dwell on them. What I have sought to do is to lay emphasis on the fact, and to present some of the evidence that it is a fact, that more and more the teaching of Christ is prevailing, that His Kingdom is coming. This, I think, no one can deny. Each added century has added to the comprehension of Christ's teachings, and to the power of His life on that of the Church. Never before were the signs of the growth of Christianity so manifest as they are to-day, or the growth itself so rapid.

CHAPTER VI

GROWTH IN PRACTICE

'There is not a secular reform in the whole development of modern civilisation, which (if it is more than mechanical) has not drawn its inspiration from a religious principle. Infirmaries for the body have sprung out of duty for the soul ; schools for the letter, that free way may be opened for the spirit ; sanitary laws, that the diviner elements in human nature may not become incredible and hopeless from their foul environment.'[1]

'A gloomy picture has unrolled itself before us. I am conscious that I have not designedly painted it too dark. . . . What we know of the moral life of Rome is derived chiefly from Rome itself. . . . The general conclusion must still be that the heathen world was ethically as well as religiously at the point of dissolution, that it had become as bankrupt in morals as in faith, and that there was no power at hand from which a restoration could proceed. . . . For Christian nations there is provided in Christianity a power which can restore the moral life again and again from the deepest degradation. The ancient world was destitute of any such power. After its palmy age—a time of comparative soundness—was gone, after corruption had once entered, it degenerated beyond recovery. Heathenism bore within itself no power of moral renewal.'[2]

---

[1] Dr. James Martineau, *Hours of Thought*, p. 181.
[2] Uhlhorn, *The Conflict of Christianity with Heathenism*, pp. 141-143.

CHAPTER VI

A S Christianity is not primarily a system of thought,
a philosophy, but rather a moral life, so the
truest measure of the comprehension of Christ's
teaching is not to be found in the intellectual appreciation of its principles, in treatises on systematic or
dogmatic theology, but in living the life and doing the
deeds Christ commanded. In this regard, too, there
has been no little growth during the centuries since
Christ called His first disciples. To treat the subject
with any fulness would require a volume instead of
a chapter. Only the briefest summary can here be
attempted. It is not pretended that the growth in
practice has been steady through the centuries, nor
that all parts of Christendom have progressed alike.
There are none more ready than the author to admit
that there have been periods of relapse, even of moral
degradation, and that there are some parts of the
Christian Church which to-day are far behind, hardly
worthy of being called Christian. Yet I think it can
be easily shown that, on the whole, there has been great
progress in living the life taught by Christ, and that
no age has made such marked progress as the present.

The distinguishing characteristic of the Christians
during the early centuries was not so much that they
worshipped one God, as that they lived earnest, simple,
moral lives. One among the five causes assigned

by Gibbon for the rapid spread of Christianity, is that of the superior morality of their lives.[1] The Andover professors, in their recent volume on the divinity of Jesus Christ, speaking of the form of Christianity during the first centuries, say : ' It is distinctly not a theology, but a life. It holds its truths not as dogmas, but as motives. It rests in a person, not in propositions. It is not concerned with philosophical questions, but with questions of character and conduct, with men and with God, with life here and hereafter.'[2] Professor Fisher, in his *History of the Christian Church*, says : ' The surprising effect of Christianity in reforming the lives of men is amply attested by Christian writers. Justin Martyr, in an eloquent passage, dwells on the fact that slaves of sensuality have become pure in morals ; the avaricious and miserly freely give to those in need ; the revengeful pray for their enemies. Origen inquires if the recovery of so great a number of persons from licentiousness, injustice, and covetousness could have been accomplished without divine help. . . . The love of Christians for each other astonished the heathen. There was a truth in the gibe of Lucian, which the humorist himself did not understand. "Their Master," he said, "has persuaded them that they are all brothers." The fraternal kindness extended to strangers, and to Christians of foreign nations, occasioned special surprise. Hospitality and almsgiving were universal among believers. Collections were regularly taken in the churches for the benefit of the poor. When a pestilence broke out, it was noticed that the Christians did not desert the sick, or

[1] *The Decline and Fall of the Roman Empire*, ch. xv.
[2] P. 125.

neglect the burial of the dead. They even took care of the heathen who had none to befriend them.' [1]

In seeking to study the growth of the application of Christ's teachings and principles through the successive periods of progress, mention should first be made of some of the leading moral and social characteristics on which Christians insisted, and which finally became prevalent throughout the Greek and Roman worlds.

1. One of the most important of these was the new sanctity of the marriage relation. Among Christians marriage became a holy thing ordained of God; concubinage was absolutely forbidden ; and divorce, except for adultery of one or the other of the contracting parties, was not allowed. The sinfulness of licentiousness and lust and all forms of uncleanness was magnified by the Church. All this was in marked contrast to the conduct of non-Christians, among whom marriage was for personal convenience ; concubinage a common practice ; divorce extremely frequent and easy, and for any reason whatever. Sexual immorality was a matter of utter indifference to the established religious worship of Greece and Rome.

2. The peculiar sacredness of human life in the eyes of Christians was another point of marked contrast between them and non-Christians. In the non-Christian world, human life in itself has never been valued or sacred. Under the Roman empire, a master was free to kill his slave, or even his children. Infanticide was

---

[1] *The History of the Church*, p. 59. For some adequate view of the moral and religious condition of the Roman world, and for the changes gradually brought in by Christianity, the reader is referred to Uhlhorn's *The Conflict of Christianity with Heathenism*, Schmidt's *The Social Results of Early Christianity*, Brace's *Gesta Christi*, and Storr's *The Divine Origin of Christianity*.

not uncommon. There was no sin involved in the gladiatorial shows. They were approved and defended by Roman moralists. But, to the Christian, human life as such was sacred; neither slave nor infant could rightly be slain. Infanticide was considered a crime. The influence of these two moral conceptions alone, enforced as they were by Christian practice, was sufficient to transform the whole social fabric. But in addition to these we should mention another, which, though not required, yet became in time generally observed by Christians ; namely—

3. The contribution of means as well as of one's own labour for the care of the sick and poor, thus leading to the establishment of hospitals, already referred to in the quotation from Professor Fisher. This led to—

4. The giving of freedom to slaves, a movement which though gradual, ultimately resulted in the destruction of slavery. By these Christian practices the ancient pagan, social, and industrial structure of Europe became in time wholly transformed. These new principles and social customs sprang from the life of the early Christians, were the natural expression of renewed hearts, hearts filled with love to God and man, and were the application of Christ's teachings and principles to practical life. When theological discussions arose and waxed fierce, and the attention of learned men and scholars was fixed on philosophy and metaphysics, and, later, when the organic Church grew to tremendous power, and its offices became filled with men more ambitious than righteous, and too often even profane and licentious, yet even then the real life and power of the Church remained as

before in the moral living of the common members. Throughout the so-called Dark Ages there were in the churches countless faithful men and women, whose lives were hid with Christ in God. The moral energy culminating in the Reformation of the sixteenth century was not due simply to the appearance of a few gifted leaders like Luther and Calvin. It was the result rather of the moral earnestness of tens of thousands of spiritual men and women, who drew their life from Christ, and who grieved over the low moral life of the rulers and officers in the organic visible Church. But for these common people, living their God-inspired, Christian lives, the teachings of Christ, and even the Church itself, would have perished long ago. But for them, the appearance of the great spiritual leaders would have been impossible. The real vital power of the Church has never been shown so much in its intellectual efforts, in its creeds, in its organisations, as in the moral life of its believers. This moral, spiritual life has ever been gaining more and more power. It has had a long deadly struggle with fleshly lusts, with defective views, with oppressive church organisations, and with intellectualism. But it has more and more gained the victory over these. The spiritual life has been growing. This growth has not been uniform. It has resembled the incoming ocean tide, wave upon wave; some waves larger and some smaller, with more or less of a relapse between the successive waves; yet the tide of the Christ-inspired life has continued to rise throughout the ages. Those who wish to know the low ebb of moral life after the Reformation will do well to study the first three or four chapters of Dorchester's *Problem of Religious*

Progress, or any of the recent histories of England. But the general fact may be confidently asserted, that great as are the moral defects, not only of the Christians at large, but even of the clergy of Europe and America, yet there has been a great advance in recent times. Sin is rebuked as in no previous age. The standard of practical living has been greatly raised. It is only ignorance of the past in its reality that makes some think otherwise. In the most recent times there has been a renewed emphasis laid on the necessity of moral life. The purity of the family, the sanctity of the home, the necessity of personal purity, honesty, kindness, and benevolence, and the inherent value of human life, are all receiving a greater emphasis than ever before. This new spirit and emphasis show themselves, not only in a general way in the lives of individual believers, but also vast numbers of organisations have been formed for the more systematic propagation of Christian views, or execution of Christian deeds. This great modern movement springs from a better appreciation of Christ's teachings, from the desire more fully to obey them, but chiefly from a more complete possession by men of His life and spirit.

We pass now from the consideration of the moral life of Christians to consider briefly some of the many ways in which the spirit of love and benevolence is showing itself in modern times and in practical ways. Of individual, personal, and private benevolences it is impossible, from the very nature of the case, to make any even approximate estimate. When, however, we reflect on the great increase of the various forms of organised benevolence and of the systematic charities, we may be assured that it indicates a corresponding increase in individual personal activities. In the following enumeration of the main varieties of organisations, which have been formed in response to the demands of the quickened Christian conscience and spirit, it is impossible always to draw the line sharply between those which are only benevolent without any moral or religious aim, and those whose sole aim is the propagation of moral truth, of Christianity, without any benevolent aim. In fact, these aims should be inseparable. In some institutions the one, and in others the other, is the main end in view. But in either case the ultimate aim is the production of a better society, by helping individuals to attain a better environment, a happier and a nobler character. These are so intimately associated that any institution which aims to improve the one, of necessity has the other also more or less in view.

1. First among these practical movements, we must mention those which provide for the sick and the suffering. This movement has its roots in the early centuries. ' Charity was not unknown before among heathen ; but the word acquired a new force of meaning from the obedience rendered to the " new command " which Christ had given, " Love one another." ' Free hospitals, though well-known forms of Christian activity during the whole Christian era, have received most remarkable development in modern times. They have become so common a form of charity that they are considered almost a matter of course. It is impossible to give any correct or complete figures on the subject ; it must suffice to say that to-day every city and even every large town of Christendom has one or more, according to its needs. In the larger places the

14

hospitals are specialised; there are hospitals for the eye, for the throat, for various kinds of disease; hospitals for men, for women, and for children.

2. Closely connected with this form of benevolence is the work of trained nurses who, supported by individual Christians or by churches, tend the sick and the poor in their homes, free of all charge, going even into the very foulest and wickedest of places. The Roman Catholic Church is especially forward in this kind of work; a fact which should not be forgotten by those who criticise it for its traditionalism, ceremonialism, dogmaticism, etc.

3. Asylums for various classes of permanent invalids constitute another form in which the modern Christian spirit manifests itself. Asylums for the insane, for the decrepit, for orphans, for foundlings, for aged and helpless men, and for women,—these and many others may be found by the hundred in the Protestant parts of Christendom.

4. Homes for the reformation of fallen women and of drunkards, both men and women, of truant boys and girls who are starting on the downward paths of sin, are another way in which the Christian spirit seeks to save the lost from further sin and suffering.

5. Still another method of Christian activity appears in the numberless charity organisations throughout England, America, and Germany, which provide work for the workless and food for the hungry, either free or at nominal prices. The amount of this work, and the sums spent in it year by year, vary with the need, and inversely with the prosperity of trade, but the sums spent are enormous. In the winter of 1893–94, it is said that $15,000,000 were spent in this kind of work

in the city of New York alone. Mr. Benjamin Kidd states that the annual revenue of the private charities of London alone is close on to £5,000,000.

6. There are also the various rescue societies. For city boys and girls are found homes in the country among farmers ; young men and women in temptation are warned, and, if possible, places of safety are found for them.

7. The Society for the Suppression of Vice should also receive mention. It is its aim to search out and to destroy, by legal process, obscene pictures and books, and secure the punishment of their manufacturers and sellers by the process of law ; the legal destruction of the implements and places of gambling, and securing the punishment of offenders is another part of its work.

8. Another most significant movement is the temperance wave that from year to year is rising higher and higher. It not only seeks by moral influence and by arguments to dissuade the young and old from drinking, but it seeks by laws and by the ballot entirely to root out one of the most potent causes of sin and error and crime and calamity in civilised countries. It has already secured the passage of laws introducing and requiring temperance education in the public schools of forty-four of the States and territories of the United States, as well as in Canada and Sweden. Scientific temperance text-books, suited to children of different ages, have been prepared, and are gaining deserved popularity. ' Mrs. Hunt's exhibit of the progress of scientific temperance instruction achieved a great triumph at the World's Fair. No part of the vast educational display attracted more attention or excited more interest than that of scientific temperance

instruction in the public schools.' This exhibit received five highest awards. The result of this instruction on the life of the nation will be seen in the votes of the rising generation. The adherents of this temperance movement are to be counted by the million.

9. The application of Christ's spirit to the circumstances of modern life may be further seen in the summer outings given to the poor in the large cities by subscription of the well-to-do; all-day steamer excursions on the cool, blue ocean, with meals furnished free, for working girls, for mothers, and for weak or sickly children.

This work in London is carried on under the 'Children's Holiday Society,' which issues a yearly report of the work done each year. The following are the figures for recent years :—

	No. of Children sent into the Country for Two Weeks.	Total Expense.	Parents' Payments.
1884 . .	4,800	£1,800 [1]	...
1885 . .	6,800	3,082 [1]	...
1886 . .	11,800	6,857	£1972 [2]
1890 . .	23,771	14,996	5245
1895 . .	28,783	18,723	6599

[1] Exclusive of parents' payments.

[2] The parents' payments are collected in very small sums, week by week, for months previous by friendly visitors. Each parent is urged to give all that is possible, so that the spirit of self-respect and self-help may be developed rather than hindered by this form of help.

10. Still another manifestation of the Christian spirit may be seen in the wide efforts of prison reform and the formation of regular associations for carrying out the work. The main aim of the prison has been changed from punishment to that of training; physical suffering and diseases arising from foul air, bad drainage, and improper or insufficient food, have been almost done away with in the prisons of Protestant Christendom.

11. The Red Cross Society, and its work of mercy among the sick and wounded soldiers of friend and foe alike, should also find mention.

12. Not least among the manifestations of the better application of Christ's teachings in modern times are the efforts being made by many large manufacturers and dealers to pay more attention to the physical and moral welfare of the workmen employed, providing them with suitable houses, wholesome surroundings, education for their children, interest for their savings, churches and libraries for their families, and even, in many cases, sharing with the workmen a part of their profits; in other words, striving in the business life to apply in its fulness the law of loving one's neighbour as oneself. The large number of Christian business men who are thus applying Christian ideals to the conduct of business is a feature that needs to be emphasised. On the revival of business in the United States in the early summer of 1895, a great many firms voluntarily raised the wages paid to the workmen. In a single issue of the July *Outlook*, firms employing 62,100 men are reported to have made such a voluntary advance; of these, 59,550 men receiving an advance of 10 per cent. on their wages. Many other

firms were also reported, the number of whose employees, or the amount of the advance, not being
given.

13. 'The College or University Settlement' is still
another way in which the Christian spirit is being
manifested in the solution of the modern social problems.
Several educated college young men take up their
home in some degraded or unfortunate part of the
city, and so identify themselves with the interests of
that special district as to be able personally to influence
the people of that vicinity, giving them higher ideas of
life and of home, as well as improving the more outward civic conditions of life. Many of these settlements
in London, in New York, in Boston, and in other large
places, have already secured very marked results. Although the first of these was started only in 1885
(Toynbee Hall), yet we already count seventy-two such
settlements, of which thirty-five are in the United
Kingdom and thirty-eight in the United States; the
number of resident workers can hardly be less than
300, and may be considerably greater.

14. Industrial and technical schools are another form
of philanthropy of no little importance. In these, the
children of the working classes are taught the most
approved methods of labour of all varieties, from the
manual trades of carpentering, masonry, bricklaying,
etc., to the gentler arts of drawing, sewing, cooking,
etc. There is hardly any kind of work that may not
now be studied in some practical manual training
school. The immense benefit of these institutions to
the poor can hardly be overrated.

15. The endowment of schools connected with the
churches is an ancient practice of Christendom. It

was thus that the large universities of Europe and England and the United States arose. They were organised and carried on by the Christian interest in liberal education. The rapid increase of this movement in recent decades; the establishment of universities by men of enormous wealth; the founding of numberless colleges and academies; and the providing, not only of capital for the institutions, but also of scholarships for needy, worthy students, is a most remarkable movement of modern times. The following is a statement of the invested capital of a few of the leading institutions of the United States :—

Girard College endowment . .	$14,000,000.00
Columbia College endowment . .	13,000,000.00
Harvard College endowment . .	11,000,000.00
Yale College endowment . .	10,000,000.00
University of California endowment .	7,000,000.00
University of Pennsylvania endowment	5,000,000.00

Leland Stanford University endowment consists of thousands of acres of more or less cultivated land. If it should all be put under fair cultivation, its estimated worth is about $200,000,000.00 ; and the income alone would be several millions. No other University in the world has such a large endowment as this. Its resources may be developed as they are needed. Three evangelical denominations in the United States reported the endowments of their colleges and seminaries at $62,631,135.00 in 1893. Were the statistics at hand, it would be doubtless found that the endowments of the strictly denominational schools, colleges, and seminaries of all the religious bodies of the United States are double or treble the sum named above.

Regarding the endowments of the universities and

Colleges of the United Kingdom, I have no precise information. Kukula's *Minerva*, for 1896, gives the total income for the various institutions as follows :—

Oxford .	. .	£326,601
Cambridge	. .	291,806
Edinburgh	. .	88,142
Glasgow	. .	62,317

In this connection, mention should be made of the establishment of public libraries—'the people's universities.' This may be considered one effect of popular education ; but it is also an effect of high ideals and of consecration of vast sums of money by the wealthy for the benefit of the people. There are in the United States 399 free public libraries, besides hundreds of private ones. In the large cities, the library buildings cost hundreds of thousands of dollars. Chicago has two buildings costing one million and half a million dollars respectively, and is soon to have a third, which, with its endowment, will cost two and a half millions.

In all the above-mentioned varieties of institutions (except the educational), the more prominent aim is benevolence, either in the relief of suffering or the providing of more wholesome environment. The sums of money that are yearly spent in the support of these many kinds of organisations and ways of work are beyond estimation. It is impossible to obtain even an approximate idea of the amount, but it must be annually many millions of pounds. It is, however, not the sums of money expended that constitute the matter of chief importance, but the purposes and aims, the wide variety of works, and, above all, the truly Christian spirit of

personal sacrifice and of love to God and man, from
which these deeds arise.

Howe's *Directory of the Metropolitan Charities of
London* gives a list of over a thousand charity organisa-
tions. Their incomes, for a few periods I have noted.
They furnish material for encouragement.

INCOME OF THE METROPOLITAN CHARITIES OF LONDON.

	No. of Societies reporting Income.	Income Reported.	For Home and Foreign Missions.[1]
1875	1050	£4,114,849	£1,340,221
1882	1003	4,313,275	1,534,238
1888	1027	5,063,137	1,807,177
1894	961	5,484,301	2,007,303

Appleton's *Annual Cyclopædia* for a few years past
has published a list of all 'notable bequests for public
purposes of $5000 each and upwards.' 'It excludes
the ordinary denominational contributions for educational and benevolent purposes, and State and
municipal appropriations to public and sectarian institutions.' None of the millions contributed for home
or foreign missions, or for denominational schools, or
hospitals, or reform homes, or charity, are here included.
Remembering this fact, how large the annual totals are!

1893	.		$29,000,000
1894	.	.	32,000,000
1895	.	.	32,800,000

[1] The figures in this column are included in those of the previous column.

It is important to observe that the greater number of these benevolent works are the product of a modern movement in the Christian Church. Hospitals, care of strangers, and nursing of the sick, descend from ancient times ; but the industrial schools, college settlements, rescue homes, the Red Cross Society, and many kindred institutions, which are too numerous to mention, are largely the product of modern ideas. In these forms of work, in these manifestations of the spirit of Christ in practical ways, we see the more and more full application of the teachings of Christ, a fulness of application that has been realised in no previous century.

It is not claimed, in the foregoing paragraphs, that all hospitals, all industrial schools, and all the various philanthropic institutions are sustained by persons who profess to be followers of Christ ; we simply say that the doing of these things is the real application of the teachings and spirit of Christ, whether done by professed Christians or not, an application more full and complete than in any previous age. The relation to this movement of the Church and the world we shall consider in the next chapter.

But the Christian zeal is seen nowhere more strikingly than in the great missionary movement of the nineteenth century, in which movement is embodied the desire to obey the final command of Christ, to proclaim His gospel to every creature. Beginning in a small way, at the opening of the century, the missionary wave has swept more and more broadly through the Churches, and has planted its workers more and more widely over the world. Among the tiny islands of the Pacific, throughout the broad continents of Asia and Africa, alike among the cannibal savage tribes, and the mighty civilised nations of the Orient; this missionary movement has made itself felt. The gospel has already been proclaimed in all lands and in all tongues; the Christian Bible has (more or less of it) been translated into 354 languages; Christian books are being used by the thousand the world over; Christian hymns are being sung in every language; Christian schools and churches are springing up in every land. To bring all this about, thousands of educated men and women, reared in the midst of the choicest civilisation, have given up their homes, have left their friends and relatives and native lands, with all their bright prospects and hopes, and have given their entire lives to the work of proclaiming the gospel, with stammering tongues, to those who, from the very nature of the case, cannot, until they become Christians, understand the motives and ambitions of those who are doing this self-sacrificing work.

This missionary work is not a new feature of Christian life; it is as old as Christianity itself. Throughout the centuries, even down to the present day, the Roman Catholic Church has had a noble army of missionary labourers, whose spirit and self-devotion we can but admire, however mistaken we who are Protestants may consider much of their teaching.

But the new missionary vigour that has arisen among the Protestant Christians, the large number of societies that have been organised, the immense sums of money raised for the missionary work, and, compared with former centuries, the great influence and the rapid results that have attended the work; the world-wide nature of the movement, the vast number of peoples, races, nations, and languages that have come within its sweep, mark out this as the peculiarly missionary century. Those who have only a superficial acquaintance with what has been and is now being done, would be amazed, could they be led suddenly to see the facts in all their fulness. Scores of islands of the Pacific have been wholly transformed from cannibal islands into Christian civilised lands. The most promising and even potent influences for morality in such lands as Africa with its savagery and slavery, and China with its superstition, and India with its idolatry and caste, and Japan with its ambitious self-confidence and worldly enterprises, are the Christian influences.

Some idea of the growth of the foreign missionary interest in the United States may be gained by a study of the following statistics of the receipts of its leading missionary societies.

RECEIPTS OF THE FOREIGN MISSIONARY SOCIETIES OF THE UNITED STATES.[1]

Date.	Total for Ten Years.	Average per Year.
1810–19 . . .	$206,210	$20,621
1820–29 . . .	745,718	74,571
1830–39 . . .	2,885,839	288,583
1840–49 . . .	5,087,922	508,792
1850–59 . . .	8,427,284	842,728
1860–69 . . .	13,074,129	1,307,412
1870–80 (11 years) .	24,425,121	1,947,738
1881–94 (14 years) .	44,390,389	3,414,645

In 1892 the sum spent by all the foreign missionary societies of the United States amounted to $5,006,283.

[1] See Dorchester's *Problem of Religious Progress.*

CHART. XXV.

Illustrating the Growth of the Receipts of
the Foreign Missionary Societies of the
United States.

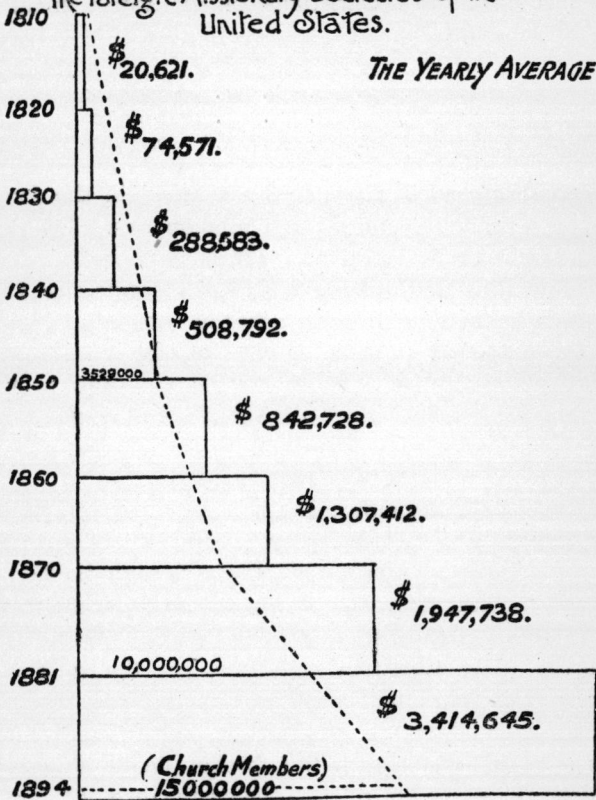

1810

$ 20,621.

THE YEARLY AVERAGE

1820

$ 74,571.

1830

$ 288,583.

1840

$ 508,792.

1850   3,529,000

$ 842,728.

1860

$ 1,307,412.

1870

$ 1,947,738.

1881   10,000,000

$ 3,414,645.

(Church Members)
1894   15,000,000

-------- The dotted line shows growth of Church Members

221

The accompanying chart (No. XXV.) shows how much faster the contributions have grown than the membership of the evangelical churches.

The Protestant Christians of the world spent for foreign missions in

1890	$12,788,000
1891	15,663,000
1893	14,713,000

For these same years they sustained in the foreign field 8511, 9110, and 11,450 missionaries. The great increase between 1891 and 1893 is noteworthy. Compared with these figures, how small seems the entire sum raised by voluntary contributions among the Roman Catholics of the whole world for foreign missions, namely, 1894,[1] 6,820,164 fr. ($1,364,033), and in 1895, 6,587,049 fr. ($1,317,410), while the total number of foreign missionaries, according to the statement of the *Missiones Catholicæ*, was 2800 in 1886.

The missionary movement, however, does not manifest itself simply in its labours for foreign nations and races. Great though its labours in these foreign lands have been, and still increasingly are, and magnificent though the results already secured have been, surpassing those of the early Christian centuries, yet the missionary activity in Christian lands—in other words, the home missionary labour—is even greater, and the results fully as assuring as those in the foreign fields. By 'home missions' we do not refer to the sustenance of the home churches by their own members, but to the efforts of these churches to propagate the gospel in their own more or less immediate vicinities. Nearly all large

[1] *Annals of the Propagation of the Faith*, May 1896.

churches now have their private mission churches and halls in the destitute, neglected, and churchless parts of the city. The active church has many visitors for work among the poor and the sick, to administer comfort and charity, and to spread the knowledge of the gospel. The children of non-Christians are gathered into Sunday schools. The number of these private mission churches and Sunday schools is very large.

In addition to this form of home missionary work, there are the regular Home Missionary Societies of the various denominations, which carry on the same kind of work throughout the entire country. These are found especially in the United States. There are many varieties of these societies. In addition to the regular ones for extending each denomination by founding new, and helping its own weak churches, there are societies for work among the various nationalities of immigrants ; societies for the establishment of Sunday schools in destitute cities, towns, and villages ; Sunday schools which in time will develop into self-supporting churches ; Publication Societies, Tract Societies, Church Erection Societies, Parsonage Building Associations, Societies for the Education of Ministers ; each society doing a broad work in many States, and supported by large and widely distributed constituencies. Thousands of ministers are supported by these agencies, who are pushing the work in its various forms ; and, beside the paid workers, there are hundreds of thousands of unpaid Sunday-school teachers who are greatly interested in the work, because personally connected with it. The last accessible report for the United Kingdom (1887) gives the number of Sunday - school teachers as 704,286, while that for the United States and British

America (1896) as 1,476,369. It may not be far astray to say that there are at present (1897) about 2,500,000 Sunday-school teachers in English-speaking lands.

The great aid to the home missionary work rendered by the various auxiliary societies can hardly be appreciated. During the ninety-four years of this century the religious publication societies of the United States, as we have seen on a previous page, have expended a total of $170,579,723.00. The British and Foreign Bible Society and the American Bible Society together had published by 1885, 149,637,171 Bibles, or portions; by 1894, 197,933,438. The American Bible Society is at present issuing over a million copies a year. The eighty Bible Societies of Christendom have in this century published and distributed over 243,000,000 of Bibles, Testaments, and portions. The Religious Tract Society (English), since its establishment ninety-five years ago, has circulated over three billions of its publications. In 1893 it issued 67,590,600 copies.

How clearly does this tremendous activity in the publication of Bibles and tracts bear significant witness to the folly of Voltaire's boastful prophecy, a hundred and thirty years ago, that ' before the beginning of the nineteenth century Christianity will have disappeared from the earth!' He prophesied of these our own times. Not only have his vain words proved a lying prophecy, but since that time the very room in Geneva where these words were spoken ' has been used as a Bible depository; and Christianity has won the greatest, the widest, and the most glorious triumphs of her whole history.' Since Voltaire's scornful remark, that the Bible would become an unknown book, it has been translated into all the leading languages of the world. What non-Christian or infidel book has been translated into more than a dozen languages? But the Bible, in whole or in part, is now to be had in 354 languages.

Though briefly referred to on a previous page, special mention should be made of several subsidiary methods of carrying on the home missionary work. In addition to the various societies and organisations, whose direct and only work is the propagation of the gospel, there are many others whose methods are indirect, such as Boys' Brigades, Working Men's Clubs, Guilds and Brotherhoods, Literary Societies, Reading Rooms, Public Libraries, Sewing Circles, Athletic Associations, Temperance Circles, Summer Clubs, Homes for Working Girls, Homes for Newsboys, Homes for Bootblacks, and many other varieties of societies. The aim of all such institutions is to give social life and entertainment, free from the usual temptations of the large cities. Though prompted and sustained largely by Christian impulse, their direct work is not to impart formal religious instruction; this latter is left to the institutions equipped for such work, namely, the churches, Sunday schools, etc.

In no better way perhaps can I illustrate the spirit and methods of this broad kind of philanthropic and evangelistic work, than by citing one concrete case. Take, for instance, the Drift Children's Mission of London, comparatively little known as yet, but doing a most important work for the children of London's submerged tenth. Here Mr. Boyer, though an American, by his tact in dealing with children, has won the hearts of the class most difficult of all to touch and hold. During his first summer (in 1888), '800 children, too

15

ragged ever to feel at home in the Sunday schools, had marched with Mr. Boyer to Victoria Park, and he was then ready to begin evangelistic work among them on a large scale, holding meetings on week evenings at the great Assembly Hall in Whitechapel Road. He had invited 600 little ones, but double that number came to the first service, and long before time for the meeting the street was so thronged that Mr. Boyer had to march them up and down to keep the highway open. A like multitude of drift children came to the second meeting, and after that tickets were used to limit the numbers.

'The first Christmas was celebrated in a humble way. With the last shilling he had in the world, Mr. Boyer bought a tiny tree, which he loaded with borrowed toys, and then invited fifty little tots to enjoy it. The Christmas festival for 1894, however, was quite a different affair. It was held in Assembly Hall, and was attended by 26,500 children; the good times filling four evenings and two afternoons. The tree was forty feet high, and was lit by 150 electric lights from a special dynamo. Every child had a toy from the tree, and also a bag of candy. The whole celebration, which cost nearly $2500, was paid for by the readers of the *Pall Mall Gazette*. Probably the newspaper people looked upon this lavish charity as practical philanthropy, and nothing more; but Mr. Boyer knows better. He is convinced that the way to make Christians out of slum children is to show them Christian love.

'The directly religious work of the mission takes the form of bright gospel services, with admission by tickets distributed from house to house by visitors; meetings in tents during the long English summer; Sunday afternoons at Cottage Grove; affiliated gatherings in outlying districts; and frequent Bible talks illustrated with the stereopticon.

'Mr. Boyer's interest in crippled children was very early aroused. At the first picnic at Victoria Park, a pair of tiny urchins had said, "Next time can we bring our Jimmie?" And next time they did. A little girl brought the child in her arms, for Jimmie was a cripple. The dutiful sister was meaning to carry Jimmie all the way, but Mr. Boyer took the child in his arms and carried him to the park and back—fully a mile and a half. He asked the little boy what toys he had to play with at home, and Jimmie confessed that he had never in all his short life played with toys. Mr. Boyer was touched. He determined to see if there were not other neglected Jimmies in London, and he directed that a search be made for crippled children. In time, the attics and cellars gave up their secrets—500 distorted little sufferers were found within easy reach of Cottage Grove. Then a beautiful work was begun. A collection of toys was lent out and kept circulating, like the books in a public library; a blind lady, whom they call Jessie, devoted herself to the task of visiting the unfortunates in their homes, with a child guide to lead her; fortnight outings at the seashore were arranged; a special school was opened; and the headquarters at Cottage Grove turned into a cripples' paradise, with a playhouse, a family of dolls, a goat, some guinea-pigs, a pair of rabbits, and a dozen other pets. Everything is done to allay suffering, and the very best surgical attendance is secured whenever it is of any avail.

'One evening Mr. Boyer took me about the streets with him to show me some of the homes his children came from. Wherever we went, Mr. Boyer was welcomed with wild enthusiasm. A pair of childish eyes brighter than the rest would recognise the beatific Yankee in the dusk of the evening, and a piping voice would cry out. "W'y, it's Mista Boya—'ello, Mista Boya!" and then a throng of diminutive admirers would come pouring after him, some clinging to his coat, some throwing up their caps, and all shouting for joy, till it made me think of the story of the "Pied Piper." A week before I had seen the "Prince o' Wiles" opening the "Tar Bridge," but he was not half so enthusiastically received in Fleet Street as was this modest American in the courts and lanes of Mile End and Bow.'[1]

The mere enumeration of these various kinds of societies and organisations for the evangelisation of non-Christians at home should convince any thoughtful person of the immense sums of money that are annually expended in the home missionary work. The statistics of the receipts of the regular home missionary societies of the United States are alone accessible. This is of course the smallest parts of the whole sum thus expended.

RECEIPTS OF THE HOME MISSIONARY SOCIETIES
OF THE UNITED STATES.[2]

Date.	Total.	Average per Year.
1820–29	$233,826	$23,382
1830–39	2,342,721	234,272
1840–49	3,062,354	306,235
1850–59	8,080,109	808,010
1860–69	21,015,719	2,101,571
1870–80	29,982,534	2,725,685
1881–94	51,402,640	3,671,617

[1] *Outlook*, Sept. 4, 1895.
[2] Dorchester's *Problem of Religious Progress.*

In 1892 the contributions to the denominational home missionary societies amounted to $6,717,558, which sum exceeds the amount contributed for foreign missions by about $1,710,000. The accompanying chart (No. XXVI.) shows how much more rapidly the contributions for home missions have increased than the membership of the evangelical churches.

It is evident from the preceding pages that I have referred chiefly to the United States. But missionary activity is not confined to the United States; Great Britain is even more conspicuously active in both the foreign and home missionary movements. British Christians support more foreign missionaries and raise more money for the foreign missionary work than do the Christians of the United States. Though, for obvious reasons, their distinctively home missionary work may not be so large as that of the United States, yet the Christians of England seem to be on the whole more awake to the religious needs of the large cities, and to be devising new methods of meeting those needs more speedily than are the Christians of the United States. The college settlements, industrial schools, recreation clubs, and many other special modern methods of work are of English origin.

The effect of these efforts for the propagation of religion among the irreligious is marked and wonderful. This is due to the nature of the religion propagated; for the Christianity taught is not mere ceremonial and church attendance, but first and foremost conversion, a change of heart and life, and the continued living of an honest, moral, upright life. None can become church members without at least living a better outward life. As a consequence, the effects of the religious beliefs

CHART. XXVI.

Illustrating the Growth of the Receipts of the Home Missionary Societies of the United States.

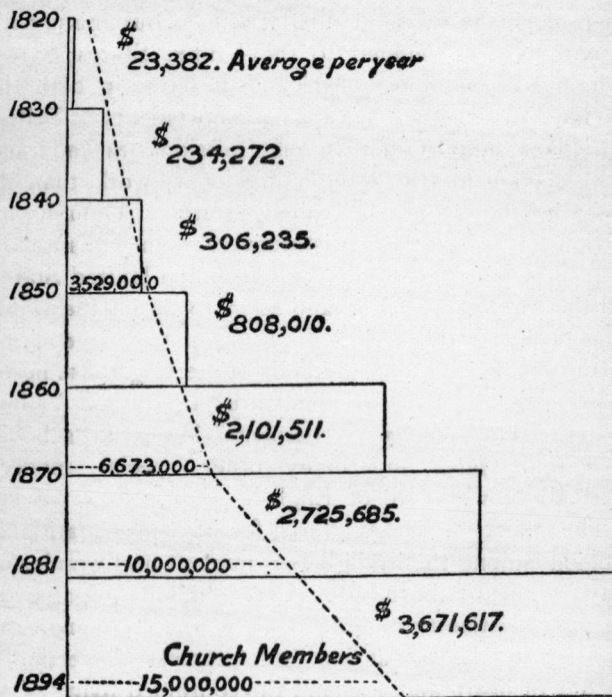

1820
$ 23,382. Average per year

1830
$ 234,272.

1840
$ 306,235.

1850 — 3,529,000
$ 808,010.

1860
$ 2,101,511.

1870 — 6,673,000
$ 2,725,685.

1881 — 10,000,000
$ 3,671,617.

Church Members

1894 — 15,000,000

------- This dotted line shows growth of Church Mem.

are seen most conspicuously on the viciously wicked. Certain districts of New York and London, once famous for their irreligious, immoral, lawless character, so lawless that it was not safe for peaceable men or women to pass through them, even in broad daylight, have become wholly transformed by from ten to twenty years of continuous missionary work. This work has been done in the form chiefly of the Sunday school. The testimony of the police to the value of the Mission Sunday schools and churches is clear and convincing.

But the most conspicuous moral and social work done for the lowest classes of society is that of the Salvation Army. By its peculiar methods and organisation it has reached, and, in connection with other influences, is helping to transform, the vilest slums of the largest cities. It takes hold of drunkards and harlots, of thieves and robbers, and, by the power of Christian love and life, transforms them into respectable, honest, pure, and trustworthy men and women. 'Probably, during no hundred years in the history of the world, have there been saved so many thieves, gamblers, drunkards, and prostitutes, as during the past quarter of a century, through the heroic faith and labours of the Salvation Army.'[1] This new movement, beginning in 1865, has made most phenomenal growth. Although in 1878 it could report only fifty corps and eighty-eight officers, in 1896 it reports 3727 corps and 12,010 officers, besides hundreds of thousands of 'soldiers.' 'It has perfected a phenomenal organisation ; created a literature of its own, circulating 33,000,000 copies of its various publications, in fifteen different languages; it has held great national and international conventions.'

[1] *New Era*, p. 351.

But in all the statements made in the foregoing pages, the main fact to which I wish to call attention is, that this missionary activity is so largely a modern movement. This is especially true of the home missionary work, having sprung up during the past fifty years. And this statement is equally true of the United States and England. A writer in 1865 remarks that 'special services for the working classes were hardly known in London before 1857.'[1] The tremendous activity of recent decades is well known to every student of modern religious life. Here is proof conclusive of the great growth made in recent times in the application of Christ's teaching, and in obedience to His commands.

Another fact which should not be lost sight of is, that the growth of this activity has been coincident with the growth in the comprehension of Christianity. The truer the comprehension of Christ's teaching, the more vigorous have been the efforts to propagate that teaching, alike at home and abroad. The movement, therefore, does not draw its main strength from superstition; ignorance is not its tap-root. Though in the early decades of the century, when the movement was comparatively young, zeal for the foreign missionary work was often stimulated by mistaken, and sometimes even by perverted views as to the nature of the non-Christian religions and the condition of the non-Christian peoples, yet progressive enlightenment on these subjects has not diminished, but has rather increased, the zeal for the work. Never was the missionary enthusiasm so great as it is to-day in England and America, though, without doubt, more

[1] *Religion in London*, p. 20.

sober, because of nearly a century of experience. Never were there such large numbers of college-educated young men and women preparing themselves for the foreign fields, knowing better than our grandfathers did both the encouragements and discouragements of the missionary work. The sense of duty to become a foreign missionary has become so pronounced as to have produced a distinct movement, having a distinctive name. The 'student volunteers' in the United States and Canada number over 3200, who are carrying on their studies in 477 institutions of higher education. Beginning in 1885, the movement has already resulted in sending 686 new missionaries into the field. More missionaries have sailed from America in the last two years and a half than in the previous five years and a half.[1]

Dr. F. E. Clark, in his address before the Christian Endeavour Convention in Boston in 1895, says: 'Nor is it too much to say that the aroused interest in world-wide missions among Endeavourers has done something toward furnishing the army of volunteers—six full regiments, each a thousand strong—who are eager to march forward into the enemies' country, to do battle for the Captain of their salvation, whenever the churches shall furnish the "sinews of war." Ten years ago the cry was for men and women. That will never be again the unanswered cry, I believe.' He also called attention to the fact that these Christian Endeavour Societies had during the previous year contributed $425,000 to the various foreign missionary boards. According to returns just published (March 1897), 1200 members of the student volunteers have already entered the foreign missionary service.

[1] See *The Student Missionary Enterprise*, pp. 62–82.

The only adequate explanation of these facts is, that modern Protestant Christians love and believe, because they understand the Lord Jesus Christ, as never before, and that they wish more fully than ever before to obey His command. This love and belief have been aroused and confirmed by the personal experience of salvation from sin. Christ and His teaching are fully believed, not as a matter of theory but of experience. There is a firm conviction, based on experience, that real permanent progress,—that of the individual as well as that of the nation, and that of the nation as well as that of the individual,—depends not so much on external as on internal conditions ; springs, not primarily from environment, but from character. This is the teaching of Christ ; and more and more is this teaching seen to be true in the experience of every race and nation and individual.

The missionary movement, therefore, is one not destined soon to pass away ; knowledge by Christians of the high moral teachings of Buddha and Confucius, or the acceptance of Western civilisation by those who do not now have it, will not remove or even lessen the missionary activity of the followers of Christ. The general acceptance by all nations and by all communities of the principles and truths of the Christ, and the change of character effected thereby, will alone bring the missionary movement to an end. For Christianity is not a mere moral scheme, an ethical system, or a system of metaphysical philosophy. It is a new life, a new dynamic, a new power which enters in and transforms man. Unlike the merely moral system, which considers sin an imperfection, arising from ignorance and bad environment, Christianity holds that sin is not unripeness, but positive flaw, positive defect, whose only cure is a change of heart. The fountain must be made sweet before the waters that flow from it will be sweet. It is this characteristic of Christianity that differentiates it from every religion or ethical teaching, and that justifies its world-wide missionary activity.

I cannot conclude this chapter without drawing attention to one more most important method in which the growth in Christian practice is working. It is the characteristic difference between Christianity and all other religions, that it combines religion and ethics, worship and morality. The Christian Church is the one institution that unites the institution for worship with the institution for the moral education of the people. In other systems and countries, the moral education of the people is left to philosophers and scholars. Since the establishment of the Christian Church, its most distinctive characteristic and duty has been just this: the moral instruction of the people. The point to which I now call attention is, that never before has the Church been so faithfully performing its duty. The great moral progress of the present century may be traced directly to the great religious revivals. So closely have worship and moral life been identified by the Christian, and especially the Protestant Churches, that they are now felt to be inseparable. The immoral man who worships is pronounced a hypocrite; for such a one, true worship is considered impossible; immorality is irreligion, is atheism. This view of the relation of worship and life has made great progress during the present century.

There are those who think that the power of the pulpit has grown less in recent decades. This may be admitted in a general way, without hesitation or even regret. Without doubt the pulpit has less influence in determining the views and tastes of the people on philosophical, scientific, literary, historical, and political matters. But this has not lessened its power in preaching the gospel, in demanding righteous living, in proclaiming God's love and the sinfulness of sin. The rise of popular education, the development of social life, the ease of wide travel, the vast number of educated speakers and lecturers on all branches of political, historical, and scientific subjects, as well as the numberless newspapers, magazines, and books, both religious and secular, have all had more or less effect in modifying the prominence of the pulpit, as well as the methods of its work; but this I count not a loss but a gain. More than ever before, 'the preacher is the teacher of righteousness. . . . This ethical function of the Christian ministry is not destined to grow less, as the social problems of modern life increase in complexity. . . . It may be said that the modern pulpit is characterised by an increasing ethical earnestness. Social ethics, especially, attracts as never before the attention of the followers of the Son of Man.'[1] In carrying out its great work, the Church has adopted, and is adopting, new methods of work. Hence have arisen the Sunday school, the Y.M.C.A., the Y.P.S.C.E., the religious press, and all the varied forms of work mentioned in this and the next chapter. The very growth of the Church itself in Protestant lands is a clear proof of its growing power in the ethical instruction of the millions who support it. The large number of powerful preachers, evangelists, and consecrated and educated laymen and

[1] *Christian Ethics*, by Newman Smyth, p. 307.

women, who may be found throughout the length and breadth of Christian lands in constantly increasing numbers, and the many hundreds of thousands who do some direct religious work, is at once a proof and a cause of the growing power of the Church, of the growing application of the distinctive idea of the Christian Church, namely, 'the institution for the moral instruction of the people.'

CHAPTER VII

GROWTH IN INFLUENCE

'When it was said in the fourth century, what none dare repeat to-day, that the doctrine of Christ is adverse to the interests of State and insufficient for the needs of society, Augustine could rightly answer, strengthening his position by an appeal to facts : "Let those who profess that the Christian religion is hostile to the Republic, give us military men, provincials, husbands, parents, sons, masters, servants, kings, judges, and administrators equal to those that Christianity has formed. Instead of resisting this doctrine, let them rather own that, if all obeyed it, it would powerfully increase the prosperity of the Republic."'[1]

'Two elements, Believers and Unbelievers, determine the practical morality of any nation. Fierce Saxons, piratical Scandinavians, pleasure-loving French, trying to manage themselves in this world by the tenets of the Divine Man of Nazareth, . . . that is what we witness in Christendom. Lay no blame, then, on Christianity for their untowardness, but rather praise it for its subduing power over tigers such as they.'[2]

---

[1] Schmidt's *The Social Results of Early Christianity*, English edition, p. 287.

[2] *How I became a Christian*, by A Heathen Convert (K. Uchimura).

CHAPTER VII

HAVING in previous chapters considered the numerical growth of Christianity, the political and commercial growth of Christian nations, the growth of organised Christianity in England and the United States, the growth in the comprehension of Christ's teaching, and the growth in the application of that teaching to the details of modern life, we proceed in this chapter to consider the influence of the Church, or, more accurately speaking, the influence of Christ's teachings, on the world, on those who make no profession of being Christ's disciples.

It is necessary at this point again to emphasise the distinction between the Kingdom of God and the world, between those persons who feel the attraction of Christ's character and life and teachings, and the need of His help in their own daily lives, and those who do not feel that attraction or acknowledge that need. Whether in or out of the organic Church, the former alone are true Christians; they are the salt of the earth; they are its light. The latter, even though members of the visible Church, are not Christ's disciples. It should also be noted that those who do feel that personal attraction to Christ, and who have realised the personal salvation from sin which He promised to all who should believe on Him, spontaneously unite in His worship, naturally combine to carry out His commands, naturally try to organise their own family life, as well as that of the town, county, and nation, on Christian principles. The organic Church is, therefore, no chance structure. It did not arise by accident. Christ Himself provided for it, though He left to His disciples no specific directions as to the details of its organisation. The Church exists both for the sake of the individuals who constitute its members, and also for the sake of those who do not. Those who in any real measure have imbibed the Christian life, of necessity feel the need of union with their fellow-Christians, for their own self-preservation, for the preservation of the gospel to later generations, and for the salvation of those still beyond the reach of Christ's influence.

It thus results that, as a rule, Christians are members of some Church, while those outside of the Church are not Christian. Ideally, all Christians should be church members, and all church members should be Christians. There should be no Christian outside of the Church. Unfortunately, this is not an ideal world. If it were, there would have been no need of Christ, Christianity, or the Church. In the past there have been bad men in the Church, and doubtless there still are. There are, doubtless, many hypocritical professors. But more common than either of these classes are the ordinary Christians, imperfect in wisdom and knowledge and character, men and women who more or less feel Christ's love and wish His help, but who have a daily struggle with sin and self. They constitute the large majority of the Church. With such members in a Church whose organisation has been produced, and is now regulated by fallible, erring, short-sighted men, the most of them living narrow, circumscribed lives, it is not strange that abuses arise and evils are tolerated; it is not strange that the Church, like its members, should be imperfect.

In this fact we may find one reason why there are some who, though they feel the influence of Christ's life and character, yet hold aloof from the Church. They see and keenly feel its defects, and the defects of its members. Instead, therefore, of being attracted to the Church, they are repelled from it. It is not my aim either to condemn or to excuse such action, but only to point out the fact, and clear the ground for the main purpose of this chapter. I admit that there are many who are members of no visible Church, who are yet more or less truly Christian; they love the Saviour as their Saviour, and more or less strive to live lives conformed to His teachings. How large the number of such persons is, none can tell, for the very reason that they refuse to associate themselves with their fellow-believers. It is impossible to count them. Many though they be, it must be admitted that, however much they receive from Christianity, as a rule they give relatively little in return. They generally fail to do their part either in preserving the gospel for subsequent generations, or in purifying the Church from errors of belief or practice, or in spreading the knowledge of the gospel to others less fortunately situated than themselves.

The important fact for us to notice is, however, that the influence of Jesus extends far beyond the church organisation. It is dominant in Christendom. Not only do large numbers of those who reject the Church feel, love, and acknowledge that influence, but all, even those who do not so acknowledge it, or even recognise it, are under its mighty power. The moral ideals and standards of Christendom are Christian, are products of Christ's teachings. It is true these ideals are far from realised in life; yet none the less are they the ideals. The influence of Jesus is so dominant that, reject many of His specific teachings, criticise His character, defame His followers, or scorn His Church as one may, none can escape that influence. And the reason is not far to seek. It is as impossible for them to get away from their intellectual and social environment as from their physical. Though they may be wholly unconscious of Christ's powerful influence over them, they are nevertheless largely dependent on Him. It is no more possible for a man who lives in a Christian nation and society to escape this influence than it is for him to escape the influence of the atmosphere he breathes, the sunshine he walks in, and the force of gravitation that holds him to the earth. He may be, and usually is, wholly unconscious of these mighty factors in his well-being; but they are none the less important to him. Speaking of the presence in our Christian civilisation of those who, though they outwardly decline to be called religious, or to acknowledge the power of the religious motives in their lives, are yet possessed by the 'highest motives' and live the 'purest lives,' Benjamin Kidd says: 'Once we have grasped the conception of our civilisation as a developing organic growth, with a life history which must be studied as a whole, we perceive how irrational it is to regard any of the units as independent of the influence of a process which has operated on society for so many centuries. As well might we argue that because the fruit survives for a time when removed from the tree, that it was, therefore, independent of the tree.'[1]

[1] *Social Evolution*, p. 242.

Fundamental principles of life, unknown to the pre-Christian and non-Christian world, have become so thoroughly accepted by Christendom, that even those men and women who pride themselves on their rejection of Christianity still cannot escape them. All who have the slightest desire to live moral, upright lives, must do so under the Christian standard of conduct. By the teaching of Jesus, the old Greek, Roman, Teutonic, Gothic, and Celtic ideals of life, in so far as opposed to Christian principles, have almost wholly disappeared. The teachings of Jesus have wholly reconstructed the ideals of life—of duty to our fellow-men, of personal and individual rights, of devotion to truth, of the position of woman, of personal purity, of the sanctity of marriage, of the mutual relations of God and man, and man and man, and of many other subjects ; and, with the change of ideals, society has been, and more and more is being, transformed.

What has brought to pass this vast change? The teachings of Christ, we say. Yet it is to be remembered that it is not those teachings in the abstract, as a philosophy, nor as held by segregated individuals. It is the influence of Jesus as preserved and handed down through the centuries, and as more or less successfully applied by Christian men and women banded together in the various organisations, the chief of which is the Church. It is the Christian Church, imperfect though it has been and still is, the product of admittedly narrow-minded and oftentimes bigoted men and women, under the guidance of fallible, erring Christians,—it is the Church, under Jesus' leadership, that has accomplished what has been done. The imperfections of individual Christians, or the defects of the church organisations, are not parts of

Christianity, not its products. They exist in spite of Christ's teachings and influence. They are indeed great hindrances to the more triumphant sway of the Kingdom of God on earth. Much of the criticism directed against the Church, as well as against Christianity, proceeds on an entirely false basis. It assumes that Christians claim to be perfect. Without doubt some few do. But the real Christian is not he who thinks he has attained perfection, but rather he who seeks it, relying on Christ for help. The becoming a Christian does not consist of a miraculous, mechanical, instantaneous attainment of perfection of the human, imperfect, sinful nature ; but it does consist in a change in the direction of life, in a change of ambition, of purpose, of will. Any criticism which ignores this fact must be unjust, must miss the mark.

Furthermore, it is to be noted that those who criticise Christians and Christianity inevitably do so entirely on the ideals furnished them by Christ. But how came they by these ideals ? By the Church, which alone has preserved them during the past centuries, and spread them throughout Christendom. For ages the Church has insisted on the ideals taught by Christ. The more these ideals and moral precepts have been pondered, it has been seen by Christian and non-Christian alike that they are reasonable ; that they are the foundations of good society, of firm yet free government, and of national prosperity. At last the non-Christian world has accepted many of them, apparently forgetful of the source from which they came.

Were the facts available, it would be instructive to compare the benevolent contributions of professing Christians with those of non-Christians living in Christian lands, and thus estimate the dynamic power of devotion to Christ as compared with its absence, among those holding, in general, the same moral ideals. For it is a well-admitted fact that ideals alone are not enough; there must be in addition to the ideals some moral force to carry them into effect. Christians assert that this comes by a personal attachment to Christ, by receiving the new life which He promised those who would believe and trust and obey Him. Such a comparative study of moral dynamics is, however, impossible. But it is possible to say, without fear of contradiction, that in all the great moral reforms and benevolent enterprises, the Church, that is to say, Christians, have led the way, and, to the end, have done the most of the work. After the reform has made some headway, after the blessings to society have begun to be seen, men who make no profession of their Christian allegiance follow their example and begin to do likewise.

The doctrine of the brotherhood of man is now familiar the world over; every educated man, whatever may be his race, not only has heard of it, but advocates it in theory. Even Buddhists, Confucianists, Brahmins, Hindoos, and Shintoists do not hesitate to urge the doctrine. In the Parliament of Religions, Rev. Shaku So Yen, a Japanese Buddhist priest, gained no little applause because of his vigorous presentation of the doctrine as the basis of his plea for international arbitration in the place of war. The great democratic and socialistic movements of the day in Christendom make this doctrine their foundation stone. Because all men are brothers, all are possessed of the same inherent rights, they argue, and argue well. But whence came this doctrine? Hinted at, possibly, by a few of the Greek philosophers (though

Max Müller says the word 'mankind never passed the
lips of Socrates, or Plato, or Aristotle'), it owes its
existence to-day, as well as its vitality, to the teaching
of Jesus, and to the belief and practice of the Church.
Though Confucius said, 'All within the four seas are
brothers,' yet, as he gave it no living expression, it has
remained a sparkling pearl among his teachings rather
than a life-bearing seed It has apparently had not the
slightest influence on the seclusion of the Chinese people.
Until within comparatively modern times none but Christians have believed the teaching of the brotherhood of
all men. An ancient satirist even makes it the butt of
his jests. Non-Christian scientific men have scorned the
simple teaching as a religious superstition. Every nation,
ancient and modern, whether Greek or Roman, Chinese
or Japanese or Hindoo, until moulded by the teachings
of Christ, believed itself peculiarly descended from the
gods, while other races were but chattering animals.
Even within the limits of a single nation the various
classes and grades of society have had no brotherly
thought for each other, have made no attempts to meet
each other's needs. The Bible and they alone who have
accepted it as their rule of life and belief have continuously taught the brotherhood of the entire human race,
and the Church has more and more successfully carried
that belief into practice. Under its teaching and impulse
all the many forms of benevolent and evangelistic enterprise have taken their rise. Gradually the non-Christian
world is learning the doctrine. In Christendom, when
Christians have led the way and set the habit, many
who make no profession of their Christian faith are
doing similar good deeds. And even in other lands the
doctrine, and some of the noble deeds it prompts, are

beginning to find advocates and doers. Surely the influence of Jesus outside of the Church cannot be questioned.[1]

But, in passing, I wish to observe that this doctrine of the brotherhood of man finds its natural counterpart and foundation in that of the Fatherhood of God. These two go inseparably together. It is impossible, as modern history has repeatedly proven, to hold for any length of time a practical, working belief in the brotherhood of man without the foundation of the twin belief in the Fatherhood of God. A great deal of the failure to give the first doctrine practical application to the problems of life has been due to the ignorance or positive rejection of the other side of the same doctrine. Without the one the other becomes distorted, visionary, unpractical. This is the one radical defect of many socialistic schemes.

The effects of this double doctrine are to be seen in almost every department of life. It will not be useless to notice a few of the more prominent manifestations or results of these central doctrines and customs of Christianity which have been more or less accepted by non-Christians. In the preceding chapter I mentioned four points of moral and social life which characterised those who embraced the Christian faith, namely—

1. The sanctity of marriage.
2. The essential sacredness of human life.
3. Benevolence.
4. The liberation of slaves.

---

[1] It is evident that in this, and all similar passages, I use the word 'Church' in its narrower sense. I refer not to the 'national' Church, nor to any visible Church or organisation, but rather to the real and spiritual Church, whose members are gladly conscious of their relation and indebtedness to Christ, the Head of the Church.

It is now pertinent to point out that these were distinctively Christian in origin and practice, and that they became predominant characteristics of European civilisation; they became so, not because the Church became predominant, but rather the Church became predominant because its members practised them. These customs and practices approve themselves to all enlightened men and women. If any doubt the origin of these moral and social beliefs and practices, let him interrogate history. Where did the wife begin to be considered the equal of her husband? Was it in Africa, where every chieftain and man of wealth counted his wealth by the number of cows and wives he owned, and where he could buy his wives in exchange for his cattle? Was it in Babylon or Egypt, or Greece or Rome, where, as in Africa, a man's wives or concubines were limited only by his means to buy them? Was it in India, or China or Japan, where, under the teachings of Buddha, woman is considered to be the source of evil, of temptation, her birth a misfortune to the family, and, unless born again as a man, to be incapable of entering Nirvana, and where the family life is esteemed a great obstacle to salvation? Excepting those nations in which Christianity has become predominant, though in many individual instances high rank may have been attributed to women and honour to the wife, marriage has been thought of as a means for perpetuating the family line, or for sexual gratification, or for securing domestic service, or wealth; concubinage has been the common practice, approved and practised even by the teachers of morality and social order; divorce has been easy, and sexual immorality a matter of course. Christianity brought in a new ideal; it was insisted on by the Church, and gradually came to be the ideal of Christendom. To-day, not only professed Christians, but even those who positively reject Christianity, hold the ideal, and in a large number of cases carry it out in life. Concubinage has practically ceased in Christian lands, and divorce has become comparatively rare (though rather on the increase in recent years). Immorality, though by no means extinct, yet, compelled to be secret, is considered a cause of shame, a blot on one's fair fame, a most serious defect of character. This is not the opinion of Christians alone, but of all; it is the moral standard of Christendom, especially of the Protestant countries, England and America. In what country or age would sexual immorality have been considered sufficient cause to blight, if not utterly to destroy, a man's political career? There have been repeated instances of late years, on which we need not more particularly dwell, in which the imputation of such immorality has been sufficient to blast the career of distinguished politicians, both in Great Britain and the United States of America. These facts speak volumes for the comparatively high moral standards held by the generality of people in these two nations. Such a thing would be unheard of in any non-Christian age or people, or even in any previous Christian century.

To avoid being misunderstood, it should be said that I by no means claim that the Christian nations, or even the Protestant nations, have nearly reached perfection in this matter. I do not say that all immoral men lose their political prospects. That is far from the case. Unblushing immorality is to be found in every large city of Christendom. Many immoral men are doubtless successful in their political ambitions. What I do say is, that now as in no previous age immorality is a recognised stain on character, and, when proved, is a most serious obstacle to success in politics, or to reception into good society; that immorality must be carried on in far greater secrecy than in former times, and in violation of the laws of the land; that these high ideals of moral life are held not by Christians alone, but by all; and that this is due to the influence of Christ outside of the Church.

The marriage relation is the foundation of the family and of the home, and thus one of the foundation stones of the nation. That the teachings of Jesus have been able to raise the ideals of marriage, and have made it sacred among many nations, gives some indication of the influence of Jesus, of the growth of the Kingdom of God even outside of the organic Church. And it must not be forgotten that these results have been very largely secured through the active agency of the organised churches.

Inseparable from the conception of the nature of marriage is that of the estimation of woman and honour accorded her as woman. It is impossible to have a high ideal of marriage and a low one of woman; and, conversely, it is equally impossible to have a high ideal of woman and a low ideal of marriage. These go hand in hand. It is a matter of easy proof that Christianity is the source of the modern idea of the nobility of womanhood. To be born a woman is not a misfortune, as taught in all non-Christian lands and times; it is rather a blessing and an honour. Whence has come this change of thought? Not from Plato, who, when he laid out a scheme for an ideal state, proposed that women should be held in common. Not from Socrates, who, when conversing sublimely with his friends about duty and death, never seemed to feel the least sympathy for his wife. She, in her distress and sorrow, came to see him in the hour of death ; but because, forsooth, it might trouble the serenity of the philosopher to see the woman who was his wife, and the children she had borne to him, they sent her away, with no word of comfort, with scorn rather than cheer ! Not from Buddha, who not only abandoned his wife, and taught others to do the same, but taught that women must be reborn as men ere they can hope to attain salvation. Nor from Confucius, with his permission of concubinage ; nor from Mohammed, with his harem ; nor from any savage religion or nation. From Christ alone came those blessed influences that have resulted in elevating one-half of the human race from a bondage more despicable than slavery, to one of highest honour, position, and power. It was Christ that revealed the nobility of humility, and gentleness and meekness, the supremacy of womanly virtues.

Not only as a matter of practice, but also in all non-Christian theory, woman is inferior to man. According to Brahminism a woman without a husband is soulless. It is the belief of the Hindoos that it is better to murder a soulless (*i.e.* female) child than not to be able to betroth her. It is the belief of all non-Christian religions which aim for holiness, that woman is a source of wickedness and temptation ; that salvation comes by refusing even to look at her.

The Christian Bible knows no difference in the inherent nature of man and woman. Both alike were created in the image of God. In proportion as Christ's teachings have been adopted and His principles practised, have women received honour, education, and rank. Only within recent times, and even now not fully, have educational advantages been given alike to boys and girls, and this is the case only in Christian lands. More and more is it being discovered by actual experience that woman, though different from man, is inferior to man in no respect. Since the opening of some of the English colleges to women, several women have wrested from men prizes of greatest honour, in mathematics, and logic, and the classics. Medicine, law, the ministry, the platform, the stage, the teacher's desk, the editor's pen, as well as the humbler walks of business, of trade, of manufacture, are being acceptably and successfully filled by women. In some respects women are found to be much more acceptable, because more capable than men. Of the 422,929 teachers in the public schools of the United States in 1890, 270,919, or 64 per cent., were women. The United States census for 1880 reports 17,392,000 persons engaged in various professional and industrial occupations, of whom 2,647,000, or 14 per cent., were women. In 1893, 2500 women were practising medicine, 6000 were post-office clerks, 275 were preaching. In the city of New York alone about 27,000 were reported to be supporting their husbands. This growing position occupied by women, this admission of her equality with man, and the growing readiness to grant her any and every position and work of which she proves herself capable, is a very modern thing, a product of Christianity. This admission of the equality of woman has in its turn a very powerful influence on the moral life of the people. The future moral development of Christendom is to be very largely in the hands of women themselves. When once they unite to suppress the foes of the home, lust and intemperance in all its forms will be doomed.

In the same way it is easy to show that the sacred regard for human life now held by all the people of Christendom, and not merely by professing Christians, is an evidence of the wide reach of the teachings of Christ. When and where did the life of a common man begin to be counted of any worth? When was it counted a wicked thing for a nobleman, a lord, or a military man to kill or even to smite the low-born or slave? When or where did it begin to be counted a sin to buy or sell human beings? Not among the Egyptians, or Babylonians, or Greeks, or Romans, or Chinese, or any non-Christian nation, not to mention the savage tribes of Africa or the Pacific Islands. In all these countries the life of the high-born, the noble, the ruler, the soldier, was indeed precious, but man as man, regardless of his birth or rank, did not differ from beasts of burden. In wars, the extermination of the enemy was no uncommon thing, and was considered quite proper. Only those were saved alive who could in any way profit the victors. The murder of a slave was no crime under the laws of most ancient nations. Crucifixion of the conquered by the victors was very common. Cæsar Augustus caused thousands of the soldiers who had fought under Pompey to be crucified.

Cæsar Augustus crucified a slave for eating a favourite quail. 'Praetor Domitius caused a slave, who had made the mistake on a hunt of killing a boar at the wrong time, to be crucified as a punishment for his offence.' Pollio gave live slaves to feed his fishes. Flaminius had a slave killed simply to show a friend, who desired it,

the sight of a man in the agonies of death. When old
and useless, slaves were either killed or allowed to starve.
Moralists argued that it was more merciful to kill them
than to let them starve. Slaves were mere 'things,
chattels, and no man who was a Roman citizen need
care what happened to them.' When the Roman
empire was at its height, slaves were trained in the
use of the sword, and made to slay each other in the
amphitheatres for the public amusement. The most
cultured even of moralists, and delicate women and
young girls, took pleasure in such sights. At the celebration over the victories of the Emperor Titus, 3000 thus
fought in Rome; 10,000 gladiators fought at the games
of Emperor Trajan. Moralists even defended the gladiatorial games. Domitian instituted a fight between
dwarfs and women. Suetonius says it would have been
cruel not to grant the request of Verona for a gladiatorial
show. Look where we may, in ancient and modern non-
Christian lands and times, the life of man as man was
and is esteemed of little or no value. Murder was the
chief characteristic of one of the religious sects of India.
Everywhere and always, murder of the low-born has
been common and almost uncondemned, and all forms
of cruelty have been counted matters of course. The
Teuton, Celtic, Gothic, and Anglo-Saxon races, before
they became Christians, were no exception to the above
indictment.

What has transformed savage, bloody, brutal, pagan
Europe into the modern, law-abiding, comparatively
peaceful nations of to-day? What has made the life of
every man safe, whether rich or poor, high or low?
What has put an end to the bloody gladiatorial spec-
tacles, and made murder a crime, alike for king and

peasant? What has made the life of every man, in theory, and also so largely in practice, of equal value? That professing Christians should accept this ideal is natural. What is wonderful is that all Christendom (except the Nihilists), even those who reject the Church, and pride themselves on their intellectual independence and freedom from superstition, accept and hold the same views, the same ideals. Except for the Church and its centuries of continuous training, such a marvellous transformation of Europe could hardly have taken place, indeed, is inconceivable.

Again, to avoid being misunderstood, it is desirable to say clearly that I by no means maintain that during all these centuries Christians, even the organic Church, has been guiltless of human blood. Alas, 'tis true that her hands have more than once been guilty of murder. I admit that much evil can be proved against her. Yet it remains true that such deeds are not the result of the teaching of Christ; they are the result of paganism still remaining unconquered in Christians and in the Church.

The sentiment of Christendom as to the iniquity of slavery is now a unit. There is no question as to what has produced this sentiment. For thousands of years, indeed from the dawn of history, slavery had been a recognised institution of Africa, Europe, and Asia. Not only was it a recognised institution, but it was accepted as a proper social state. Slavery as a proper and normal institution was not even questioned by ancient pre-Christian moralists of any race or religion. Slavery was entrenched in Greece and Rome. It has been estimated by modern historians that in the most brilliant days of Greece one-third of her population

17

was in slavery, while one-half of Rome's millions were in the same sad state at the period of her greatness. At one time there lived in Athens 400,000 slaves, but only 10,000 freemen; one freeman to forty slaves. How has it come about that to-day there is not only not a single slave in Christendom, but that all are strongly opposed to it, as a great moral crime? What has changed this entrenched social custom of the ages? What has induced those whose very wealth apparently depended on its continuance to give it up? This is one of the most interesting and profound changes that has come over the Occidental nations. What has caused it?

Christ gave no specific teaching about slavery, yet the general principles which He taught involved its destruction as surely as the sunlight drives away the darkness. Only gradually the Church came to a realisation of what Christ's teachings involved; this depended on growth in comprehension. For long centuries after the rise of Christianity slavery existed, not only within Christendom, but was practised, and even sometimes defended, by Christians. Only slowly did the Church carry out in practice what it came gradually to perceive in theory. Nevertheless, more and more the Christian Church did set itself against the evil; more and more did Christians liberate their slaves; more and more did public opinion condemn the slave trade and its defenders. At the cost of billions of money and hundreds of thousands of lives, slavery has been swept out of the United States. To-day one powerful, if not the only, motive, as well as the sufficient justification for the division of Africa among the nations of Europe, is the zeal to exterminate the slave trade, with all its inevitable horrors. If ever the military seizure of one country by another has been justifiable, that of Africa by the nations of Europe has been; and it has already begun to bear fruit in the successful limitation of the dreadful slave trade, so appropriately named by David Livingstone, 'the open sore of the world.' It is safe to say that the twentieth century will know nothing of its horrors by experience. Slavery is doomed. For thousands of years the scourge of the human race, slavery, is at last on the point of extinction. Satan is being bound hand and foot by the gentle and loving, yet powerful, Jesus of Nazareth. In this, too, is Christ's influence outside of the Church very manifest. The Kingdom of Heaven on earth is growing far faster than many think, far faster even than the visible Church.

Arbitration in the place of war is distinctly a modern development of Christian thought. It has been not only discussed, but has been actually tried on many occasions by those nations whose people are confessedly the most Christian, by England and America, and with marked success. A recent conference of some of those in the United States interested in urging on the International Arbitration Movement took place not long since at the house of Mr. Smiley, on the shores of Lake Mohunk. Below is the declaration of principles adopted by this conference. 'The feasibility of arbitration as a substitute for war is now demonstrated. In the last seventy-nine years at least eighty important controversies between civilised nations have been peacefully adjusted in this mode. Thirteen of these were between the United States and Great Britain. Arbitration is now the American practice. To perpetuate peace, a formal Act should make it henceforth the rule of national life. The present time is ripe for such a step. In 1887 an English delegation of thirteen men, all prominent in public life, brought to this country a memorial signed by 233 members of the House of Commons, addressed to the President and Congress of the United States, and expressing the wish that all future differences between the countries be settled by arbitration. In response to this memorial, our Congress in 1890 unanimously requested the President to open negotiations to this end with all countries with whom we have diplomatic relations. In the same month the Republics of North, South, and Central America, by their representatives in the International American Conference, declared their adoption of arbitration as a principle of American international law, in the settlement of difficulties between these republics. And in October of the same year a treaty drafted by that conference was submitted by our State department to the governments of all civilised nations for their consideration and concurrence. In June 1893 the British House of Commons unanimously expressed its approval of the movement. . . . Expressing, as we believe, the judgment of the American people, we urge the Government of the United States to negotiate a treaty of arbitration with Great Britain.'

Since the above paragraphs were penned, the cause of international arbitration has made much headway. The black war cloud that loomed up so suddenly in December 1895 between the United States and Great Britain has proved to have had more than a silver lining, for it has been the occasion for the preparation of a general treaty of arbitration between these two great nations, which has called forth the heartiest expressions of good-will from the best elements of these two great nations. Though the proposed arbitration treaty may fail of ratification, as now seems likely, yet there can be no longer any doubt as to the opinions and desires of the greater and most intelligent elements of the two nations on this point. It has also become clear that it is the Church and the Christ-spirit that have been the strongest influences making for international peace and good-will on earth. Although the proposed treaty may fail to become law, yet it is the promise of one that will before many years have passed. The point of interest for us, however, is not merely the fact of this proposed treaty, but the source of the influences that have made it possible, and the universality of the joy in the prospective relation, felt not only by those who acknowledge, but also by those who reject all thought of their relation to Christ. International arbitration is one of the conspicuous signs of the influence of Christ, reaching far beyond the limits of the Church.

So beautiful and so reasonable is the thought of universal arbitration, that not only Christians, but all enlightened men, of all religions, in theory at least, are beginning to advocate its universal application. This is another indication of the wide influence of Jesus.

NOTE ON SLAVERY IN THE EAST.

(See pp. 257 to 259.)

It is a mistake to say, as some do, that slavery never existed in the East, for it has existed for centuries, and still exists in full force, in Korea. It also practically existed in ancient times in Japan, as recent investigations prove. Yet we freely admit that there has been a great difference between the East and the West in this respect. The cause for this great difference is well worthy of profound study. The author knows too little of the facts to warrant a positive statement, yet he would venture two suggestions on the matter.

1. The comparative non-appearance of slavery in Eastern lands cannot be attributed to moral or religious considerations, for the doctrines of the brotherhood of man, of the inherent value of human life, and of the equality of man as man, have been and still are unknown to all Eastern nations and individuals who are unacquainted with Western civilisation and religion. The low esteem of the life of the low-born, and the frequency of their murder, are facts which have already been noted. It should be also borne in mind that the buying and selling of women is even yet, though now forbidden by law in Japan, a not uncommon thing in all the East.

2. The reason for the comparative non-appearance of slavery in the East is due, I think, to the fact that the social conditions for it did not arise. In the West the captives made during inter-tribal and international wars furnished the slaves, and the industrial civilisations furnished the demand for them. Neither of these social states have existed to anything like the same degree in the Eastern as in the Western lands.

CHAPTER VIII

GROWTH IN INFLUENCE—*Continued.*

' The great characteristic of Christianity, and the proof of its divinity, is that it has been the main source of the moral development of Europe, and that it has discharged this office, not so much by the inculcation of a system of ethics, however pure, as by the assimilating and attractive influence of a perfect ideal.   The moral progress of mankind can never cease to be distinctively and intensely Christian, as long as it consists of a gradual approximation to the character of the Christian Founder.   There is, indeed, nothing more wonderful in the history of the human race than the way in which that ideal has traversed the lapse of ages, acquiring new strength and beauty with each advance of civilisation, and infusing its beneficial influence into every sphere of thought and action.' [1]

---

[1] Lecky's *History of Rationalism in Europe.*

CHAPTER VIII

CONTINUING in this chapter our inquiry as to the influence of Christ and His teachings, I would again call attention to the fact mentioned in a previous chapter, that practical benevolence is to be found to-day in manifold forms—caring for the sick, feeding the hungry, clothing the naked, giving work to the destitute, and in fact devising every possible means for raising up and establishing in self-support all those who need it. The question at once meets us, When and where did this spirit arise? Did Athens with three-fourths, and Rome with three-fifths of her population in slavery build hospitals for the sick, the lame, the blind, the insane, the leper? Did these humanitarian feelings and customs of benevolence arise in India or China or Japan, with their highly praised, elaborate system of morals? Do the savage tribes of Africa have pity for the suffering, and strive to relieve the distress of the sick and those who mourn?

These questions answer themselves.

Among pagan nations there has been high culture, art, and eloquence, but little humanity. Greece and Rome had shrines for numberless divinities, forty theatres for amusement, thousands of perfumery stores, but no shrine for brotherly love, no almshouse for the poor. Millions of money were expended on convivial feasts, but nothing for orphans, or for homes for widows.

'In all my classical reading,' says Professor Packard, a lifelong professor of ancient languages in Bowdwin College, 'I have never met with the idea of an infirmary or hospital, except for sick cats (a sacred animal) in Egypt.' Dr. Schneider, forty years a missionary in Turkey, said he knew of 'only one hospital in the whole Moslem empire. . . . In India, monkeys are worshipped and provided with gorgeous temples, as much as $50,000.00 being sometimes expended on the marriage of two sacred apes. Boa-constrictors are maintained in state, but no provision is made for suffering humanity.'[1]

So unfamiliar with the idea of philanthropy was the popular Buddhism of pre-Mejii Japan, that Nobunaga was commonly credited with the saying (whether actually uttered by him or not we cannot say) that the Christian (Roman Catholic) work in Kyoto, on account of its marvellous benevolence, was certainly worthy of suspicion; for though it was common for the people to contribute to a temple, never yet was it heard that a temple contributed to the help of the people.

Not till Christ had taught the duty of perfect love to God and equal love to fellow-men, of whatever race or class; not till Christ had taught, and Himself had practised, the duty of loving and praying for even one's enemies; and not until the followers of Christ had taken these lessons to heart, and had more or less fully tried to practise them—not till then did hospitals arise; not till then did the spirit of benevolence appear, which is to-day so beautiful a flower of the human race. What an astonishing spectacle—one that angels may well rejoice to look on—is that afforded by the freewill

[1] *Problem of Religious Progress*, p. 508.

gifts of the millions of dollars, by the safe and the well
for those that suffer—by fire, as at Boston or Chicago ;
by flood, as in the Ohio or Mississippi valleys, at
Johnstown or in China ; by earthquake, as in the
Carolinas, Japan, and Greece ; by famine, as in Russia
some years ago, and just now in India ; or by epidemics
of cholera, yellow fever, or the plague ! What a
noble idea it gives of the human race, that prosperous
America should send shiploads of grain for free distribution among starving Englishmen or Russians or
Koreans or Chinese, and that Englishmen should subscribe their tens of thousands of pounds for the sufferers
by famine in India ! How Christ-like that men of one
land and race should send untold thousands of dollars
to relieve the distress and sickness and hunger of
brother-men, though of other races and other lands !
Truly, the godlike in man is beginning at last to
blossom forth. This spirit and these deeds are now by
no means limited to professed Christians. Many there
are in Christian lands who make no profession of their
faith, who perhaps think and assert that they have no
religion, who nevertheless give liberally of their means
for organising and carrying on such forms of work. So
sweet and reasonable have these institutions and methods
and principles been seen to be, that all men praise and
approve them. So important are many of them for
the welfare of the community, that even governments
do not hesitate to contribute public money for their
establishment and support. Not only the governments
of Christian lands, but even of non-Christian lands,
have quickly caught the spirit, and are following the
examples set them.

Yet it still holds true that the great majority of

those who give either their means, and especially themselves, to benevolent work among the poor and the
wretched, the vile and the wicked, who establish not
only free hospitals for the sick, but rescue homes for
the fallen, who labour not only for temporal and physical
comfort, but also for the mental, moral, and social improvement and welfare of the lower and vicious classes
of society, are earnest Christian men and women. Yet
the wide sympathy and financial help in its support
that this form of the Christian's work and ideal find
among non-Christians, shows how pervasive is the influence of Jesus, how far it has spread beyond the limit
of those who profess to be His disciples. It is the
relatively modern growth of this spirit and these deeds,
outside the Christian Church, to which I call special
attention.

In the matters of genuine democratic government,
too, and popular education, and political and religious
liberty, the proofs are abundant that they are products
of Christ's teaching, the natural development of the
doctrine of the inherent and equal worth of man as
man. From the beginning, the Church has been
democratic in many very essential respects. Genuine
democratic principles first came to self-conscious existence at the time of the great Reformation, especially
in the Calvinistic and Puritan systems of thought and
government. With them, too, arose the idea of universal popular education. These two thoughts have
gone hand in hand, each strengthening the other. It
was under the lead of earnest professing Christians that
they found their first applications. Gradually they
have grown. All enlightened progressive men, regardless of their personal relation to Jesus, now not only

believe in, but take their personal part in sustaining, the democratic system of national government and popular education. The nation itself is seen to have a duty in the line of popular education ; many of the Christian nations now expend millions yearly to carry it on.

To avoid being misunderstood, it may perhaps be wise to guard the above statement by saying clearly that I do not for a moment say that Christ taught these things directly ; but I simply say that democratic government and popular education are enfolded in the principles that Christ taught, as the branches and flower of the apple tree are enfolded in the seed. It required time and a suitable environment to produce the flower. The Teutonic, and especially the Anglo-Saxon, race, seemed to be the necessary environment for the blossoming of the seed planted by Christ. Democratic government and popular education did not come from Greece or Rome, or Babylon or Egypt, or China or India or Japan. With the exception of Greece, they have never, even to this day, dreamed of them, and the dream of Greece properly described was oligarchy. Four slaves to every free man was the Grecian realisation of liberty, democracy, and popular rights. The nearest approach to democratic government and popular education outside of Christian lands is to be found in China.

In this remarkable land, as is well known, education, of the Chinese type, is highly esteemed; official promotion is based on success in passing the government examinations. In no country is it more possible for the sons of poor parents, by sheer ability in classical learning, to reach positions of high rank in the government, and great influence in the community. Perhaps less known is the fact that occasionally free schools are sustained by benevolent persons, in order that the children of the poor may have an opportunity to secure an education. It is nevertheless true that China never has known, and does not even yet know, the very first principles of genuine democratic government, nor has she any conception of what really popular education is. It may be asked how the above statements are compatible. How can it be justly said that she has no knowledge of democratic government, while it is admitted that her poorest sons, even of the lowest ranks, may rise to high positions in the government? How can it be possible that she has no conception of popular education, so long as it is freely admitted that education is highly esteemed and honoured by all classes, and often attained even by the poorest?

In reply, I would point out the fact that the fundamental principle of genuine democratic government is its constitutional character, in which equal rights are conferred and equal duties are laid alike on all the members of the nation, regardless of differences of wealth, rank, title, etc. Under genuine democratic government, legal methods are provided for the making known of grievances and the securing of relief in a peaceful manner. Law is not the will of one man or of a few, or even of a class, but of the majority. This conception of law and government is entirely foreign as yet to the Chinese mind. Confucius had no such ideas. His whole school of thought 'regards the people as little children that must be fed, protected, and taught their duties.' The only method known to the ancients of China, as well as of other lands, for redressing their wrongs, and for securing relief from oppressive rulers, was that of rebellion. Confucius himself made no other provision. Says Dr. Ernest Faber: 'Confucius, praising Yao and Shun as the highest patterns of moral accomplishment, points principally to the fact that both rulers selected the worthiest of their subjects to become their co-regents and their successors. This high example has not found a follower among the 244 emperors of China, from Confucius' day to the present. This is the case, in spite of Confucianism being the State religion of China. Confucius himself appears to have regarded with favour rebellious movements, in the hope of bringing a sage to the throne. Mencius is certainly outspoken in this respect. He justifies dethroning, and even the murder of a bad ruler. No wonder, then, that rebellions have occurred on a large scale over fifty times in about two thousand years, and local rebellions are almost yearly events. Neither Confucius himself, nor one of his followers, ever thought of establishing a constitutional barrier against tyranny, and providing a Magna Charta for the security of life and property of the ministers and people of China.' On a very slight consideration, nothing can be more manifest than that, in spite of all the democratic features in her communal and national life and government, China never has had any conception of really democratic government,—government 'by the people, for the people.'

In like manner, it would not be difficult to show that with all her emphasis on the study of the classics as a necessary requisite to government promotion, the conception of popular education has been far from her. Education of all the children, of girls as well as boys, that each one as he or she grows up may be fitted for the actual duties of life, — education in practical matters, and not merely in the classics,—this is the meaning of the phrase, 'popular education.' Of such education China has never had the slightest conception, nor has it yet dawned on her darkened mind.

Genuine democratic government, therefore, and, absolutely essential to it, popular education, are distinctly the products of Christianity, and especially of Protestant Christianity.

In the foregoing paragraphs on democratic government, I have called attention to the fact of the rise of these ideas in Christian lands, and I have stated that these ideals and practices were 'enfolded in the principles that Christ taught, as the flower and fruit of the apple are enfolded in the seed.' It is not my purpose to dwell on the process whereby these Christian ideals and principles gradually worked themselves out into actual life, and took the form of democratic government. But I cannot forbear to call attention to what Mr. Kidd in his suggestive work repeatedly says, namely, that the enfranchisement of the lower classes of society is primarily due, not to their wresting it from the power-holding classes, but, on the contrary, to the altruistic feeling with which, through the Christian religion, the power-holding classes have become increasingly equipped.[1] This enfranchisement of the lower classes of society has brought new millions of individuals of those nations where Christian ideals have had the greatest effect, into an equality of opportunity; it has stimulated their ambitions, and made them feel that they are men. It has thus raised those nations to the

[1] *Social Evolution*, pp. 139, 155, 165, 179, 181, 185, 186, and 201.

highest degree of social efficiency which the world has ever yet possessed.

Still another of the blessings secured to the world by Christ, when His teachings are practically worked out in a Christian civilisation, is, religious liberty; in other words, liberty of conscience. This is perhaps one of the crowning blessings of a Christian civilisation.

But whence did it arise, and how? Not in Athens, which killed Socrates for being an atheist, and whose most brilliant philosopher, Plato, would punish with death disloyalty to the State gods, in case five years of solitary confinement could not reform the criminal! Not in Rome, which put to death countless gentle, peaceable, confessedly innocent men, women, and children, for no other crime than that of refusing to worship the State gods. Not in India, or China or Africa, where even now, to abandon the national and tribal religion and become a Christian is too often to take one's life in one's hand and to endure great suffering and social persecution. The doctrine of religious liberty did not come from great atheistic, infidel, or materialistic philosophers of ancient, or even of modern times. Not until the new conception of religion, as a personal relation of each man with his Maker, of 'religion as a matter of conscience, and not of the magistrate,' did or could the idea or practice of religious liberty arise. As an historical fact it actually arose for the first time in the world in the Protestant country of Holland, and was soon introduced into England and the United States. Nay, the United States, or rather New England, came into existence because of the power of this new conception and the difficulty of carrying it into practice among those who

18

vigorously tried to destroy and crush it. And even in New England time was needed for the full development and liberation of the conception.

Now, however, that the idea has been produced, and the long bloody battle has been fought and won, none are so loud and noisy in their advocacy of it as those who reject Christ and His teachings. Truly the Christian origin of liberty, both religious and political, the wide acceptance of the fundamental factors of civilisation beyond the bounds of the Church, and now, in the last decades of the nineteenth century, their extension even to non-Christian lands, are beyond dispute.

The fact that these principles have become so popular, and have been more or less adopted by all governments and by all nations which seek to be civilised, not in the least deprives them of their essentially Christian nature. It only shows how far the influence of Christianity has extended beyond the organic Church. Yet, it still is a remarkable fact, that private education for the uplifting of the low and ignorant and superstitious ; unselfish, disinterested education of other grades of society, or other nationalities, is a work, even yet, done only by Christians, and chiefly by Protestant Christians. Popular education by the State, including the State universities, is a thing of very recent growth, whereas private schools and colleges and universities, endowed and sustained by Christians, are very old. No non-Christian society, no organisation of men inspired only by philosophy and reason, have ever done such things.

Within very recent times there has arisen in many quarters outside of the Christian Church a deep interest in, and concern for, the welfare of the masses of the people. It is beginning to be perceived that all classes of society are inseparably linked together ; that in this democratic age the superstition of the ignorant, poor, and struggling masses, cannot long exist with continued safety to the higher and wealthy classes ; that the disease-producing filth of the crowded slums carries death into the homes of the rich as well as into those of the poor; that vicious voters, whether ignorant or educated, cannot be trusted with the reins of power ; for if poor they sell their votes, and if rich they buy their way to office, and seek their own advantage, not that of the nation. Honest, upright, peaceful government in the hands of unprincipled men cannot exist. These facts are becoming very clear in modern times ; many educated men and women, who make no claim of having a Christian faith, are studying the social problems and discussing the remedies with no little anxiety. The problems of immigration, of labour, of city life, of municipal and national government, of temperance, of the coloured race, of illiteracy, of corrupt methods of banking, of railroads, of illegitimate business combinations, to say nothing of gambling, intemperance, prostitution, and countless other subjects, are all being discussed in the public press from the moral standpoint as never before. The remedies generally suggested are additional and more stringent laws. Without doubt these are very valuable and essential, because of the new conditions of social and industrial life which the introduction of steam has brought about within the last fifty to seventy-five years. But the most significant fact is the growing interest itself in the moral aspects of these problems; men perceive, as never before, the real solidarity of each city, and of the nation; that no class of society can suffer, be ignorant, or vicious, without bringing danger to the entire city or state or nation; that each part, each family, each individual even, has a vital relation and interest in each and in all.

Nor is this interest merely that of scholars concerned with an abstract problem in science or philosophy; it is a practical interest, one that leads to action. Many of the daily newspaper companies, though absolutely non-religious in character (as well as companies organised for the purpose), have established the custom of starting subscription lists for special objects of need as they arise, and of administering the funds thus secured. For many years the *New York Tribune* has collected and expended a 'Fresh Air Fund,' under the management of Rev. W. Parsons, in the interest of children who live in the tenement districts. Forty thousand persons, for several years past, have enjoyed the benefits of this beautiful charity. From ten to fifteen thousand children are sent into the country for a two weeks' vacation. A great number are sent out for single-day excursions. . . . Hundreds of lives have undoubtedly been saved every year as a result of these outings. The New York Association for Improving the Condition of the Poor is also engaged in a most interesting fresh-air work. It maintains a free home for convalescent children at West Coney Island, and a people's sea-side home at the same place; its special solicitude in the fresh-air work is for poor people whose physical condition requires a change from the tenement houses. Its ocean parties are taken to Coney Island every Monday, Wednesday, and Friday, where a dinner and bathing facilities are provided.

' In Chicago, the *Daily News* is entering on the sixth season of its fresh-air work. The report for the summer of 1894 is a gratifying one. More than 10,000 sick babies, more than 14,000 mothers, and other children, enough to bring up the total to 62,374, were entertained at the sanitarium of the *Daily News* in Lincoln Park, on the lake shore. This charity, like those of New York, is well organised, with suitable medical attendance and various facilities for recreation and enjoyment.' The leading papers of all the large cities in the United States are doing more or less of this kind of work. Those named above are cited only as typical illustrations. These works of charity are not done in the name of any religious organisation or church, but simply in the name of humanity, and prompted by the practical brotherly interest in the suffering poor felt by the tens of thousands who are able to contribute their dimes and their dollars.

Whence has come this interest? Whence has come this tremendous moral earnestness? Without doubt, the drift of the times and the evils of modern life have helped much to arouse it. But the times, the environment, only arouse, they cannot produce it, for it depends primarily on high moral ideals and moral character. The industrial, social, and moral evils of China or India or Africa are vastly more terrible than those of Europe or America, yet they do not produce moral earnestness in those lands and nations. Not the external, but the internal, not the accidental, but the essential, character is of prime importance.

It must be evident that the growing moral earnestness of modern times in Christian lands is one of the products of Christianity. It is the Church that more or less constantly and consistently has held high the ideal of truth and duty and fidelity, in public as in private life. It is the Church that has given Christendom its moral ideals and standards. It is the Church to which all owe their ideals of life, their moral vigour, the moral atmosphere they breathe, whether they recognise it or not, whether they claim or reject the Christian's faith in Christ.

This moral earnestness is to be found in no other part of the world. Heathendom has none of it. Even in so-called Christian nations there is a great difference in the degree of its vigour, for the Protestant nations far surpass those under the Roman Catholic, the Greek, and the other Eastern branches of the Christian Church.

A most significant and promising feature of modern civilised life is the appearance and rapidly growing power in English-speaking lands of what may be called the public conscience. This conscience is the combined product of high moral ideals, Christian character, intelligence, and knowledge of the daily experiences of the nation, of its classes, and even of its individuals. Wrong or injustice of any sort may appeal to the public conscience with the assurance of finding sympathy. When the public is satisfied of the reality of any wrong or injustice, through the public press, and, if need be, through the democratic forms of governments of both England and America, it speaks with no uncertain sound. If new laws are needed, they are enacted. If bad men are to be driven from office or power, the way is surely found. The abolition of slavery in all the English world many years ago; the great American civil war for the abolishment of slavery, in more recent times; the expulsion of the Louisiana lottery from the State of that name; the vigorous moral uprising in New Jersey, New York, and elsewhere, against the gambling evils of the race track; the moral indignation that always arises on the clear exposure of corruption in municipal or national government, such as those of the Tweed ring, and, more recently, of Tammany, and the New York police protection of immorality; the success of many labour strikes whose justice the public recognises; the common failure of those in which violence and wrong are done by the strikers—these are some of the many ways in which the public conscience speaks and acts. In Great Britain this public conscience has often spoken with tremendous effect, overthrowing men and measures, however power-fully supported by the Government, that in some more or less flagrant way had violated its sense of righteousness or morality. The abolition, again, of slavery throughout the British empire many years ago, and the passing of many reform measures in more recent times, with the intense feeling on the question of the Armenian atrocities, and England's duty in view of them and her treaty responsibilities,—these are all manifestations of this public conscience. Though sometimes called the 'Nonconformist conscience,' it is by no means limited to the members of the Non-conformist churches, but is shared alike by all earnest Christians, vast multitudes of whom are members of the Established Church.

Though it has received no special name in the

United States, this national conscience is none the less really operative. It is to this public conscience that all reform movements appeal ; only by its action can they hope to succeed. This public conscience is in the process of development, of education. This educational process needs time; each new phase of a subject needs careful study, and receives it. It is the existence of this public conscience, and its manifest growth in the latter part of this century, which are the hopeful signs of the moral growth of the country.

A recent editorial in the *Outlook* says: ' There has never been in this country such a revival of the civic conscience, as at present; such an effort to introduce righteousness into all departments of society ; such a resolute and persistent determination to make the nation, not only nominally but actually, what it should be. . . . The distinctions between right and wrong, the reality of moral order, the fact that righteousness alone constitutes true prosperity, are appreciated as they have not been for many years.' The recent repudiation of Tammany and Hill, the revolt throughout the United States against machine government and corrupt or doubtful political methods, are indications of the growth of the public conscience. ' Public conscience is a public force in America. It may be, and often is, somnolent. It may be, and often is, hoodwinked for a time. But it cannot be safely defied. And the politician who disregards it, and depends on corruption, management wiles, or cunning, is sure, sooner or later, to be discovered, and absolutely sure, when discovered, to be defeated. The American people will have none of him. . . . Public conscience is a greater power than public corruption.'

But time would fail me to speak of the countless little

ways of speech and life over which the gentle Jesus has exerted, and still is exerting, His kindly influence. The brutality which seemed characteristic of the ancient Roman, Gothic, and Teutonic races, though by no means wholly conquered, yet has been wonderfully overcome. Not only has ruthless murder been very effectually stopped, but all forms of torture in the examination of supposed criminals has been done away. And even in the case of criminals condemned to death, the most painless method of execution is coming more and more to be adopted. Needless pain and wanton cruelty are being banished by the rising public conscience. Not only have laws been enacted on the subject of cruelty, but private societies have been organised to insist on the execution of those laws— Societies for the Prevention of Cruelty to Children, and even Societies for the Prevention of Cruelty to Animals. Those societies yearly spend large sums of money in carrying on their humane work. Whence, again I ask, has come this spirit of gentleness, of sympathy, of horror for pain as such, not simply in one's own body or that of one's bone and flesh, but even when experienced by others, by those with whom one has none but the remotest relations, even by dumb creatures? What influence has made bloody Teutons and Celts, who used to burn hundreds of human beings before their dreadful Druid gods,—what power has transformed them into the peace-loving, cruelty-hating peoples of modern times? No mere teachings of ethics and moral rules could have done it. It was the work of Christianity, the influence of the gentle Jesus, whom so many of them have slowly learned to love, and more and more fully to understand and obey.

It is not here claimed that the Church has from the beginning been wholly free from cruelty, that it has set its face like a flint againt needless pain, for, alas, it is not true. Too often has the Church, adopting the heathen spirit and the methods of the times, taken and used the sword, the thumbscrew, and the rack, forgetful of the teachings and example of Jesus. But these were the work of the pagan spirit. Nor is it claimed that there is now no cruelty in Christendom. Were that true there would be no need of such societies as those named above. But it is claimed that cruelty is on the decrease, that the face of Christian civilisation is finally set against all forms of cruelty and needless pain; that this tendency is a product of Christian teaching, a result of the wide influence of Jesus, reaching beyond the limits of professing Christians; and that it is a modern movement, one of the signs of growth of the Kingdom of God in the world.

A few more signs of the increasing influence of Christ outside of the Church demand our attention.

I mention first, the growing popular interest in the observance of the Lord's Day. The modern industrial revolution has done much to break down its former strict observance in England and America. Immigrants to the latter country have brought in the so-called 'Continental Sabbath'—a day of sport and business rather than of rest and worship. With this method of regarding the day, the number of those who labour on the Sabbath has of late greatly increased. But with this increased disregard of the Sabbath have come in great evils. The fierce struggle for existence, the intensity of industrial and commercial life, the long hours of the closest attention, the increase of the strain

of labour due to increased specialisation,—all these
have contributed to a keener realisation of the absolute
need of rest one day in seven. Multitudes who care
nothing for the religious uses of the day demand its
observance, on the ground of the physiological, social,
mental, and moral needs, both of the individual and of
society.

The 'Sunday problem' is receiving the most careful
scientific study. Not only as a matter of theory, but as
a matter of experience, is it being studied in each
department of labour. The advantages and disadvantages to the labourer and to the business man
are receiving most careful and impartial consideration.
It is seen that the physical health of the employed
demands rest, because of the intensity of modern
industrial conditions. Agitation and legislation to
enforce Sunday rest are becoming common. International conventions for the one purpose of the study of
the problem have been held. The working men themselves are becoming intensely interested. Labour
unions in Europe and America are urging its wider
observance. The representative of over 100,000 railroad
employees in the United States, at the late International
Congress of Sunday rest, held in connection with the
Columbian Exposition at Chicago in 1893, spoke in the
most emphatic terms of the desire of the men for, as
well as their absolute need of, regular and complete
Sabbath observance. Over 500,000 members of labour
organisations in Great Britain opposed the Sunday
opening of museums in 1892 ; while between 1872 and
1891, 719,000 signers of petitions to the House of
Commons opposed, and only 80,000 favoured, their
opening. Although in general the Sabbath observance

of England and America is far ahead of that of Europe, yet in some respects Europe is ahead. ' In Belgium, postage stamps have printed on them, " Not to be delivered on Sunday." . . . In Holland and Switzerland, no Sunday newspapers are issued. In Italy, a congress of workmen's societies held in 1892 voted in favour of obligatory rest.' In the United States, in the army, the navy, the Government, and in all postal offices, work is reduced to a minimum. In most Protestant, and in some of the Roman Catholic, countries, societies for the further study of the problem, for popular education and agitation, and for seeing that the Sabbath legislation is observed and enforced, have been organised in recent years, and are doing much to create public intelligence and sentiment on the subject.

There has been much recent legislation on the subject both in Europe and America. The Fletcher prize essay for 1892, on 'The Hallowed Day,' says that 'only one of the States of the United States has no Sunday law; the most of the States of the United States have good Sunday laws.' . . . After a careful examination of them all, the author deliberately says they 'are not the old Puritanic laws of colonial times, but the revised statutes . . . providing for the proper observance of the Lord's Day in these closing years of the nineteenth century.' The immense importance of the Sabbath in the eyes of the American people may be measured in part by the fact that the petitions for Sabbath closing of the Columbian Exposition represented a constituency of forty millions in the denominations, labour unions, and other bodies represented by special vote, besides millions of individual signatures. Only liquor dealers' associations and two labour bodies voted for Sabbath opening, and altogether did not represent more than a million individuals. The national Government voted to grant the Exposition two and a half million dollars, on condition that the grounds should be closed on Sundays. Though the Sunday closing movement did not succeed, because of the foreign character of the majority of Chicago's citizens and Exposition committees, yet the failure of the masses of the visitors to attend on the Sabbath caused Sunday opening to be a great loss. The largest attendance at the Fair grounds was usually on Saturdays; the largest on a single day was 716,881 persons, who paid an admittance fee. The total attendance was 27,377,733, being an average of over 150,000 for each day of the six months during which the Exposition was open. The Sabbath attendance was, however, very small, not exceeding, it is safe to say, 20,000 a day. On August 6, 1893, 16,000 persons visited the Fair. The average Sabbath attendance at Mr. Moody's religious services was 50,000, being a far greater number than went to the Fair grounds.

In England the Sabbath is more held on to by the working classes, as their only hope, than in the United States. Throughout Great Britain there is not a single daily newspaper published on Sunday. There is abundant Sabbath legislation. As already mentioned, there is great opposition among the working classes to the opening even of museums on the Sabbath.

On the Continent, the recent growth of the Sunday rest agitation and legislation is marvellous. Each nation, from Russia to Portugal, and from Greece to Sweden, has awakened to the subject during the past decade as never before. Much new legislation has been enacted since 1890. Sunday rest is rapidly growing. After a careful survey of the recent Sunday legislation and its observance on the Continent, E. Deluz, in the *Sunday Problem*, says: 'The above facts show that the cause is making important progress on the Continent of Europe, and encourage further effort.'

But the Sabbath is a Christian institution. Its adoption as an essential of modern civilisation by non-Christians is a noteworthy sign of the growth of the influence of Christianity.

I mention, in the second place, the recent growth of the White Cross Society, and the evidence it affords of the great emphasis that is being laid on having and enforcing the same standard of morality for man as for woman. 'A white life for two' is becoming a well-known phrase. This is a most promising movement in the moral world. But it is safe to say that its moving power, no less than its origin, is Christian. I have yet to hear of a single 'social purity' society wholly outside of Christian influence.

Another significant sign of the times is the demand, made even by those who reject Christianity, that others shall follow the Christian standards when they come into relation with themselves. This is a virtual admission of the truth and authority of Christ's teachings.

There seems to be an impression that, more and more, scientific men are leaving the Christian ranks. The relation of education to religion has been briefly considered in a previous chapter (cf. pp. 147-155). Here I only wish to deny the correctness of the above-mentioned impression. It is impossible, from the nature of the case, to present any statistics on this subject ; yet the following facts are not unimportant :—In 1865, 617 scientific men, members of the British Scientific Association, many of them of the highest eminence in Great Britain, drew up and signed a statement declaring their belief in the authority of Scripture, and the harmony of the Scriptures with natural science. This document is now in the Bodleian Library at Oxford. Again, at the annual meeting of both the British and the American Scientific Associations, the holding of prayer meetings is a recognised custom, which meetings large numbers of the members attend. It is evident that the scientific mind is not of necessity anti-Christian, though there are some famous scientists who may be.

It is a significant sign of the return of scientific men toward the theistic view of the world that the Marquis of Salisbury, in his recent address as President of the British Scientific Association, and as giving a dispassionate and accepted summary of the present view of natural science, could assert, in the words of Lord Kelvin (Sir William Thomson), 'that the argument of design has been greatly too much lost sight of in recent zoological speculations. Overpoweringly strong proofs of intelligence and benevolent design lie around us ; . . . with irresistible force they show to us through nature the influence of a free will, and teach us that all living things depend on one everlasting Creator and Ruler.' It is safe to say that the scientific mind of the civilised world is as fully convinced of the truth of all that is important in Christianity as it ever was, and that it is also as devoted as ever to the attainment of real Christian character. The number of anti-Christian scientists is without doubt comparatively small, though they attract much attention by the extreme nature of their views, and the constancy with which they assert them.

A paragraph from a recent editorial in the *Outlook* (February 23, 1895) is worthy of quotation in this connection.

One of the most significant signs of the times is the change of attitude among scientists toward religious questions. Those who keep pace with scientific thought, and are familiar with the atmosphere and spirit of scientific investigation in the universities abroad, have been struck by the radical change which has taken place in the last twenty years. What now strikes one, in the attitude and spirit of a great many scientific men, is a spirit of reverence toward the religious side of life. This does not mean that there is a return to the old dogmatic statements, or to the ecclesiastical explanation of things ; but it does mean that there has come a deeper percep- tion of the facts of religious experience, and a deeper realisation of the immense part which the religious element plays in human life. It is very generally felt that the explanations of religious phenomena offered twenty years ago, and accepted at the moment as final, are inadequate ; that religion is something deeper, more pervasive, and more influential than many scientific men took account of two decades ago. The feeling is growing that the religious phenomena of history are not to be explained by the mythological and anthro- pological explanations once offered. Mr. Kidd's striking book, so widely read and so earnestly dis- cussed during the last year, is a striking revelation of the attitude which many scientific men are now taking toward religious questions — an attitude of free but reverential investigation. There are of course a number of old-time scientific men who still hold to the somewhat arrogant agnosticism of two decades ago ;

but the younger men are inspired by a very different spirit.'

The evidence presented in the preceding pages of this work has had all but exclusive reference to the increasing influence of Jesus within the limits of Christendom. In closing, I wish to call attention to the spreading of that influence to non-Christian lands. I have, in a previous chapter, spoken of the growing efforts to propagate the teachings of Christ in foreign lands. I should also refer to the effects of those efforts. Scores of islands in the Pacific Ocean have been transformed into wholly Christian lands. India and Japan have been wonderfully modified, and in no slight degree, elevated by Christian ideals. Hundreds of thousands of believers and church members have been gathered in those countries. But the influence of Jesus is by no means limited to the Churches. Millions in those Eastern lands, who acknowledge no connection with the visible Church, know and admire, and, more or less consciously, have accepted the teachings of Christ as the best the world affords. It is safe to say that the gospel of Christ, and love for the Saviour of mankind, are spreading more rapidly among non-Christian communities during the nineteenth century than at any previous time, not even excepting the first and second centuries. As was well said, not long since, in the *Boston Advertiser*: 'They who do not know what they are talking about, still say that missionaries have made no impression in heathendom except upon a relatively small fraction of the lower orders of mankind. They who speak from knowledge, say that in Japan, to take that one case, Christian ideas have already permeated the institutions and populations of the

19

country to such an extent, that, from the Mikado to the humblest labourer at four cents a day, there is no man in the island-empire who does not, directly or indirectly, feel the influence of the new religion, if not as a spiritual force, at least as a creative energy in politics, industry, and learning. Statistics can never do more than dimly shadow forth the truth of such a matter.'[1]

This brief survey of the growing influence in the world of Christ and His teaching would be faulty indeed, were there no reference to the mighty power of His personality in purifying, in ennobling, in refining, and in inspiring all our literature, poetry, painting, architecture, sculpture, music, and oratory. These are sensitive thermometers of the advance of civilisation.

For nineteen hundred years, the most ennobling poetry, the most magnificent architecture, the most exquisite painting, the most thrilling music, and the most moving oratory, has been that which has been most intimately connected with devotion to Christ's person, and with efforts to present, in beautiful forms, some phase of Himself or His teachings. The development of all these arts, expressive of men's æsthetic sense, has received its best and most permanent stimulus from the efforts fitly to express loyalty and devotion to the Saviour of mankind. And to this very day, no one who would aspire to take the first rank in any of these departments would venture to ignore Christ's teaching. Indeed, it is safe to say that he could not possibly attain to the first rank without having first received the impress of Christ's character upon him. Public sentiment renders absolutely impossible to-day such

[1] *Boston Advertiser*, October 15, 1894.

literature, poetry, and music as is common in all pre-Christian and non-Christian and semi-Christian lands and times. The purest and best and most ennobling of Greek and Roman poetry is filled with passages which are expurgated in all modern editions intended for the public eye. It is safe to say that no man in all history has given so powerful and ennobling a stimulus to all the arts expressive of man's æsthetic nature as did the lowly Man of Nazareth. But the point of special importance for us is the fact that Christ's influence along all these varied lines is growing century by century. Never was fiction so pure, or poetry so inspiring and spiritual, as during the latter half of the nineteenth century. What previous century can claim such a galaxy of noble men as this? Whittier and Lowell and Longfellow, Wordsworth and Tennyson and Browning, Beecher and Moody, Spurgeon and Parker, Cobden and Bright and Gladstone—to name no others, are fitting representatives of the nobler movements of modern thought. But they are what they are through the influence of Christ and His spirit.

Enough has been said, I think, to indicate the growing influence of Christ outside of the organic Church. The Christian need not despond, but rather should rejoice, for, after all, that for which every Christian cares is not the growth of the Church, but of the Kingdom; not the dominance of the ecclesiastical organism, but of the Christ-spirit. That the wide-reaching influence of Jesus is truly growing, who can doubt?

CHAPTER IX

THE SIGNIFICANCE OF THE GROWTH OF CHRISTIANITY AND OF CHRISTENDOM

'The victory (of Christianity) was no mere outward triumph, but the defeat of heathenism in its inner principles. Hearts were won, consciences convinced, the heathen were made Christian in disposition; the views, life, conduct, and customs of the people were changed from within.'[1]

'The Christian religion must be ever regarded as the crowning glory, or rather the life and soul, of our whole modern culture.'[2]

'There can be no good government without law and order; nor that, without authority; nor that, without justice; nor that, without God.'[3]

'The true and permanent interests of man can be promoted only in connection with religion.'[4]

---

[1] Uhlhorn, *The Conflict of Christianity with Heathenism.* English ed., p. 385.

[2] Carlyle, *The Signs of the Times.*

[3] Cardinal Gibbons.

[4] Mark Hopkins.

CHAPTER IX

WE have now completed our study of the first and fundamental question with which we started— the question as to whether or not the Kingdom of God is growing. I trust that the answer to that question has been both clear and convincing. Let us take a rapid glance over our course. We have seen how rapid has been the growth of the number of the Christian adherents during the last two centuries. We have seen how enormous is the growth of the Christian nations, in populations, in political power, in wealth, and in civilisation. We have seen how, during all the centuries, and especially in recent times, there has been an ever-growing understanding of Christ's teachings, and a fuller application of them to the problems of life. We have seen how the influence of Christ's teachings is spreading beyond the limits of the organised Church ; how all classes and individuals, even those who reject Christ for themselves, are yet guided and blessed by His teachings and influence. And we have seen how rapid is the modern growth of the active membership of the Christian churches, of the allied organisations, and of the whole religious life in Protestant lands.

It may be said by the critic that I have presented only the bright side of the picture ; that I have ignored many important facts, the consideration of which would give a very different estimate of the moral state of

Christendom. I am not concerned to deny the charge, for it has not been my aim to set forth a complete view of the moral condition of Christendom. My one primary purpose has been to show that there has been growth, that the Kingdom of God *is coming*. I think this has been done. In doing so I have not denied the imperfections of the Church, of Christian individuals, or of Christian nations. I am not ignorant of the sordid selfishness of tens of thousands of so-called Christians ; or of the fearful social and moral conditions of millions of the working classes of Christendom ; nor of the oppression and wickedness of many manufacturers ; nor of the scores of thousands of children, and hundreds of thousands of women, working in factories and in 'sweating' houses under the most unwholesome circumstances, and for a bare living ; nor of the venality of much official life ; nor of the corruptions of municipal governments ; nor of the worship of mammon, so common where commerce and business prosper ; nor of the enormous fortunes fraudulently made by speculation in banks, in railroads, in corporations, in 'corners' on the necessaries of life, and in government contracts ; nor of the race antagonism existing in the Southern States of America toward the negroes, manifesting itself in political oppression, and disfranchisement of hundreds of thousands of legal coloured voters, as well as in the frequent mobs and lynchings of recent years. Nor am I ignorant of the immense sums of money worse than wasted on strong drink and gambling ; nor of the crimes and poverty that spring from intemperance ; nor of the unblushing prostitution permitted, and often even protected by the police in many of the large cities of Christendom ; nor of the large amount of secret vice and sensuality throughout all the Christian lands; nor of the indifference of the Church as a whole to these evils, and the comparatively little effort that is put forth by Christians individually or collectively to remove them.

All these things I admit and deplore. Were it necessary and desirable for our purposes, statistics on these foul factors of modern life could be given, which, by themselves, would sicken any pure soul, and might discourage even the most hopeful. It would not be difficult to prove that many of these evils have come to their present dimensions during recent times, and that some, perhaps many of them, are even on the increase. Those who are interested to see the dark side of Christendom or the Church will find no difficulty in getting the facts. Dr. Josiah Strong's *Our Country*, and some of the writings of Professor Herron and President Gates, present the dark side of civil and church life in the United States, the dangers that threaten the Church and the State. Indeed, to those who stand in the midst of the conflict and see the evil, the crime, the passion, the jealousy, the corruption, the injustice, the licentiousness, and the many varieties of sin that exist on every side in such varied form, and with such malign effects, it often must seem that the world is surely growing worse. The purpose of this book has not been to conceal or deny these evils and dangers. But neither has it been its purpose to present them. What I have tried to do is to present the abundant evidence that the Kingdom of God *is* growing, both within and without the organised Church. The partiality, therefore, of our view is not due to ignorance or desire to convey a false impression, but only to the limited range of our subject.

Before considering, however, the special topic of this chapter, the significance of the growth of Christianity, I wish to make a few remarks with reference to the great industrial and moral evils of the present age, which, it is hoped, will aid the reader the better to estimate them in their relation to the Church, to the State, and to the individual.

1. The industrial conditions of Christendom are of very recent development. They are due to the discovery of steam power and its wide use in manufacturing. The introduction of steam and electricity into the industrial world has compelled a reconstruction of society which none could foresee. It has made possible, not only the immense manufacturing establishments, many of which employ thousands of workmen, but also the immense growth of the cities, by (*a*) providing work for the thousands in the cities ; (*b*) insuring a sufficient food supply for all in the cities ; (*c*) and thus making it more possible than in former ages to satisfy the social demands of human nature.

2. But many of the evils of these modern times are a direct consequence of this new industrial period—the new distribution of the labouring forces of the world, the massing of the millions in small areas, and the corresponding diminution of the farming populations. Two points should be specially noted : (*a*) Power is put into the hands of individual men as in no previous period of the world's history ; power to make immense fortunes, while fully conforming to the standards of business morality hitherto accepted by all; power also to rob the millions or to take usurious gains from them, and to deal unjustly with thousands of employees, while yet being legally guiltless. This power has developed

the cupidity of all, the desire to be rich, the worship of mammon. (*b*) The new social and industrial conditions into which the labourers have suddenly been brought, their crowding into cities, their struggle for life ; the limitation to their personal growth by the specialisation of their occupations; the loss of personal manhood and responsibility, consequent upon their living on weekly wages, and ownership of no real property ; the ease of earning money and the corresponding ease of gratifying fleshly appetites. All these and other unfavourable factors of modern industrial life have had, and still have, most disastrous effects on the wage-earning classes.

3. The new material civilisation, with its inventions and wealth, plays into the hands of the ignorant, the wicked, the vicious, and the depraved, as well as into those of the wise, the righteous, the upright, and the honest. It is natural, therefore, that the wicked should grow more wicked, the licentious more licentious, the unjust more unjust. This is in accord with the principle of Christ's teaching, that he that hath shall have more abundantly. It is to be expected that the wickedness in the world will develop, showing more and more its real inherent nature, its hideous flower and corrupt fruit. This is the law of development. But because wickedness is developing its true nature, those who love truth and purity need not despair ; they should rather rejoice. For thus will it work its own final destruction.

4. This new industrial period has come on so swiftly and silently, and the new forms of industry, the new discoveries, the new occupations for men of ability, have arisen so rapidly, that, preoccupied by these, the attention of the nation's brain and conscience has unconsciously been turned away from the moral and social

problems involved. The old standards of moral action have been so thoroughly accepted, as well as the laws and precedents that were their outgrowth, that the legal and moral restraints placed by society on grasping men have proved insufficient for the times. Legislation has not kept pace with the industrial evolution. But this means that the public was unconscious of the new evolution that was taking place in society, that the moral consciousness of the nations and of the Christian churches was not awake to what was coming about.

5. Though this is still true of the churches as a whole, yet it is to be noted that is not true of all. A consciousness of the new situation has arisen in many quarters. The new conditions and problems are being studied in every possible way. Statisticians are tabulating the facts. Social science is only just coming into existence. Christian churches and Christian individuals are giving their means, their sons and their daughters, to lives of loving labour among the poor, down-trodden, and ignorant labouring masses. University settlements are arising; they are only in their infancy, however. The legislators are enacting new laws to meet the new conditions, determining new standards of right and duty on the basis of the fundamental principles of Christian democracy. Philanthropists are founding industrial schools for the children of the wage-earners. The labouring classes themselves are combining, with increasing intelligence and wisdom, into brotherhoods and unions for the better preservation of their rights and their manhood. In a word, the consciousness of the new industrial age is fairly dawning on Christendom, and the moral and religious conscience is awaking and is already beginning to work, in the last decades of this

century, to right the wrongs of the oppressed, and to enforce the principles of the Christian democracy on all even upon the most grasping and un-Christian of men and corporations.

6. While, therefore, for the purpose of stirring up still greater activity in the work of individual reform, in legislation, in popular education, in social reorganisation, and in philanthropic labours, it is desirable to make known to all the evil aspects of modern civilisation, the corruption of the money-worshipping society, and the defects of the Church, which such earnest men as Drs. Strong, Herron, and others are doing, it is also desirable clearly to present the noble elements, the hope-inspiring factors, of modern life, both in the Church and in the State. It is this latter work that I have aimed to do in the preceding chapters.

Briefly to summarise what we have learned, I may say that the one hopeful, because fundamental, element of modern life, is the growing influence of Jesus. Not only is the number of those who openly profess allegiance to Him growing, as we have seen, but they are increasingly gaining insight into the meaning and spirit of His life and teaching ; they are more and more perfectly carrying out His instructions, living His life. The influence of Jesus also is more powerfully felt beyond the ranks of professing Christians than ever before. When thousands of working men will hiss the parson and the Church, but applaud the name of Christ, when the meetings of an intense political campaign are frequently opened by prayer, as was the case before the recent elections in the United States, is it not evident that Christ's influence is felt and He himself is loved by multitudes who, for whatever reason or however mistaken, refuse to connect themselves with the Church? *Christ is King in His Kingdom to-day, and is recognised as such as He never was before.*

Bearing in mind the substance of all that has been thus far presented, let us now consider the significance of the moral, political, and material development of Christendom, and especially of the Protestant world.

Science, popular education, democratic and constitutional government, material civilisation, knowledge of many of Nature's secrets, and ability to make use of her forces; medical and surgical skill, political supremacy, the faculty of self-government as well as of ruling other races; together with a growing comprehension and application of Christ's ethical and religious teachings—all these have appeared simultaneously in a remarkable degree among the Christian nations. What is the meaning and explanation of all these phenomena? It is one of the fundamental assumptions of science that for every result there must be, not only a cause, but an adequate cause. This is true not only for such physical phenomena as the falling of an apple, the revolution of the planets, the movements of the stars, the myriad forms of fauna and flora, but for the great outstanding movements of history. If there is meaning and intelligence involved in the evolution of the animal and vegetable kingdoms (which meaning and intelligence only an intelligent being can comprehend), so, too, is there meaning and intelligence involved in the mental, moral, spiritual, social, and industrial development of the human race. The great onward movements of humanity, consuming centuries of time for even a partial result, are not caused by chance, are not the product of blind fortune, mere luck. These are the words of ignorance. There is no such thing as chance. And, on the other hand, 'fate,' or 'necessity,' has no meaning, except it refers to the universal and unalterable law of cause and effect. As there can be no effect without the cause, so there can be no millennial progress without a meaning, without revealing a purpose. History, therefore, is full of meaning. The rise of one race and the downfall of another, the predominance of one style of civilisation at the expense of another, the progressive growth of one religion and the decay of all others,—these are not meaningless or causeless events.

As has been well said by another : 'Nations and races, as well as individuals, are called of God, ordained and set apart to a specific work for the furtherance of His Kingdom upon earth. Endowed with special fitness for the appointed task, they are also providentially trained, and in due time are inducted into their high office, their divine calling. This accepted and fulfilled, they become notable instruments in the accomplishment of His beneficent and sublime designs in behalf of a lost race. With this fact in mind, of which history affords so many striking illustrations, mention is often made of three peoples in particular of the ancient world, which with gifts and tasks exceedingly unlike, yet played each its essential part, and all wrought wondrously together, both to prepare redemption for the world, and the world for the redemption. Thus, among other things, through the Scriptures, was supplied the knowledge of the true God, and of that righteousness which is acceptable to Him. The Greek contributed a magnificent language, and a civilisation in which the gospel could find expression. And the Roman, with his world-wide empire, made communication easy, brought peace everywhere, from the Euphrates to the Atlantic, and made a great advance to the unity of mankind.'[1]

The Creator and Upholder of the universe has His purpose in it, and He is surely though slowly bringing that purpose to pass. By the effects of men's ideas and ideals upon themselves; by their effects on their surroundings, on their social, commercial, and national life; by their effects on the health of their possessors, on the size and vigour of their bodies, on the keenness and the accuracy of their minds;—by all their varied effects, acting on their total conditions, external and internal, subjective and objective, perfecting and developing their original endowments and capabilities, God is teaching His children which of their ideas and ideals are worthy; what kind of conduct and customs are moral—in a word, what is really good and true and beautiful. Those whose eyes and minds and hearts are open to see and understand and believe and practise what He thus teaches, receive the blessings; they multiply in numbers and power. But this is the law of the survival of the fittest. And since God's providence extends not only to ancient nations and races, since the special call of special nations to special work is not a thing of the past alone, but also of the present, it is the duty of those who would comprehend the meaning of the universe, who would know the purposes of God, to study not only physical nature and its immutable because divine laws, not only human nature and its innate consciousness of truth and of moral law, but also the grand movements of history, and especially of modern history, in which we are playing a part. It is the duty

[1] *Missionary Review of the World*, Oct. 1894, p. 748.

of the wise both to recognise the facts and to comprehend their meaning.

If, then, we apply this principle of the survival of the fittest to the facts brought out in the previous chapters, we may make the following assertions with scientific accuracy and certainty :—

1. Religion has a very and an increasingly important place in the history and development of the human race. It is a factor of the utmost importance in determining the moral, the intellectual, the material, and the political status of the nations. In view of the nature of religion, this is what we might expect, and, as a matter of fact, we find it to be so historically. There are some who write and speak as if religion had far more power in ancient times than now. No doubt superstitions and fears had more influence then than now. But never did true religion have so powerful a hold on the human mind as to-day ; never has ethical truth and belief in God, the Creator and Upholder of the universe, the Maker of man, the Father and Saviour of sinful men, had such moulding force in society as in modern days. Never before have the demands for justice, and for equality of opportunity for all the classes of society, been so clearly made and admitted by all. Belief in, and action according to, ethical religion, is a more potent factor in the entire social development of man now proceeding than ever before, and is increasingly operative.

A striking and widely read book of recent times is Benjamin Kidd's *Social Evolution*, from which we have already made several quotations. Its main argument is, that religion is the one all-important factor in the social evolution of the human race. The argument, being presented in the terms and spirit of evolutionary

20

science, has attracted a good deal of attention. At the close of two chapters of great interest on the character of 'Western Civilisation,' Mr. Kidd draws the following conclusions :—' First, that the process of social development which has been taking place, and which is still in progress in our Western civilisation, is not the product of the intellect, but that the motive force behind it has had its seat and origin in that fund of altruistic feeling with which our civilisation has become equipped. Second, that this altruistic development, and the deepening and softening of character which has accompanied it, are the direct and peculiar product of the religious system on which our civilisation is founded' (p. 198). 'In the religious beliefs of mankind,' says Mr. Kidd, on a previous page, 'we have not simply a class of phenomena peculiar to the childhood of the race. We have therein the characteristic feature of our social evolution. These beliefs constitute, in short, the natural complement of our reason ; and, so far from being threatened with eventual dissolution, they are apparently destined to continue to grow and develop' (p. 126).

2. All forms of Polytheism are doomed to extinction. At one time Polytheism was the belief of all the nations of the world. But the extent of its rule has been constantly diminishing. To-day there is no polytheistic self-governing nation of any size on the face of the globe. The reason is apparent. Polytheism is the mother of superstition and ignorance, of which in turn it is the product. It does not stimulate education, thought, or individual character. In a word, the real reason why Polytheism is dying out is because it is not fitted to survive. It is not the truth, nor does it beget love of the truth. Polytheism is unable, therefore,

to give that solidity or unity to a nation which shall enable it to govern itself in righteousness, and all its classes with impartiality, or to meet and conquer the foe, whether external or internal. The belief in Polytheism which remains to this day in such countries as China is one important cause of the misrule and inherent weakness of that great nation.

3. Christianity is the religion of the dominant nations of the earth. Nor is it rash to prophesy that in due time it will be the only religion in the world. This is not equivalent to saying that all non-Christian countries will become tributaries to Christian nations, but only that non-Christian countries will in the course of time become Christian. As Rome could not resist either the logic or the noble lives of preachers and believers, so it will be in India, and even in China. That day may be centuries hence, and the forms of church organisation and creedal statement may differ considerably from those which now prevail ; but the day will surely come ; and the religion will be essentially Christian, only purer and nobler and more loyal to Christ, we may hope and believe, than that which is now prevalent in Christendom. By the intellectual, moral, commercial, and political blessings—in a word, by the civilisation which God has given and still is giving to those nations which have adopted Christianity—He has indicated His approval ; it is evident that He intends that these Christian nations shall have the predominant and moulding influence in the world at this stage of its development. The real reason why Christian nations are predominant is because they, more than others, have discovered and loved and lived the truth, the eternal principles on which God has created this world. And if we ask how

they have come by this truth, there is only one answer, and it is exceedingly simple. Jesus Christ has given it to them, not explicitly, but implicitly; not by direct, specific detailed teachings, but by planting the seed ; by starting the leaven, by implanting a fervid love of truth and purity and righteousness ; by inspiring love of God as Father, of man as brother ; by the giving of a new life, a new character, a new hope, and a new ambition ; and, not least, by inspiring those who believe in Him with loyalty to Him and to truth. The seed Christ planted has sprouted, the leaven has spread slowly, Christian civilisation has developed. It is still far from perfect. Nevertheless it is here, doing its work, bestowing its blessings ; those nations who accept it heartily, and adopt its inmost principles, are ever to prosper, materially, mentally, morally, and spiritually.

It may be well at this point to turn aside from our main topic to consider for a moment a very natural criticism. It is sometimes said that the so-called Christian nations are dominant in the world, not because they are Christian, but because they are not ; that they rule the world because they are grasping, are over-reaching, are regardless of the rights of weaker nations ; in a word, because they ignore in practice the religion they believe in theory. Not a little can be said, and truthfully, to sustain this view. I do not defend the ruthless, and oftentimes bloody, policy of the so-called Christian governments in their relations either to the non-Christian world, or even among themselves. By many deeds of treachery and wickedness and blood have they plundered the defenceless savage tribes and the weaker nations. Often, though by no means always, they have waged unprovoked and uncalled-for wars. I do not defend the bloody victories over American Indians by Spaniards, French, and English. I do not defend or excuse much of the treatment by the United States of the North American Indians. I do not defend much of the English treatment of Hindoos or Africans. I believe most emphatically that all these deeds were culpably wicked.

But I do contend (*a*) that the violence of the so-called Christian nations has been a hindrance, and not a help, to their world-wide predominant influence. Who doubts that the influence, if not the actual power, of England in India and Africa, or of Spain in South America, or of the United States over the American Indians, or any of the Christian countries on China and Japan, would be tenfold greater than it is now, if the uniform policy of these Christian governments had been controlled by the Christian principles of truth and righteousness and love? The past conduct of the so-called Christian governments has been a great hindrance, not a help, to their predominant positions.

(*b*) I contend, in the second place, that the governments of Christendom are not properly called Christian. They make no effort to be. This is a sad confession to make, but it is true. It is the so-called 'Christian nations which have armed and drilled the Japanese and Chinese who are fighting in Korea. It is Christendom that is perfecting its instruments of slaughter, building pneumatic guns which will hurl heavy charges of dynamite a couple of miles, and that is perfecting the Maxim flying-machine, which is to extend the area of slaughter to the air above.' Europe is an armed camp. The peace footing of the twenty leading nations of Europe in 1892 was 3,240,000 men, and the war footing 12,564,000 men. When the recent laws have gone into effect, the war footing will be 22,621,000 men. The present annual cost of the 'peace' armies of Europe is about $1,638,000,000, not to speak of the loss of production due to withdrawing such vast hosts of capable men from their natural fields of industry. Truly, with all this terrible machinery in preparation for mutual slaughter, Christendom is still far from Christian.

The explanation is, however, simple. Christ taught a few general principles. The Christian community is working them out, applying them to the developing needs of life. Christianity, as a system of practice, is in the process of development. Christendom has tried the experiment of subordinating the civil government to the organic Church, and has found it a failure. She is now trying several other ways of relating the Church and State. This is not the place to describe them. I can only say, that in the past the teachings of Christ have been too largely interpreted in their bearing on individual salvation and individual future life, and too little in their bearings on the national governments. But the progressive elements of Christian society now see that Christian principles are wider than the individual, and must be embodied by, and have control over, both local and national governments, over the entire social organism. The efforts for honest and impartial state and national government, for honest elections, for honourable treatment of American Indians, and the movement for international arbitration, are some of the signs of the growing Christianisation of the governments. But the newer view is not yet in the ascendant. It still is true that the governments of so-called Christian nations are not Christian.

(*c*) I contend, in the third place, that, defective as has been the adoption of Christ's teachings by the State and the individual, yet those teachings have been the main element in producing the civilisation of Christendom, by fostering a better, truer regard for, and estimate of, the rights and inherent value of the individual, a truer estimate of morality, by developing the conscience, and by producing a devotion to duty and truth for their own sake. The acceptance of Christ's teachings, and efforts to practise them, have laid the foundations of upright, and so of strong self-government. This esteem of the individual, and the consequent power of self-government, by large nations, together with the material civilisation which these nations have produced, have made the nations strong, have made them able to conquer with ease and rule with little trouble the millions of India and Africa. In the last analysis, the fundamental cause for the difference between England and China, is the difference in their religions. Christianity has made England enlightened and powerful. Confucianism, Buddhism, and Taoism have left China ignorant, superstitious, and weak.

(*d*) I contend, in the fourth place, that, though the nations of Europe and North America are called Christian, yet we must not forget that there are still millions in each land who make no profession of being Christians, and that millions more have only a nominal interest in Christianity. As we have seen in the case of the United States, out of sixty-two millions, only some twenty millions (Protestant and Roman Catholic combined) are actively connected with the Churches. Of the voters in the United States, only 30.4 per cent. are members of Evangelical Churches, and 7 per cent.

of the Roman Catholic Church. It would be interesting to know how many voters in the United Kingdom are personally interested in the growth of Christ's kingdom, and confess their individual dependence on and indebtedness to Christ for all their higher, truer life. It is not strange, then, that the governments are not managed on Christian principles, seeing that it is the entire nation which constitutes and regulates the government.

4. Returning again to our main topic, and with the principle of the survival of the fittest still as our guide, let us inquire as to the relative truth and power of the various prevailing types or forms of Christianity. These differ in such important respects that we are compelled to ask which is the truer. Here, too, the tendency of history is not vague, the divine answer to our question is not dubious. The progress in material civilisation, in numbers, in general intelligence, in commerce, in national wealth, in political powers, and in general prosperity, are found to belong, in their highest measure, to those nations which have pressed onward in their interpretation of Christ's teachings; who have not bound themselves to the limited religious attainments of their ancestors, either in theological views, religious customs, or church organisations; but who have pressed onward in their Christian liberty to a profounder comprehension of the teachings of Jesus, and to a fuller application of those principles to the needs of modern society. In other words, they are found to belong, in the highest degree, not to Roman Catholic or to Greek, but to Protestant countries; not to Spain or Italy or Austria, in which countries, for hundreds of years, the Bible has been a forbidden book, freedom of conscience

denied, and the Inquisition has flourished, but rather to Germany and England and the United States, in which countries the Bible has been the most honoured and read and studied of all the books ever produced, where each man has been free to study and interpret the truth, whether of the Bible or of nature, according to the measure of the ability his Maker has given to him.

It is no accident of history that, since Northern Europe broke away from the Roman Church at the time of the Reformation, material, mental, and spiritual civilisation, and thus national growth and national prosperity, have found their most favoured home in Protestant lands. It is no accident that truer comprehension of Christ's teaching, greater love for the truth, greater insistence on character, and greater zeal in doing the work of the Samaritan, should go hand in hand with the marvellous growth and the unprecedented blessings that the Ruler of the universe is bestowing on the Protestant nations. It cannot be an accident, but rather is a matter of profound significance, that the leading powers of Christendom are no longer Roman Catholic Italy or Spain or France, as in former generations, but Protestant Germany and England and the United States. When the New World was discovered, Spain and France were far ahead of the rest of the nations in civilisation and power and size. They ruled Europe. They conquered the New World. They planted their religion by force among the natives in South America. But these Roman Catholic nations have now lost their predominance, both in Europe and in America. The new nations in South America, which have grown from their conquests and which adopted their religion, have proved comparatively weak. What can be the cause of this? It can be none other than the nature of their interpretation of Christianity. They spurned the Bible, hindered popular education, denied and rejected religious freedom, upheld a hierarchical church, persecuted other faiths, laid no emphasis on personal faith in and devotion to Christ alone, and thus encouraged ignorance and superstition and mere traditional religion. It was an inevitable result that the people of such countries could not develop so well in self-control and self-government and general civilisation; it was consequently inevitable that they could not establish successful colonies, or steady, national, free governments, or even keep the lead they already held among the nations of Europe. They fell behind, because, more than others, they failed to see or obey the laws of God which govern the rise and fall of the nations, because they failed to take the new light that came into the world with the Reformation.

A matter of the greatest significance is the fact that all the Roman Catholic nations have comparatively recently rejected many of the distinctive claims of the Roman Catholic Church. They reject her political control and her insistence on religious intolerance, and have repeatedly confiscated her property and banished her most zealous priests, the Jesuits. In other words, even the nations most earnest in their adherence to the Roman Church, such as Spain, Austria, and Italy, have within a few decades adopted some of the most important principles of the Protestant Reformation, such as religious and political freedom, and popular education. These new principles are already working wonders in the nations adopting them. More than a hundred years ago, France rejected the Roman Church as a political leader, and as a consequence she has much more nearly held her leading place in the world than any other Roman Catholic nation. Spain and Italy have endured the Roman yoke the longest, and have suffered the most. The article on the Reformation in M'Clintock and Strong's *Cyclopædia* has the following striking passage :—' Although the Catholic Church has still a larger membership than all the Reformed Churches combined, the power and commanding influence upon the destinies of mankind are more and more passing into the hands of states and governments which are separated from Rome. In the New World the ascendency of the United States and British America, in both of which Protestantism prevails, over the states of Spanish and Portuguese America, is not disputed even by Catholics. In Europe, England has become the greatest world-power, and, in its wide dominions, new, great Protestant countries are springing into existence, especially in Australia and South Africa. In Germany the supreme power has passed from the declining Catholic House of Hapsburg to the Protestant House of Hohenzollern, and the new Protestant German empire marks an addition of the greatest importance to the aggregate power of the Protestant world. The combined influence of the three great Teutonic peoples, the United States, Great Britain, and Germany, continues to be cast in a steadily increasing ratio for the defence of that freedom from the dictation of Rome which was first won by the Reformation. That freedom is now not only fully secured against any possible combination of Catholic states, but the Parliaments of most of the latter—as France, Austria, Italy, Portugal—are as eager in the defence of this principle as the Protestant states. Thus, it may be said, after an existence of about three hundred and fifty years, the Reformation has totally annihilated the influence of Rome upon the laws and the government of the civilised world.'

It is Protestant Germany and especially Puritan England that have grown in influence and power. No peoples have been so controlled by the religion of Jesus Christ as the Anglo-American. No peoples have absorbed it so fully into their national life, and have so embodied it in their language and literature and government. No peoples, as a natural consequence, have so succeeded in establishing prosperous, self-governing colonies and nations. As we have already seen, the English language is to-day more nearly than any other the world language, and is rapidly growing more so ; German comes second, with Russian a close third ; while Roman Catholic French and Spanish and Italian are hardly worthy of mention. This is not accidental. God means that the type of religion and civilisation attained by the Anglo-Saxon race shall have, for the present at least, the predominant influence in moulding the civilisation of the world. And everything points to the growing predominance of the Christian religion and Christian civilisation.

The Protestant nations are far from perfect, as has been repeatedly admitted. There still remains too much that is non-Christian, that is pagan, in their governments, in their churches, in their social customs, in their individuals. Yet it is nevertheless true, that the measure of the truth they have attained is the real cause of the progress they have made. It is the knowledge of the truth that gives freedom, says Jesus. This is true in every sphere of life. But all the spheres are intimately connected. Increasing knowledge and practice of the truth of chemistry, of physics, of mathematics, of mechanics, of architecture, of social science, of commerce, of government, are making man free in all the various walks of life. But more important and fundamental than all the rest, are the knowledge and the practice of moral and spiritual truth, the attainment of noble, pure, loving, truthful character. The attainment of truth in other departments of human welfare depends in no little or indirect way on the attainment of character. Attained and preserved together, they surely bring the blessing of God. But the attainment of this moral truth, this vital life and moral character, come through Christ and His teachings, as from no other source. The verdict of history on this point is beyond the shadow of a doubt. 'If ye abide in My word, ye shall know the truth, and the truth shall make you free.' Men for hundreds of years have been testing this assertion of the greatest religious Teacher the world has ever known ; and more and more have they found it true, in proportion as they have understood and followed His teaching.

Jesus, however, took no rose-coloured view of the growth of the Kingdom. He did not expect the Kingdom of truth to prevail over, and utterly drive out, the kingdom of wickedness and falsehood. He well knew that there would be a long, fierce struggle, in which persecution and the sword would be freely used. In the Parable of the Tares and the Wheat He clearly foretold the common growth, side by side, of good and evil. The two kingdoms will exist side by side, even to the end, and each bring forth its legitimate fruit. We need not wonder, then, but rather should expect the evil to appear with the good, even in the Church, the tares with the wheat; for the Lord of the harvest has Himself bidden us expect it. Nevertheless, there is to be a harvest; the tares will be there, but the wheat will also, and the harvest will be worth reaping.

This, then, is the answer to the question which we asked ourselves at the beginning of our study. Is the Kingdom of God growing? Who can doubt it? Who that has eyes to see and a mind to perceive can fail to understand the answer of history? Yes, the Kingdom of Heaven is growing, and never so fast as in the last decades of the nineteenth century. Whoever wishes may clearly see that, through all history, 'one eternal purpose runs,' that the influence of Jesus is spreading in every land and on every shore; that the Sun of Righteousness has arisen on this dark world, to set no more; and that this Kingdom of God, of Love, of Truth, of Heaven, of Jesus, shall ever more progress 'with the progress of the sun.'

As we look back over the course of our thought thus far, as we reflect on the incalculable blessings that have come through Christ and His teachings, not only to the poor, the afflicted, the diseased and sorrowing, but to all society, even to the noblest and strongest and most illustrious and intellectual,—blessings that have come by the gift of lofty ideals, graces of character, and noble ambitions, secured through Christ and His Church,—we do not wonder that all Christians and all Christendom unite in singing the praises of Him who was at once Son of God and Son of Man. Why is it that Christianity alone of all religions of the earth is pre-eminently a religion of song and praise, does someone ask? It is solely because of what Christ is and does to-day for all who know and love and obey Him. And those who know Him the best love Him the most passionately, and sing His praises most sincerely.

In Christendom the loftiest, most soul-stirring music is Christian. No such songs of devotion and love as are rising to Christ from all lands are offered to scientists or poets or philosophers, or philanthropists or religious leaders, much less to military heroes, or tyrants or infidels. But throughout the world, wherever those are found who read and love the Bible, of whatever race or tongue, the human heart spontaneously sings its thanks and prayers and praises. It would almost seem as though the power of human language and human song had been exhausted in men's efforts to find appropriate strains with which to offer their worship to Him who gave Himself to the world, that the world through Him might know the surpassing love of God, in calling all men through His only begotten Son to become children of the living God. As we think of the Kingdom of the lowly Jesus, now at last, after two thousand years of waiting, only just beginning to establish throughout the world its benign reign; as we strive to appreciate all it is and does for those who become His willing and joyful subjects; and as we realise the fact that Jesus does in truth satisfy the hunger of the human soul to know its own origin and destiny, and its relations to the great Unknown who is in and over all this marvellous universe; and as we see that, through Jesus, finite men do actually come to know in a real way the heart of the Infinite, and to have daily communion with Him, we do not wonder that the followers of Jesus unite in all lands and in every tongue to sing the glorious anthem—

> ' Jesus shall reign where'er the sun
> Does his successive journeys run ;
> His kingdom stretch from shore to shore,
> Till moons shall wax and wane no more.
>
> For Him shall endless prayer be made,
> And praises throng to crown His head ;
> His name, like sweet perfume, shall rise
> With every morning sacrifice.
>
> Peoples and realms of every tongue
> Dwell on His love with sweetest song ;
> And infant voices shall proclaim
> Their early blessings on His name.
>
> Blessings abound where'er He reigns ;
> The prisoner leaps to lose his chains ;
> The weary find eternal rest,
> And all the sons of want are blest.
>
> Let every creature rise, and bring
> Peculiar honours to their King ;
> Angels descend with songs again,
> And earth repeat the loud Amen.'

THE END

Date Due		
OCT 23 '8		
MAR 17		
XXXXXX		